John Todd

The Sabbath School Teacher

Designed to Aid in Elevating and Perfecting the Sabbath School System

John Todd

The Sabbath School Teacher
Designed to Aid in Elevating and Perfecting the Sabbath School System

ISBN/EAN: 9783337772291

Printed in Europe, USA, Canada, Australia, Japan

Cover: Foto ©Lupo / pixelio.de

More available books at **www.hansebooks.com**

THE

Sabbath School Teacher;

DESIGNED TO AID IN

ELEVATING AND PERFECTING

THE

SABBATH SCHOOL SYSTEM

BY JOHN TODD, D.D.,

AUTHOR OF "LECTURES TO CHILDREN," "STUDENT'S
MANUAL," ETC.

AUTHOR'S EDITION.

NORTHAMPTON:
BRIDGMAN AND CHILDS.
1869.

PRINTED BY
GEO. C. RAND & AVERY.

PREFACE

Few things strike the Christian traveller with more force than the fact, that let him go where he will, the Sabbath School has gone before him, and meets him on his arrival. The Church of God, however her separate branches may differ on small unefsentials, has come to the firm conviction, that this is a mighty inftrumentality, which she cannot forego without heavy lofs, and which she cannot faithfully use without great succefs. And this succefs, like everything else that is valuable, must be the child of patient toil and earnest effort. The whole plan of God in redeeming, enlightening, and training men up for heaven, involves individual responsibility and individual labor.

Were it in my power to mark out a plan for a Sabbath School, which would promise great success with little or no labor and anxious responsibility, my little book would be hailed through the world as a great benefactor. This I cannot do. I know of no way to rear a beautiful flower, or a fruit-bearing tree, but by careful planting, till-

(3)

ing, and training. I have not, in this unpretending volume, undertaken to diminifh labor; but to show how it may be most available. Not how the tree, full grown, may spring from the ground, at the touch of the teacher's wand; but how he may plant the seed, and watch its growth, and rear it to be a tree, that shall eternally grow in the garden of the Lord.

The author cannot feel too thankful that this little work has found so much favor on the other side of the waters, and has pafsed through so many editions. It is now reduced in size and price, and sent forth again into the world, with the hope that many will find in it hints that will aid them, or facts that will encourage them to rely on the great promise, "In due season we shall reap, if we faint not."

PITTSFIELD, March, 1856.

CONTENTS.

CHAP. I. — First principles in Christian Education.

CHAP. II. — Superintendent — Character and Duties.

CHAP. III. — Qualifications of a Good Teacher.

CHAP. IV. — Other means of Doing Good besides Teaching.

CHAP. V. — Acquiring Information in order to Teach.

CHAP. VI. — Communicating Religious Instruction.

CHAP. VII. — Infant Sabbath Schools.

CHAP. VIII. — Singing in the Sabbath School.

CHAP. IX. — Connection of the Missionary Cause with the Sabbath School.

CHAP. X. — Duty of the Church and Pastor to the Sabbath School.

CHAP. XI. — Encouragement to Faithfulness.

(5)

SABBATH SCHOOL TEACHER.

CHAPTER I.

FIRST PRINCIPLES IN CHRISTIAN EDUCATION.

In every science, and in every department of knowledge, there are certain points, or what may be called First Principles, which must be definitely understood, and which must be used as starting-points by all who would succeed. These are not theories which each one adopts for himself, but they are discoveries of the combined wisdom and experience of all who have examined the ground. Some of these first principles I wish to present to the Sabbath School teacher. I take pains to present these clearly and distinctly, because I deem them of great importance.

1. Lay it down as a first principle in Christian education, *that the first object of the teacher is to form right* HABITS *in the scholar.*

Were you to give the most solemn and impressive instruction possible, to a company just as they were about going into the theatre, it would do no good. The impressions would all be gone in an hour, and

other and deeper impressions would take their place.
The same feelings awakened in an audience who
were in the *habit* of daily prayer, would be likely to
abide, and to bring forth the fruits of eternal life.
Those children who are prodigies of learning and at-
tainment in early life, often prove to be very ordinary
men; and the surprise is, that a tree so full of blos-
soms should produce so little fruit; while, in other
cases, a child giving but faint promise of mind, in
early life, frequently becomes great, and wise, and
good, in mature years. This difference is not merely
to be attributed to the slowness with which these
minds were developed, but to the *habits* formed in
early life. A child may acquire thought slowly, yet
if he has formed the habit of acquiring each thought
fully and distinctly, and of retaining it when acquired,
he will eventually become a wise man. On the other
hand, that boy so bright before you now, who commits to memory so readily, or who is so prompt in
undersanding and so quick in answering your questions, may be forming habits which will more than
destroy all that he now obtains. All great men have
attributed their success more to the mental and
moral habits acquired in early life, than to any thing
else. Even the temper,—the disposition, is formed by
acquired habits, so that one who is naturally irritable, may become a calm man.

Let it be impressed on the mind of the teacher,
that it is not so much the *amount* of knowledge which

you communicate to each scholar, that is to make your teaching a blessing, as are the habits which you aid him in acquiring.

He may or may not have gone over much ground, —but has he subdued it? Have you created in him a taste for patient thought and investigation, till he has thoroughly understood every idea, and mastered every subject presented? Here was one great error in the old system of committing an amazing amount to memory, when the child was praised or blamed according to his success or want of success in loading the memory.

You will frequently meet with a man who in early life was left an orphan. You see that he has risen up from obscurity, through difficulties and trials, till he has become successful in his pursuits. The facts, on investigation, would be found to be, that on being thrown upon his own resources in early life, he was compelled to form *habits* of sober thought, of prudence, foresight, economy, and diligence, which in more indulgent circumstances he could not have acquired. These habits made the man. And it is of unspeakable importance that the child now under your care form right habits. Do you not yourself daily lament that you have some wrong habits hanging about you which you acquired in childhood? I have not unfrequently met with men who would readily acknowledge that thousands of money would be no object, could they, with it, purchase such habits, mental and moral, as might and ought to have been formed in the days of childhood.

It ought never to be forgotten, that right *habits* are indispensably necessary to enable a child, or even a man, to meet and resist temptation. Piety and courage were prominent in the character of Daniel; but after all, I should tremble to place any man in his circumstances, with the lion's den before him, who had not Daniel's *habit* of daily prayer. "The man," says the venerated Porter, "who is so much the slave of circumstances in *common* affairs as to forego his regular food, and exercise, and rest, may *live*, but cannot enjoy life; he cannot for any length of time possess vigorous health of body. He who has so little firmness of religious principle as to intermit his regular, secret devotions, from indolence or hurry, or complaisance to friends, may be a Christian still, perhaps in a state of temporary but woful backsliding. But certainly he is not a decided, consistent Christian. He does not "keep his own heart with all diligence." He is not prepared for his upward flight,to live in heaven, like Enoch, who "walked with God." Nor yet is he prepared to live in Babylon, like Daniel, who "kneeled upon his knees *three times* in a day, and prayed and gave thanks." The *habits* so beautifully described above, are as essential to the well-being of the child, as to the man and the Christian.

The habit of *perseverance* should be cultivated with unremitting assiduity. It is what every child, and I may add, every teacher, needs. The habit, once acquired, is invaluable, though exceedingly difficult to be attained. Take every method to encourage the child, and to show him the possibility of producing very *great changes* from slight beginnings. I cannot better illustrate this point than by telling the short story, from the London Quarterly Review, as related by Lochman. ' A Visier, having offended his master, was compelled to perpetual captivity in a lofty tower. At night his wife came to weep below his window. " Cease your grief," said the sage, " go home for the present, and return hither when you have procured a live, black beetle, together with a little *ghee*, (or buffalo's butter), three *clews,*—one of the finest silk, another of stout pack-thread, and another of whip-cord; finally a stout coil of rope." When she again came to the foot of the tower, provided according to her husband's commands, he directed her to touch the head of the insect with a little of the ghee, to tie one end of the silk thread around him, and to place the reptile on the wall of the tower. Seduced by the smell of the butter, which he conceived to be in store somewhere above him, the beetle continued to ascend till he reached the top, and thus put the Visier in possession of the roll of silk-thread. He then drew up the pack-thread by means of the silk;—the small cord by means of the pack-thread, and by means of the cord, a stout rope capable of sustaining his own weight,—and thus he escaped from the tower.'

2. *That the teacher should endeavor to fix the great principles of God's truth in the mind of the child.*

What I mean by this, is, that while you lead the child to commit to memory, do not fear that he cannot be made to comprehend and embrace the great principles of revealed religion. The fashions, the plans, I had almost said, the rage of the present day, is to bring every thing in mechanics, literature, morals, and religion, down to the test of present effect, and present apparent good. As if God had not wisely ordained that good shall always flow from the embracing great, fixed principles. We feel that it is a loss of time to pause long enough to give or receive deep, solid instruction, or to endure the task of thinking. How difficult to get men to sit down and read a sober, original, deep book! Our ideas must all be thought out for us, and poured into the ear just as a song would be. In our preachers, we demand men who have popular talents,—who can electrify, lighten and thunder, sweep like a whirlwind, carrying men into the kingdom by violence and before they know it, and move them on in the growth of grace by successions of powerful impulses. Our teachers must be men of popular address, with the power of communicating knowledge, which can be obtained in the least possible time, and at once be applied to use.

As if men, in this agitated state of the world, could come up amid the rockings and the storms of the age, without deep, fixed principles for a sheet-anchor. The waves of excitement already run high, and will run still higher; and he who acts as a teacher in the theological School, or as an author, as a teacher in the day or Sabbath School, who does not try to lay the foundations of character on fixed, definite principles, even the everlasting foundations of truth, falls far short of his duty. You might as well neglect to place anchors in the bow of your ship, as you send her from her moorings, because she does not *now* need them, as to neglect to fix deep and definite principles in the mind of the child, because he has not immediate use for them.

This leads me to take this opportunity to answer the question so frequently asked in Sabbath Schools, is it best to teach *Catechisms* in these schools?

Till within a short time, Catechisms of all kinds have nearly been proscribed in most of our schools, and the impression seemed to be gaining ground, that they were to be laid aside with the rubbish of other times, with things and modes, good, perhaps in their day, but not adapted to the day in which we live. The objections seem to be, that the memory alone is cultivated by learning catechisms; that the child cannot understand them, and that they are sectarian in their tendency.

After looking at this subject long, and in various

lights, I am not altogether certain that these objections are not directed chiefly, if not solely, against the Assembly's Shorter Catechism; and that a sort of tacit compromise has not been made, that all catechisms should be laid aside for the sake of getting rid of that.

In regard to the two first objections, I believe they may be reduced to one and the same: viz., that the memory is burdened, *because* the child does not comprehend what he tries to learn. The answer to these objections, is two-fold. First, that it is one very important part of education to exercise and cultivate the memory; and few things will do it better or faster than the Catechism. Secondly, that it is not true that the child cannot be made to understand the Catechism. Till within a few years it was thought that a mere child could not be made to understand Arithmetic, Grammar, or Geometry. He was told to commit the rules to memory, to be applied to use at some future time. But all this is justly exploded. The child of six years old can now be taught Arithmetic on the plan of Colburn. It is only the substitution of *things*, for the signs of things. I do not believe there is any greater difficulty in teaching a Catechism, than in teaching many parts of the Bible. The book of Romans, for example, is a very difficult part of the Bible; and yet I have never seen a school more interested in any study, than in this book. The great obstacle with which I have met,

Mrs. Sherwood.   Assembly's Catechism.   Third principle—*power of example.*

has been, that the teachers seemed to make up their minds that the Catechism must be difficult to teach, and thus made it difficult.   But let any one begin and proceed just on the plan of Colburn's Arithmetic, and I will warrant success and pleasure. Let any one read Mrs. Sherwood's beautiful stories on the Church Catechism, and he will be satisfied that even catechisms can be made bewitchingly interesting.   The man who shall make the Shorter Catechism equally interesting, will do a great work for his fellow-men.*

Then as as to their being sectarian,—if this be so, let each sect select its own catechism.   While I frankly say that I prefer the Assembly's Catechism before any other, and, indeed, before any other uninspired compendium of revealed religion, I should indeed sink low in my own estimation, did I not feel willing that every one should enjoy the same liberty of choosing; and I trust I should love no one the less for the exercise of such a right.   Perhaps those schools which have the Catechism taught in short lessons once a month, are wise in their course; for it ought not to be taught every Sabbath.

3. *A process of education, from* EXAMPLE, *is continually going on in the mind of every child.*

---

* By the experiment of delivering a few lectures on the Shorter Catechism, I am satisfied that it may be brought down to the comprehension of every person, though I had many doubts when I commenced.

Example of a real Christian

The parent who supposes the few lessons of instruction which he bestows upon his child, constitute any considerable part of the education of that child, is greatly mistaken. The child is at play in the corner of the room, with his blocks or his toys, and the parents are talking together without heeding him. But ever now and then the little prattler stops talking to himself to catch the tones and thoughts of his parents, and he is there receiving impressions which form his character, and which will abide with him through life. It is on this principle that example is so powerful a teacher; and that a real Christian can do so much for his Master. " God has not permitted the world to despise a true Christian; they may pass by him with a haughty and supercilious coldness, they may deride him with a taunting and sarcastic irony; but the spirit of the proudest man that ever lived will bend before the grandeur of a Christian's humility. You are at once awed, and you recoil upon your own conscience, when you meet with one whose feelings have been purified by the Gospel. The light of a Christian's soul, when it shines into the dark den of a worldly heart, startles and alarms the gloomy passions that are brooding within. Is this contempt? No: but all the virulence which is excited by the Christian graces can be resolved into envy—the feel ings of devils when they think on the pure happiness of angels; and to complete their confusion, what is

that moment the feeling in the Christian's heart?
Pity, most unfeigned pity."

Those influences hardly noticed or thought of, the
every-day acts of parents, and teachers, a word, or a
look even, may permanently and mightily influence
the character of the child. What then? Must we
so reverence that little one, as to be always subject to
painful restraint and anxiety in his presence? The
little mimic would be sure, in that case, to "catch
the truth" of concealment, and would never grow up
with an open countenance, or an ingenuous mind.
There is no way but to *be*, habitually and permanently, such as the child ought to see you *appear*.
You must be *in* the law of justice, truth, love, holiness; not *under* it. It must be the perfect law of
liberty to you; so as to manifest its presence, not as
an outward, restraining power, but as an inward,
well-spring, whose waters flow out freshly and pleasantly in all the channels of social life and Christian
duty.' A teacher who has not carefully noticed the
fact, will be surprised to find how narrowly he is
watched, how every part of his character, and almost
every habit of his, becomes a part of his pupil's. You
will frequently see a class eyeing their teacher as he
delivers an exhortation, or tries to impress a truth of
great importance upon them, just as a child will eye
a father when he receives a command,—not because
he does not fully understand the *words* of the command, but because he wants to know just how much

2 *

his father means. A congregation will look at their minister in the same way, and are impressed, not more certainly by *what* is said, than by the looks and appearance of the preacher. These little folks cannot reason about great principles of action,—cannot make allowances for the temperament of their teacher, but they judge of character and of religion by looking at small things, and receiving repeated impressions. A word too much, or a word too little, may be forgotten; but impressions made upon a child by example are at once moulded into his character. What Adam Clark so pertinently says of a minister, is wonderfully applicable to a Sabbath School teacher. 'It is impossible that he should *ever* be a *private* man; even in his most trivial intercourse with others, it is never forgotten what his office is: the *habit* of every one's mind, is to expect information or example from his company and conduct; he is constantly living under the observation of mankind, and he who is always observed, should *never* venture on dubious conduct, or suppose for a moment that what he does in the view of another can ever for a moment be a matter of indifference, or be regarded as a trifle. I will tell you a curious circumstance that happened to me some years ago. In a day or two from the time that I refer to, I was about to set off from London to Ireland: a friend desired me to take charge of a young lady to Dublin, to which I readily agreed, and she was sent to me at the coach. I soon found from

Moral honesty to be observed.

her conversation that she was a Roman Catholic, and also quickly perceived that she had been led to entertain a very high opinion of me. After we had travelled some distance, talking occasionally on various subjects, the day-light began to sink fastly away, when she took out of her reticule a small Catholic book of prayers, and commenced seriously her evening devotions. While she was reading, such thoughts as these occurred to me,—' I believe this lady to be sincere in her religious creed, which I think to be a very dangerous one; she appears to be of an ingenuous temper, and to feel much personal respect for me; is there not here, then, a good *opportunity*, as well as subject, to exercise my influence, and to deliver her, if possible, from her erroneous creed?' But, continued I in my thoughts, ' was she not entrusted to my care? would her friends have so entrusted her, had they ever suspected that an attempt at proselytism would be made? Would not the attempt be a breach of trust, and should I, even were ultimate good to accrue to her, be a *morally honest man ?*' I instantly felt that *my own honesty* must be preserved, though the opportunity of apparent good might be apparently lost. In a short time Miss —— closed her book with this observation, ' We Catholics, Dr. Clarke, think it much better to believe too much than too little.' I replied, ' But, Madam, in our belief, we should recollect that we never should yield our assent to what is *contradictory in itself*, or to what *contradicts other*

ascertained facts.' This was the only observation
that I made that looked at all towards Catholicism. In
process of time we arrived at our journey's end, and
I deposited her safely in the hands of her friends.'

'From that time till about two years ago, I never
heard of her, till we met in the following way. I
had been preaching at Chelsea Chapel, and on entering the vestry after service, a lady followed
me, shook hands, spake with much emotion, and
said: 'Do you not recollect me, Dr. Clarke? I am
Miss ——, whom you kindly took care of to Ireland:
I was then a Catholic; now I am a Protestant, and
have suffered much in consequence of the change.'
I inquired how the alteration in her views was
effected, and she gave me in detail the account which
I will shortly sum up to you. When she heard to
whom she was about to be entrusted, she resolved to
observe and watch closely this eminent Protestant
minister; she was pleased with the conversation and
friendliness shown her; and was so struck with the observation I had made in the coach, that she said it
afterwards absolutely haunted her, caused her to
examine and think for herself, aud at last led her to
freedom from her thraldom: ' but,' said she, ' I should
never have been induced to examine, had it not been
for the previous examination I had made of *you*.
From the first moment you entered the coach, I
watched you narrowly; I thought, now I have a fair
opport·nity of knowing something of these Protest-

ants; and I will judge if what I have heard of them be true. Every word, every motion, every look of yours, Sir, was watched with the eye of a lynx; I felt you could not be acting a part, for you could not suspect that you were so observed; the result of all was, your conduct conciliated esteem, and removed prejudice; your one observation on belief, led me to those examinations which the Spirit of God has blessed to my conversion; and I now stand before you, the convert of your three days' *behavior* between London and Dublin.' You see from this account, how all ministers should ever feel themselves to be public men; how cautious should be their conduct, and how guarded their conversation. Had I attempted to proselyte this lady, all her prejudices would have been up in arms; had my behavior been unbecomingly light, or causelessly austere, she would have been either disgusted or repelled, and her preconceived notions of Protestants would have been confirmed; she saw and heard what satisfied her: thus, even in social intercourse, the public teacher should always be the Christian instructor.'

If the above account cannot be commended for the modesty of the narrator, it certainly contains sound sense, and ought to be well weighed by those who, *in any sense*, are teachers of God's word. The reader should observe too, what is always true, that a Christian is more likely to do good, if he has earned a good reputation by his life and conduct. It is thus that " a good name is better than precious ointment," and the example of such an one grows more and more influential till he reaches the grave, and has finished his work on earth. A *young* man might make the remark, and probably hundreds of young men might make the remark, and it would be forgotten,—' that every man makes his own character;' and it makes no deep impression. But see the father of the late Dr. Rice leading his son, just as he entered manhood, and introducing him to the venerable Patrick Henry, that he might receive some impression that would do him good. The father introduces his son, and the venerated Henry turns his kind and powerful eye upon the stripling, and in tones full of benevolence says, " My son, remember that every man is the maker of his own character !" This falls from one who made his own character,— from one whose life entitled him to speak with meaning. The sentence sank deep into the soul of young Rice, and was probably the means of leading him to make his own beautiful and symmetrical character.

4. *Religion should be taught from the very earliest dawn of intelligence.*

Among the many crude notions which prevail among men, we often hear it gravely advanced, that a child ought to grow up unbiassed, without having his head filled with creeds and religious impressions; so that when he becomes mature in after life, he may make his own choice in religion. I verily believe I have heard people advance these sentiments who would be exceedingly mortified to have views imputed to them on any other subject, equally superficial and puerile,—views as far from common sense, as they are from the Bible. The mind of every child must and will be growing and strengthening every day; and daily, too, will it receive new impressions and new thoughts. *These* must educate that mind; and a child who sees his parents and teachers careless about religion, and ignorant of God and of his government, is not left to choose for himself,—*he is educated to forget his Maker, and to trample on his laws and commands.* But without stopping to discuss this point, and without more than alluding to the severe reproof of Coleridge, who showed one of these wise ones his garden full of weeds, saying ' he was leaving it without bias, and letting it choose for itself,' I would mention a few familiar reasons why religion should be the first thing taught to a child.

(a.) *It is the most important thing with which the child becomes acquainted.*

The warrior feels that war is the highest end of man, and the noblest employment of a being bearing the image and likeness of God, is to destroy his fellow-man. This highest end of man he wishes his son to pursue, and for this he educates him. Now how does he begin, and *when* does he begin? He would rear that child up to be a man of blood, a terror to men, and a destroyer of all that is fair and beautiful and good. We know how he does it. He makes the very play-things of the nursery to consist of drums, and plumes, and mimic guns, and the splendid glitter of the warrior. He teaches him to lay his hand on the cannon, to shout at its roar, and to have his soul speak through his sparkling eyes at the sight of the sword and the weapons of death. The son of Buonaparte was walking his post as a centinel, in the ranks, as a common soldier, at the age of seven years. And Hannibal made his son swear on the altars of his gods, at the age of twelve, that he would be the everlasting enemy of Rome. These men understand what they do; and they begin the work in early life.

We look upon the character of God, the government under which he has placed us, the services in which he proposes to employ our souls for eternal ages, as the most important subject ever presented to the mind. We would educate the soul for immortality, we would train it up to be a burning and a shining light here while passing over the globe, and when removed hence, to shine as the sun in the firmament forever and ever. We cannot begin too early,—we cannot be too anxious to make the proper impressions upon the soul, before it is otherwise occupied.

(b.) *The command of our Savior is, "preach the Gospel to every creature," and especially, "feed my lambs."*

There can be no doubt that children, even from a very early age, are included in this command. They are immortal, they are sinners, they need the washing of regeneration, and the renewing of the Holy Ghost. By preaching the Gospel to such, or by feeding such, must evidently be meant, communicating religious instruction according to their capacity and age, giving "line upon line, and precept upon precept." Of such is the kingdom of heaven; and we are to bless God, that out of the mouths of babes and sucklings, he has perfected his own praise. Never, perhaps, did the blessed Redeemer appear more interesting than when he paused at the threshold of the temple, while the daughter of Zion shouted for joy, fulfilling the words of holy prophets, and doing it by the mouth of the children who shouted Hosannah in the Temple.

(c.) *The mind of the child is tender and susceptible to impressions.*

Who has not seen the old man, who could hardly remember what he saw or felt during the last year, sit down and distinctly and vividly recal the scenes of childhood? Who does not remember things which took place when he was but little more than an infant—the words of a parent—the example of a sister—the gate on which he swung—the brook in which he played—the pond on which he used to slide—the tree under whose shade he used to sit—the grove through which he used to walk—the trees that

3

stood by his father's door—the very countenance of the stones and rocks on which he used to gaze in childhood? And how is this so? Because he then received *deep* impressions from every thing around him,—impressions which will probably last as long as the memory lives, even forever. *Then*, every impression, every look, the words and tones of our parents and teachers, sank deep into the soul, and all left their image there. The soul of the child is empty, and you may fill it with the treasures of life. It is confiding, and you may imprint your own soul upon it; it is yielding, and you may train it up for the skies. You speak to that youth who had little or nothing of these religious impressions made upon his soul in childhood, and how little do you move, or restrain, or affect him by religious motives! Speak to that man who has grown up without religion, and whose *habits* even from childhood have all been formed for this world, and why do you not move him by conversation, or by the solemn sermon? Because his soul has been educated to habits which almost forbid religious impressions; and I sometimes feel that instead of wondering why no more of such men, in manhood's strength, are not converted to God, it is rather a matter of astonishment, that any are permitted to receive impressions which lead them to God and to holiness.

(d.) *The effects upon the community are such as to demand that religion be the first thing taught.*

Nothing ever expanded, enlarged, quickened, and

as it were, created mind, like the truths of the Bible. They make wise the simple. A nation of people who were taught religion the first thing, and who had grown up under the impressions of religion, would be more enlightened, intelligent, free, than any which the world has ever yet seen. They could do almost any thing towards enlarging the bounds of investigation and knowledge, they could give an example which all other nations would feel and acknowledge, and they would show what men could do, when virtuous enough to govern themselves. The earlier, the deeper religious truth is impressed on the mind of the child, the more intelligence will he possess, the more influence will he have in life, and the greater blessing will he be to the world. Let the Sabbath School instructer think how much vice he will prevent, from how many temptations he will shield, how much strength he will create for the hour of temptation, how much the world needs men sanctified even from the cradle, and he will feel that it is impossible to begin too early. I make these remarks, because somebody must take the youngest classes, and cheerfully and faithfully instruct them in religion; and the teacher will find it a laborious piece of work, unless he first be convinced, that this is the very time to begin. The wax is more soft, and you may mould it as you will. The mind is curious and thirsty: you may give it the waters from the wells of salvation. Never repine that your class are young, perhaps the youngest in the school. They may become trees in the garden of the Lord, they may be vessels of mercy to this world, they may give you more joy beyond the grave, than the brightest crown ever worn here, could give its possessor.

(e.) *Once more, religion ought to be the first thing aught, because it will add to the everlasting happiness of the child.*

The promise is that if you train up a child in the way he should go, when old, he will not depart from it. The character will be formed in the morning of life, and it will be fitted to be a glorious spirit in eternity. You have seen men converted to God in manhood,—and in old age; seen them live and die in peace; but did you ever see a character equal to that of Joseph,—of Samuel,—of David, who did not in early life receive deep religious impressions? We have seen men live and die, such as Payson and Evarts, and many others whose sun went down in glory, and whose bright spirits could almost be traced as they went up to the rewards of heaven; but such men were instructed in childhood. Their earliest, deepest impressions were made when they were children. And will not their eternal condition be altered in consequence?—their songs be louder and sweeter?—their robes purer, and their crowns brighter? Those who are early and faithfully instructed, will shine brighter in heaven, because they will have fewer sins to be forgiven;

they will have made the service of God the business of life; they will have turned many to God, who shall go with them to the hill of Zion above. Perhaps it is not speaking beyond bounds, to say, that a child of ordinary capacity and destitute of property, but converted to God in childhood, is frequently worth more to the church than ten wealthy men converted at the noon of life.

4. *A child is more averse to receiving religious instruction than any other.*

Those for whose benefit I am writing, do not wish me to stop to prove this point. Their ingenuity has been too often tasked, their patience too often and too severely taxed when trying to fix and keep the attention of their class, to doubt the truth here laid down. Instead of spending time on its proof, therefore, I prefer to mention some of the causes of this aversion to religion, in order to aid you in overcoming it.

(a.) *Every one naturally dislikes to contemplate the character of God.*

All who teach religion feel the difficulty, though all do not confess it. Some try to escape it in one way, and some in another,—but all meet it. Some deny it in words, but acknowledge it in practice; for they are forced to draw the character of God widely different from that drawn in the Bible. They hold him up dressed in robes of mercy and love, indifferent to the violations of law, winking at

3 *

sin,—a representation of God about as correct, as
a beautiful picture of the ocean sleeping in the
silvery light of the moon, is a true and faithful representation of that awful bed of waters. Others do
not, and dare not bring the true character of God
before the mind of the child, but, instead of it, they
give beautiful illustrations of this and that duty.
What need of this? Why is the character of God
an object of aversion to every unrenewed heart,
whether in a child or in the full-grown man? I answer, that when the mind fully sees the greatness of
God, it receives the full impression of his awful and
holy nature,—of his unchangeableness,—of his power
and right to govern and command us,—of our consciousness that we have sinned, and are daily sinning
against him,—and the soul is at once open to fear and
forebodings. Tell the child that God is almighty and
can protect him, and he knows too, that this almighti-
ness may be used to crush him,—and he is afraid.
Tell him that God sees him and knows all things,
and therefore will forever shield him from injustice,
and he knows that this very knowledge has counted
up his sins, and will bring every thing into judgment.
Tell him to rejoice, for ' the Lord God omnipotent
reigneth;' and he cannot do it,—for he knows that
his government extends over *him*, and will to eternity
bind him to obedience.   .

Now what shall be done? Shall we avoid leading
the child to contemplate the character of God, be-

cause it is unpleasant to him? By no means. Take every possible method to make the child understand the whole and the true character of God;—his eternity, is time and years continued forever : his skill is seen in the painting of the rain-bow, and in every limb of the child; his power is seen in all creation, the flood, the mountain, the ocean, the wind : his holiness is seen in the Red Sea becoming the grave of Egypt, the wilderness becoming the grave of all one generation of Israel, and in judgments upon individuals and nations; his mercy in sending his Son, giving the Bible, and the assistance of the Holy Spirit, in preserving the life of the child, surrounding him with friends, and the means of grace;—and then try to show the child the guilt of carrying a heart which does not rejoice under this government. If he trembles and is unhappy at the idea of having the eye of God continually upon him, it is because he is constantly doing wrong. This will open the door to teach him the doctrine of repentance, and to lead him to Christ.

(b.) *The same consciousness of guilt in the pupil which makes religion irksome, is more or less felt by the teacher*, and makes him cold in presenting truth.

Hence religious instruction is not given by the teacher or by the parent with that cheerfulness and interest which they ought to feel, and which perhaps they would feel on any other subject. If the teacher feels chilled or lukewarm, he will certainly add to the distaste which the child naturally feels in regard to religion. He will present all he has to communicate in a very dry light.

(c.) *Ignorance of the best methods of reaching the heart and conscience will add to the aversion.*

There is a tact, a kind of skill, which some have, and which brings a circle of children around them at once, and continues to hold them. This tact is in some apparently natural; but it may be acquired to almost any degree. The great thing wanted to create it, is a strong love for the souls of men. Let the heart be filled with this love, and you will have benevolence seen in the countenance,—have it felt in the tones of your voice, and so spread over your character, and all that you do, that the children will love you at once. This will lead you to think much on the subject of the best methods of doing good. You will study to simplify and make plain the truths of the Bible,—to illustrate and fasten them upon the memory. No man can hope to gain the confidence and affections of children who does not try to let himself down to their condition, try to conceive how he should look upon this or that thing, were he a child. I shall probably resume this topic again. I introduce it here, because I am confident it is one cause of the aversion which children have to religious instruction. If you give it with hesitancy, with reluctance, and as a task, you may be certain that it is received in the same way.

(d.) There is one thing beyond all this, which renders religion irksome to the unrenewed heart,—*its own unhappiness.*

Every one knows by experience, that an unsanctified heart is unhappy. The soul may be sunk near the state of the beast, it may live in an ideal world, —it may revel in sin,—it may fly from flower to flower, and from fountain to fountain, for peace and happiness, but cannot find it. It is unsatisfied, it is uneasy, it is unhappy. It must throw away thought, and be a mere trifler, or it is wretched. Every child has more or less of this feeling. The restraints of conscience and the voice of conscience are now a burden. But having no clear idea of religion, (and *can* he have, before feeling its power?) he feels that religion will only increase the restraints of conscience, give her voice new power, and give her new fetters, and this is all! He thinks he shall have the same wicked heart *after* conversion as before, and all the addition he will obtain, is, that conscience will have new power over him, and the clashings between his conscience and feelings will be seven-fold increased;—consequently, that every addition of piety is another addition of gloom, and of wretchedness. He has hitherto known nothing that looks so much like religion as conviction of sin, and he imagines that real religion is only adding to these convictions till the soul stops sinning, and this is religion! Is it any wonder, then, that there is naturally an aversion in the mind of all, whether children or adults, to religion?

They conceive it to be only an accumulation of iron in the fetters,—only an addition to the bad feelings which already fill the heart. How shall this difficulty be met and overcome? I would advise the teacher to become familiar with the workings of his own heart, and to become well acquainted with the religious experience of other Christians. Let him learn the manner in which those who are now Christians, once looked at this subject, learn what misapprehensions and distortions their feelings and imagination gave them, and in this way learn to pour light into the heart that is darkened by sin, and that aches under a sense of its unworthiness. I illustrate this point by a conversation which is similar to many which I have had since I have been in the pastoral office. Nothing is altered but the name of the individual.

" Mr. G., I am glad to see you of late at our evening meetings, at our Bible-class, and even out three times on the Sabbath. I have long been hoping that you would be brought into the fold, and that I should have the pleasure of seeing you a decidedly religious man."

" Thank you, Sir; but I am not certain that I shall continue to attend these meetings much longer. I have often thought I would *have* religion, but the more religion I obtain, the more gloomy and unhappy I feel."

" I am surprised, Mr. G.,—for I did not know that

you had 'obtained' *any* 'religion!'   Do you mean
to say, that you have repented of your sins, forsaken
them all,—that you are now trusting in the blood of
Jesus Christ, with a heart contrite for your past life,
full of gratitude for mercy and pardon, and full of
holy resolution for the future?"

" Not exactly so ; but I mean, I have attended your
meetings, and have heard all you have to say,—that I
have given my thoughts somewhat to religion, but the
more I have done it, the more dark it seems, and the
further I am from being happy.   If conscience now
gives me so little peace, what should I do, were I to
give up all my thoughts to religion, and let conscience
have full swing?"

" My dear Sir, conscience will have 'full swing,'
as you call it, to all eternity, even if you are lost, and
have your portion with unbelievers and hypocrites.
But this is not religion.   Pharaoh and Judas had this
kind of religion, and it drove them to madness."

" I don't wonder at it."

" You have mistaken the lashings of conscience for
religion.   It *is* true, that the more of *such* religion
you have, the more wretched you will be.   But have
I not often explained to you from the pulpit, that
religion is something widely different from this?"

" I don't know ; you often seem to preach contra-
dictions.   I cannot understand why the very first
movements of the soul towards religion should make
me more and more unhappy.   You tell me it is a'

gold, and when obtained it will render me happy. How can a great quantity of gold make me happy, when the first small piece I get renders me so miser-rable?"

"Mr. G., you recollect, some days since, you gave me an interesting account of your boy. You said he ran away from school, and spent three days in the company of vicious and idle boys. You recollect that you told me, that when you called him to account, you shut him up in a chamber without food, till he would acknowledge his sin, ask your pardon, and the pardon of the school. Am I right?"

"Yes, Sir; but I don't see what this has to do with the subject."

"Did you not tell me, that he held out for three days, and that every time you went to the door he seemed more stubborn and hardened?"

"Yes."

"Do you suppose he was growing happy during this time?"

"No, he grew miserable; and my going to his chamber and asking him if he would submit, seemed almost to render him distracted."

"Was that submission to you?"

"No, to be sure not."

"Well, did he not grow more and more miserable and wretched, till at last he was brought to submit, bow his will to yours, ask your pardon, and the pardon of the school?"

" Yes."

" Well, he undoubtedly looked upon the feelings of *submission*, just as *you* do upon religion ; the more he thought of these feelings, the more he dreaded them, and supposed that the feeling of submission would be intolerable to bear ; whereas, you said that the moment he submitted, the cloud all rolled off, and he was perfectly happy. So it is with you. God is coming and calling you to repentance ; you are stubborn, refuse to repent, and dread to be a penitent, because you think your present unhappy feelings will continue, and the present agony be increased seven-fold ! Sinners frequently think that a change of heart consists in nothing but an increase of their present feelings, till they become almost insupportable. That which your boy finally felt, and which we call submission, was not an increase of the feelings which he had when you shut him up, but an entirely new feeling. And if you ever do really ' obtain religion,' it will not be an increase of your present feelings, which you call ' religious,' but which in fact are awfully wicked, but feelings entirely new. It seems to me that God permitted your child to do as he did, that you might have a glass in which you could plainly see your own character. You are wading in miry waters in order to lay the founda‧ tions of your hopes, and complain that God suffers the waves to dash over you, to show you their bitterness, and their filth."

CHAPTER II.

In almost all communities it is better to have one mind preside and direct, than to have more, if we can safely trust so much power to one man. But as in most cases, this power is in very great danger of perversion and abuse, we are careful not to delegate it. The government of God is the government of one mind, and is the most perfect conceivable. An earthly monarchy is, in theory, the most perfect of human governments; but human nature is too selfish and too wicked, to make it desirable in practice. The family government is that of one presiding, directing mind, and as the power is not very liable to abuse, it is by far the best possible. The Sabbath School is like it; and every Sabbath School must have one directing, presiding mind at its head.

The church is one body: the members are not all alike, though all may be useful. One is the eye, another the mouth, another the hand, the foot and

38

the like. She can furnish many willing hands, and ready feet, but they want the eye to guide them. In other words, there are multitudes of good people who can do good, become very useful, but they want to *lean* on some one for direction. Some are too young, and lack experience; some are, by habit and education, diffident of their own powers; some are comparatively ignorant; and some are naturally timid and indifferent. These are all willing to labor to do good,—are desirous to do so; but they want some one to guide, direct, and to lead.

The best army has been routed, and the tide of victory rolled suddenly back, by the fall of a leader. The army remained the same, the courage the same, but they could do nothing without the presiding, directing mind. What Xenophon says to his generals, may be said to those whom God has raised up to be the leaders among his people. " All the soldiers direct their eyes to you.—If they behold you dispirited, they themselves will be cowards. But if you appear preparing to attack the enemy, and encourage them onward, be assured they will follow you, and attempt to imitate you. And it is fit that you should excel them."

So many qualities of the very highest order need to be united in a Superintendent, that I feel afraid of beginning to enumerate them, lest the reader say, ' he has drawn a character neither to be found nor attained.' I am afraid too, of so estimating some parts of his character as to lead to the impression, that they may be sought and cultivated, to the loss, or to the neglect of others. The prosperity, life, character, and usefulness of a school, depend more upon the Superintendent than upon any, and perhaps all other things united. Thus, you will at one time see a school flourishing, full, and prosperous. It is the glory of the congregation. You call a few years after, and find it small, drooping, and almost lifeless. The reason of this difference, in most instances, is to be traced to the different men who superintend it.

I will first mention the DUTIES which belong to the office, and then the traits of character needed to meet and fulfil these duties. What I shall try to say in a few pages, ought to be drawn out and illustrated through a whole volume.

I would here remark that the teachers ought to be annually elected by the church; and the meeting of election ought to be one of examination of the school, review of the past, prayer for the teachers and school, and of plans for aiding the teachers. This makes the teachers feel that they are elected by somebody, have a trust committed to them, and are accountable to the church. It will give their characters and instructions weight in the sight of the children. Should new teachers be needed during the year, the Superintendent ought to nominate, subject to the acceptance of the teachers. I would, then, have the Superintendent annually elected by the teachers; and for

THE SABBATH SCHOOL TEACHER. 41

How Superintendent to be elected.   Importance of the office.

these reasons; that if he does not do well, a change
may be easily made; that he may feel that he is
called into office by the teachers, and is responsible,
in a measure to them; and especially, that being
elected by the teachers, he may seem, in the eyes of
the school, to represent all the teachers, and embody
their views, feelings, and plans. His office expires
at the end of a year; and, if re-elected for a suc-
cession of years, the greater is the testimony to his
worth, and the more is he held in honour by the
whole community. Let him be the very best man
in the church; a man of age,—that the teachers may
feel that they are not under the direction of youth,
that the parents may feel that they are committing
their children to experience; and that the children
may feel that they are guided by worth and respectability. "A good name is better than precious ointment," and what falls from the lips of such a man
has weight with the school. Under the present system, the office of the Superintendent is the most important office in the church, next to that of the Pastor; and every pains ought to be taken to secure the
best man possible, and the man who enters upon that
office, should feel that he is assuming a very heavy
responsibility.

Another reason why the school should be under
the supervision of the church, besides the desirable-
ness of having the church cherish it as the apple of
the eye, is that if the teachers are *not* elected by

42   THE SABBATH SCHOOL TEACHER.

Supervision o the Church.   Proper place of the Sabbath School.

the church, if they organize by themselves, and stand alone, distinct from the church, there is danger lest they feel that they have a distinct organization, distinct interests, and may lay their plans, and pursue their ends, not only without consulting the wishes of the church, but without consulting her interests. I shall, in another place, describe the duties of the church towards the Sabbath School; but I wish distinctly to say here, that I should lament most deeply to see the day, when the teachers in our Sabbath Schools shall be found acting independently of the churches, and in array against them. There is not, cannot be, in nature, any separate interests in the two bodies. But should the day come when the fashion shall prevail, that Sabbath Schools shall be organized and carried on, as independent organizations, then will heart-burnings commence. Then will many of the church withhold their children, the church and the minister stand aloof, or become subordinate to the school, the power of the church will pass into the school, and the church, in fact, take that particular shape. Then will the school control the election of the Pastors of the churches, and do all that which is now done by our churches, as such. No man can think more highly of the Sabbath School system than I do. I trust these pages will prove that point. But woe the day, when they shall strive to "lord it over God's heritage," and concentrate every thing pertaining to the church of Christ in the Sab bath School. Christ did not organize his church in the shape of the Sabbath School, nor can she ever assume that shape without destroying her proportions, and her existence. The attempt so to shape the church can never succeed; and I trust it will never be made. I am not, however, making war upon a man of straw; nor would I make these remarks without intending to have them mean something. I proceed to the duties of the Superintendent.

1. *It belongs to him to govern and direct the school.*

Men, and indeed, all created beings, must be under law, and government. You cannot find the spot, whether it be the family, the church, or the Sabbath School, in which constant supervision and government are not necessary. Some schools will require more of government than others,—those in cities more than those in the country,—but all require it, and no school can be prosperous without it. It is a wise provision in this system, that the Superintendent is the Executive, and that the teaching and the governing, are, in some measure, disconnected. The very first ingredient in genuine government, is, that the Superintendent govern himself. Without this, he can never exercise a wise control over the school. If he speak harshly, or quickly, or peevishly, to the teachers or scholars, if his color comes and goes, and the school is expecting some out-breaking of impatience, he has not self-government. This he must have, and this he is inexcusable for not having. The teachers should feel that the government of the school is in his hands, and they are to sustain his decisions. At the same time, it is well to remember, that the more he can conceal his authority, and not make it prominent, and continually *felt*, the better. He should have his plans matured, whether they are, or are not, drawn out on paper before the school, and silently, steadily, and un hesitatingly, see them carried out. As corporeal punishments are properly excluded from this system, he must have an accurate knowledge of human nature, that he may ingeniously contrive modes and substitutes. He needs ingenuity to plan, and cool judgment to execute. I have been fearful that the good effects of government and discipline in the Sabbath School are not sufficiently appreciated. In most instances, it will correct evils, and what is better, will prevent them in future. Many instances might be cited in which boys, who were vicious, disorderly, troublesome, and corrupting, have been reclaimed, and have become, in after years, efficient, and devoted teachers. I will illustrate this by an example or two, from undoubted testimony.

" In a flourishing school connected with one of the churches in the city of Washington, there was a very rude and unmanageable boy. As all mild measures failed to make him better, it was determined that he should be sent away from the school. To make a deeper and more lasting impression upon himself and all present, it was also determined that this act of discipline should be administered in a formal and solemn manner. Accordingly, whilst the exercises of the school were going on, the Superintendent knocked upon the table and called for attention. He directed the teacher of the class to which the little culprit belonged, to take him by the hand, and lead him out into the view of the whole school. This done, the Superintendent, in a solemn manner, told him, that he had been so bad a boy, the teachers were under the painful necessity of sending him away from the school, and go he must. After a few words of admonition and advice, he gave out an appropriate hymn, and the whole school sang it standing. The teacher, by the direction of the Superintendent, then took the boy by the hand, led him out of the school, through the vestibule, through the enclosure, and through the gate; then closing the gate upon him, let him go. The boy wept; the teachers and scholars wept; the whole scene was most affecting. A salutary influence was exerted upon the whole school by this transaction, and it is hoped a lasting and most beneficial effect was produced upon the little exile himself. For who should come the very next Sabbath morning, but the same little boy, entreating with tears that he might be taken back, and promising that he would henceforward be a good boy. The teachers were not unmoved by his tears of penitence. They received him again into the school, and since his restoration he has been altogether another boy. He gives no trouble to his teacher since."

Another instance of discipline will show the sympathy of the school. "It appeared that two of the boys had misbehaved, and were, of course, injuring the rest of their class. The school was called to order, and the usual exercises suspended by the Superintendent. He then informed the children that something was about to take place quite unusual among them, but which, he regretted to say, was exceedingly necessary. After some very appropriate remarks, the two boys were called up to the head of the room, in view of the whole school. The teacher was then requested to state the offences of which they had been guilty; and every other teacher in the room desired to give his views of the matter. Afterwards the Superintendent spoke some time on the nature of their conduct, and the consequences that might result from it. "And now, children," said he, addressing the whole school, "what shall we do with these boys? Shall we expel them? I want every child who is in favor of their expulsion to rise." The children in favor of this course arose, and strange to say, there were nine only out of about one hundred and eighty, who were in favor of expulsion! The Superintendent then enquired what was to be done with the two boys,—they ought not to be suffered to injure those around them. "*Try them a little longer*," was the answer;—and accordingly they were permitted to remain on trial for six weeks longer."

In all such cases, the Superintendent requires judgment, firmness, and persuasion mingled with authority. But discipline of this kind, judiciously administered, will always do good. The whole school, teachers and pupils, will feel it.

It belongs to the Superintendent to direct the school. It is pretty well ascertained that seldom more than six scholars should be committed to one teacher; but to classify these, to put the right children together, to give the right scholar to the right teacher, belongs exclusively to the Superintendent. Here his wisdom will all be needed,—else he will be liable to place the stupid and the quick in contact,— the timid, trembling learner, under the bold, off-hand, decided teacher; and the rough, headstrong boy, under the gentle, timid teacher.

The Superintendent ought to arrange the classes, become acquainted with each class, individually, and make his supervision, as far as possible, extend to each member of every class. A general supervision, and a general care, are not enough. It is his business to open and close the school promptly;—to conduct all the exercises of the school, and to give all notices. He should open the school with prayer,—select the hymns for singing,—make the prayers and devotional exercises short, to the point, fervent, and reve-

rent. He should not address the school more than
once each Sabbath, by way of application or exhortation ; and then, he should not speak, as Witherspoon
used to tell his pupils, " before he has something to
say, and should always stop when he is done."   He
should not have more than *one point*, selected from
the lessons, upon which he tries to pour light, or with
which he tries to make an impression.   The greatest
difficulty with these exhortations is, that they are apt
to be too long,—far too long; and to become tedious
by sameness.   To avoid the latter evil, some read
stories and anecdotes; but stories and anecdotes are
very uninteresting, unless introduced to illustrate
some point of instruction.   To read and tell them
without illustrating some important weighty instruction, is to make your dinner of the spices which are
designed as a seasoning to your meat.   Always remember that the great art of public speaking is to
be short.   You can easily weary an audience of men,
and almost crucify one of children, by prolixity.
Even clergymen, who ought, of all men, to understand this, are often complained of for being too long ;
and any man is in danger of falling into prolixness,
in proportion as he is unaccustomed to public
speaking.

   2. *The second duty of the Superintendent is to
advise with the teachers as to the interests of the
school, and especially to aid in forming their characters.*

One of the deepest impressions which I should like to have made upon the Superintendent, is, that he has almost the whole responsibility of the prosperity of the school resting upon him, while he must have the help and co-operation of others to do the work. Let him feel that the most decided influence which he can exert upon the school is through the teachers,—not by direct precepts and teachings, or reproofs, perhaps, but by the general spirit which he creates and diffuses around him. Some of these teachers may be young and inexperienced: they want the example of one who knows how to let himself down to the heart of childhood. They will have their characters materially shaped and formed by the general character and spirit of the Superintendent. These teachers must at times be aroused,—for they have forgotten the object at which they aim;—the end for which they commenced their journey. He must do this by his spirit of prayer, and by an example that reproves, warns, and encourages. It will often be desirable to have a kind of review of the ground, with the teachers, by themselves,—to advise with them as to the progress made, the evils noticed or growing into notice, the plans pursued, and the improvements desired. Has the Superintendent, or any of the teachers, found any new light, or received any new hints from any source? Have they seen or read of improvements which might be introduced into their school? Have the teachers a habit of observation, so

5

that they can gather materials for teaching from every thing—or do they need hints on this point? The Superintendent ought not merely to notice who among the teachers is absent, and note it down, and at the next meeting, kindly, but decidedly ask the reason, but he ought also to be able to know the absences from each class,—to know the reasons of them from the teacher or the absentee,—to know as far as possible, the temperament, habits, and feelings of each scholar. And I would here suggest to a Superintendent to do,—what I am in the habit of doing, in regard to each member of the church under my pastoral charge. I keep a book in which I write the name of each person on the top of the page when he enters my church. The whole page under the name is left blank. This blank page is to be filled up at a future time,—by such memoranda as these;—when the person left us,—where he went,—when he died,—traits of character,—influence, &c. &c. By this means, I know what has become of all who have been under my charge. Such a private record, would, in the course of years become not merely interesting, but invaluable to the Superintendent; and its review would recall the past, and suggest much for improvement. It is the duty of the Superintendent to see that the scholars are visited stately by the teachers. In some schools this is done monthly, quarterly, or yearly. The most faithful and most successful teacher I have ever known, visited his class, or saw each scholar, every week. This duty must be insisted on by the Superintendent in his visits to the classes, and in his private conversations with the teachers. I say *statedly*, whether the visits be more or less frequent; for what is done by impulses is seldom well done. I need hardly say that in order to train the teachers to habits of regularity, and punctuality, the Superintendent must be a pattern himself. He must also insist on this as an indispensable requisite for the teacher. He can give hints, more or fewer, almost every Sabbath. One new hint and valuable suggestion dropped by the Superintendent each Sabbath, will soon make an impression that will be felt in the school.

Some Superintendents are frequently making innovations, introducing new plans, and making new discoveries of a more excellent way. Not unfrequently, indeed, we find a school in which a great improvement is said to be made, and with vast success. Awhile afterwards, you find the improvement laid aside, and the school fallen to its original state. I would not speak against improvements; I believe that they are yet to be made; but in most cases, the advantage consists solely in the increased zeal and effort with which the teachers apply their supposed improvement. The school is benefited so long as the novelty keeps alive exertion, and no longer. Hence, the great thing needed in this, and indeed, in every department of the Church, is an increased zeal, and an untiring energy in applying the means already in our hands. And laboring for the Church, whether as a minister at the altar, or as a teacher in the Sabbath School, I should study more to have the means already provided for our use, faithfully applied, than to invent new. This general remark, of course, applies to the whole movements of the Church; and if it be said that I am voting to keep the Church in the dark, and to have her grope her way in twilight, instead of walking in new and clearer light, I answer, that the history of the Church clearly shows, that changes, are not, of course, improvements;—and that she has lost more by experimenting upon theories, than in any other way. *Labor, hard, persevering, untiring labor, will make any Sabbath School prosper;* and without this, changes and inventions will soon be found to be useless. Let this thought be well understood by the Superintendent, and it will frequently prevent his wasting time in seeking to improve his school by new schemes, when the difficulty lies too deep to be reached by any such changes.

The school ought to be examined statedly,—and publicly,—once a month, or certainly once a quarter. These examinations will be conducted by the Superintendent; but he will wish to consult with the teachers in relation to them,—to have their advice, co-operation, and aid. They should be spirited, short, and with no desire of display. To meet these,—to make them pleasant to the school, satisfactory to the teach-

ers, instructive and useful to the parents and specta-
tors,—there must be previous training, and adapted-
ness in the teaching.

3. *Aid in the teachers' meeting, and feel responsible for it.*

Perhaps my own views may be singular, defective,
or erroneous; but my impression decidedly is, that
the teachers ought to meet weekly, for the purpose
of obtaining a good knowledge of the lesson, and of
mutual benefit by prayer and conversation; and that,
as a general rule, the Pastor of the church ought to
be the instructer, when the teachers sit down to get
their lessons.   My reasons are these:—

1. The Pastor is responsible for what food is given
to the lambs committed to his charge.   The Sabbath
School takes the children, in a measure, out of his
hand, and that becomes the Pastor to the little flock;
but it does not, and it cannot, release him from the
responsibility of seeing that the word is "rightly divided."   He can see that this is done only by sitting
down weekly with the teachers, and going over the
lesson familiarly, and teaching them just as he would
have the lambs taught.   This will release his mind
from any fear lest wrong interpretations are given to
Scripture,—lest wrong impressions are made upon the
mind of childhood, or lest modes of thinking or of
teaching prevail, such as he cannot but feel are mistaken, useless, consuming time, if not in themselves,
dangerous.

5*

2. The Pastor is, as a general thing, the best qualified to aid the teachers to understand the lesson. He
is, or ought to be, familiar with the tenor and spirit
of the Bible, knows its great plan, and has that in
mind when looking at its several parts; he has long
been in the habit of studying it, for the purpose of
understanding and explaining its meaning, has helps
and aids by which to understand it, which few possess; and, he has the habit of communicating thought,
and ought to be able, in a given time, say an hour,
to communicate more thought than any other man.
To " be apt to teach," is one essential ingredient in
his character. What would cost another man days
of hard study, and perhaps weeks, not knowing on
what books to lay the hand for information, the minister can at once communicate; for the ground is
familiar to him, and he has been over it all repeatedly.

3. The Pastor should aid the teachers in their
meeting, because it will give him a deeper interest in
the school. I have known teachers to shut out the
minister from all their meetings, from giving his
views on the lesson, and then bitterly complain because he took no deeper interest in the school. But
who can feel interest in a factory in which he never
entered,—in a stock of which he owns none,—or in a
business with which he has nothing to do ? I never
have known any schools so well conducted, so efficient
and spiritual, as those in which the minister exerted
his influence by means of the teachers' meeting. It

binds the Pastor and the teachers together; it prevents all feelings of jealousy and complaint, and it makes the school the nursery of hearts whose piety is kindled at the very altar. There are, undoubtedly, exceptions to these remarks; and perhaps I am speaking too much of my own delightful experience.

But besides, or in addition to this hour devoted weekly to obtaining a correct and familiar knowledge of the lesson, perhaps at its close, there should be a meeting under the direction of the Superintendent, to review the last Sabbath,—to lay plans for the future, to talk over difficulties and discouragements, cases of discipline, irregularities observable in the teachers and in the scholars, the state of religion, and the means to be used to advance it, &c. This meeting should be a sort of " to-do-good meeting," for mutual improvement, and for the benefit of the school. It might be short; and if there was little to say, at times, the season would be no less profitably employed in prayer, and in seeking aid and wisdom from God. But even without such meetings, for the purpose of going over the lesson, and of laying plans and the like, your school cannot prosper. As a general thing, *teachers with whom I have been acquainted, have no adequate conception of the amount of furniture necessary in order to teach a class in the Sabbath school.* Some schools have never had these meetings with a view to study the lesson; others have but part of the teachers present. Those schools, and

those teachers, who are neglecting these meetings, are
suffering a loss,—to say nothing of enjoyment,—which
is unspeakably great. I have seen teachers who felt
too wise or too indifferent to attend such meetings,—
when they came to teach the lesson, find it hard work
to fill up the hour, and have had to fold their hands,
and be silent for the last few minutes,—wondering
why the time to close the school had not arrived.
The Superintendent ought to be as particular in inquiring for absences from the teachers' meeting, as
from the school on the Sabbath.

The increase of the school is a very important part
of the duties of the Superintendent. Unless great
pains are taken, every school will diminish,—by the
removal of scholars,—by deaths,—by the indifference
of parents,—by the age of pupils, and by other
causes. The Superintendent will find his little congregation diminishing from year to year, unless he
make this an object of special attention. There will
be new families moving into your precincts, new children growing into the age to attend, but who, through
negligence, do not enter the school, and there will always be materials to fill up the school, at least equal
to what are withdrawn from it. The object of the
teachers is not merely to keep the school full, but to
bring every child in the community under the influence of religious instruction. Let the Superintendent
advise, encourage, and co-operate with, the teachers,

Superintendent should not be dogmatical.

and have one, and in cities two, special efforts made every year, to fill up the school with new scholars.

But let the Superintendent be careful lest he become dogmatical; 'lest in consultation,' to use the somewhat obscure, but powerful language of John Foster, ' his manner indicate, that when he is equally with the rest in possession of the circumstances of the case, he does not at all expect to hear any opinions that shall correct his own; but is satisfied that either his present view of the subject is the right one, or that his own mind must originate that which shall be so. This striking difference will be apparent between him and his associates, that *their* manner of receiving *his* opinions is that of agreement or dissent: *his* manner of receiving *theirs* is that of sanction or rejection. He has the tone of authority deciding on what they say, but never of submitting to the rejection of what he himself says. Their coincidence of views does not give him a firmer assurance of being right, nor their dissent any other impression than that of their want of judgment. If his feeling took the distinct form of reflection, it would be, ' mine is the business of comprehending and devising, and I am here to rule this company, and not to consult them: I want their docility, not their arguments; I seek not their co-operation in thinking, but to determine their concurrence in what is already thought for them.' Thus many suggestions which seem important to those who make them, will be disposed of by him with so slight in attention, that it will seem very disrespectful to those, who may possibly refuse to admit that he is wiser than all men, or that they themselves are idiots.' All this must be studiously avoided.

It may sometimes become a question whether, in a single village, for example, the same set of teachers shall have one school, or several; i. e. one large, central school, or several different branches. It is impossible, in answer to all such questions, to do any thing more than to lay down general principles. There can be no question that a large school has many decided advantages over a small one, or several small ones. These advantages are obvious. There is more excitement and interest in the teachers and in the scholars in a large school, than in a small one. The Library is managed to better advantage, every thing is on a larger scale, and is more animated. If the responsibility of the Superintendent is increased, so are his means of doing good, and so are the motives to exertion. There is something in sympathy, mysterious indeed, but exceedingly powerful, and which, in a large school, may be used to great advantage. We know its influence upon the Senator, upon the Advocate, and especially upon the pulpit orator. The man who is effective, powerful, and almost beyond what is human, before a large audience, is tame when speaking to a score of people. Probably the man has never yet lived, who could long be an orator before a small assembly. Even Cicero could not detiver his famous Oration in behalf of the Poet Archias, though addressed to a single man, without having all that was learned and great in Rome to hear him. People in the country know that their minister speaks more eloquently, and the meetings are more interesting in the summer, than in the winter,—because the meetings are more fully attended.

Having made allusion to a certain principle, perhaps I shall not have a better place than this, in which to give my views and feelings to those who guide our Sabbath Schools, on the possibility of perverting the human sympathies in promoting religion.

I have long been of the opinion, that regular philosophical principles are as really employed in revivals of religion, under the direction of the Holy Spirit, as in any other case. The whole Jewish system of worship was designed and arranged to meet the social sympathies of man. Read the sublime description of the march of the children of Israel as they followed the cloudy pillar, which the luminous, but too sceptical pen of Jahn has drawn. Read the songs of Degrees in the Psalms of David, which the gladdened tribes sang, as they went three times a year up the hill of Zion, to meet the scattered nation, and to bow before God in solemn worship. They met on the sacred hill of Zion,—mingled their songs, their sacrifices, their prayers, their joys and sorrows, formed new acquaintances, revived old friendships, and learned the condition of every tribe and corner of the land.

John the Baptist made use of the same principle; so did Christ, and so did Paul, in that remarkable instance when he held up his clanking chains, and wished them all Christians like himself, " except these bonds !" The iron of those chains went to the heart, and the king and all the court rose up hastily. One more such appeal would have opened the flood-gates of sympathy, and the king would have felt that he was a man. The most remarkable instance of the use of the social principle by Christ, was when the curious, gazing crowd were for a short time all in raptures, cutting down branches of trees, and even stripping off their garments to do him homage, as he gloriously entered Jerusalem on the borrowed ass, to fulfil the words of prophecy. The Hosanna-Rabba began on the mountain east of Jerusalem, and ran down the mountain's side like wild-fire, passed over the valley of Jehoshaphat, till it had gone even through the crowd of market-men in the court of the temple, and reached the little children within. ·

Scarcely any thing among men is so awful and appalling as is this principle, when highly awakened and wrongly directed. Let any one read the fearful history of the Reign of Terror in France, when men wore the ears of their butchered fellow-citizens in their hats for cockades,—and women were stripped to the elbows, and ancle-deep in blood, butchering the multitudes as they were brought out of prison,— and when the painter David, with a soul refined by the most refining art, for days together, assisted to condemn and execute victims, that he might see how the blood gushed, and how the livid countenance of sudden death looked,—so that he might transfer these to the canvas! Could the history of the dark world be written by the pen of the archangel, it would seem impossible to exhibit more awful scenes of guilt and sin. Read the history of the charges made and received in the battle of Waterloo, and inquire if you could gather fifty thousand slain upon an area of two miles square, were it not for the awful power which sympathy gives, when once excited, and so fearfully directed.

Mather's Magnalia, and the history of the Salem Witch-craft, will afford abundant and notable examples of what I mean. It seemed as if common sense and conscience were thrown away, when they most needed these commodities. The whole, or almost the whole, may be traced to the power of sympathy.

We all witnessed its-power, harmlessly exhibiting, and expending itself, when Lafayette came to this country on a visit, a few years since. A minister of the Gospel told me that he was on the common in Boston when Lafayette arrived,—amid the rushing, the enthusiasm,—and the wild waves of sympathy. "I could not help weeping," said he, "and all around me were weeping."

"Pray, Sir, for what were you all weeping?"

"O, I don't know. I hardly got near enough the

General to see his figure distinctly; but the bells were all ringing, the cannon roaring, the people shouting,—it was *such* a time! and every body was so much delighted, that all were weeping, and so I wept too!"

A very philosophical reason, if not a very good one! Probably few could have been by his side without feeling the power of sympathy, and weeping too. But why were they weeping? Because the rest did,— and this is reason enough.

Who has not been amused at Dr. Franklin's description of the effects of Whitfield's eloquence upon himself? The Doctor had gold, silver, and copper, in his pocket, but resolved that he would not give a copper. He sat, heard, sympathised: first resolved that he would give the copper; then the silver; and when the time came, in went copper, silver, gold and all.

Now we use this principle very abundantly, and, in general, rightly, in religion. Let any one attend the great anniversaries of our benevolent Societies for the first time. He sits and hears the glowing, thrilling, overwhelming appeals there made, and is captivated, melted, and almost delirious. He resolves that he will now do more for the salvation of men in one year, than he has done in any ten preceding years. He goes out, thrilling, aching, weeping. The next day he feels lassitude, and undoubtedly has some feelings not greatly unlike those which the votaries of the theatre have. This was not religion; it was

sympathy wrought up to a high pitch of excitement.
Just suppose this man to be destitute of religion. Let
him see all this, feel all this, and have all his sympathies highly awakened; let him there resolve that he
will hereafter live and act as a Christian. He leaves
the meeting with this solemn resolution: *is* he a
Christian? Possibly he may be; but most probably
he is not:—it is only an unsanctified feeling kindled up.

This sympathy may be used, and must be used, in
the Sabbath School. I introduce the subject to
guard against making it a standard of action, and
mistaking its power for the power of the Holy Spirit.
In a school where the Superintendent and teachers
are faithful, there will be seasons of special tenderness, susceptibility, and seriousness. The teachers
will unconsciously, and unavoidably, and very properly, make use of the principle of sympathy. There
will be ardent feelings among teachers and among
pupils; these will be kindled to a glow. A teacher
finds a scholar tender, or awakened. He urges him
to submit to God,—gets him to go home with him,—
prays with him, and tells the scholar to delay no
longer,—now is the time,—and he must now kneel
down, and pray, and give his heart up to God. He
himself feels as if a crisis had come; and that the
salvation of the scholar turns upon this hour; the
scholar feels so too. He is highly,—unspeakably ex
cited. The whole system trembles. He kneels,

prays, makes the consecration, and says he gives himself up to the service of God.

"Do you feel any differently from what you did
before ?"

"O yes, widely different."

"Well, do you now solemnly resolve to be a Christian from this hour ?"

"Certainly I do. I never felt so before ;—I *will*
serve God, come what may."

Now I do not say that this scholar is *not* a Christian, or that this is not conversion; it may be, and it
may not be. And here is the danger of such machinery. Like steam, it is powerful, and may be made
to do almost any thing, if properly directed; would
it were as easy to direct and manage human sympathy when excited, as to manage steam.

Could this sympathy always be under the direction
of devoted, discriminating, judicious, well-balanced
minds, there would be comparatively little danger.
But as this is a day of excited sympathy, as the
young are easily excited, as multitudes have thus
been aroused and have mistaken this excitement for
conversion, the Superintendent should understand it.
The teachers should understand it. Just in proportion as the passions are excited, let the cause be what
it may, the judgment is unfitted for its office. In this
state, no man can judge correctly and surely of himself or of others. It seems to be a settled principle
of action with some teachers, that if they can only

get men excited, they have no fears but all will be well, and the more excited they become, the sooner conversion will take place. I cannot too earnestly recommend that every Superintendent should own, and often read, Edwards on the Affections. The reader will understand me to say that I have but little fear of the abuse of this principle, except on one single point;—viz., *that of mistaking excited feeling for the conversion of the soul to God.* How often was this mistaken by the old church! Read the history of their joy on the banks of the Red Sea, when Pharaoh was destroyed,—of their solemn vows at the receiving of the law, and in multitudes of similar cases. Might I specify evils which I have seen result from the abuse of the sympathies,—what I have said above, would seem any thing, rather than an unmeaning digression.

4. *It belongs to the duties of the Superintendent to lay plans to raise up new teachers.*

In the late arrangement of the United States' government to send several ships in an exploring expedition to the South Seas, they had to build a number of new vessels. Why did they? They had ships enough, good ships, and of the right size; but they were not built for this business, nor adapted to it. It is so with every thing. The Indian constructs the canoe which is to be used on the swift river, differently from what he does, if it is to go on the smooth lake. The horse, the dog must have early and careful training, if they attain

6 *

their highest perfection; and we all know that a boy becomes perfect in any business very much in proportion to the age at which he began to apply himself to it. There will be a very great gain to the power of the Sabbath School, when we can have teachers who are raised up, and trained for years for this express purpose.

The Superintendent should early and constantly lay his plans for this. For this purpose he must know each scholar personally, his habits, modes of thinking, talent of communicating, and, above all, the condition of his heart. Were there no other reason why he should strive earnestly for the conversion of his school, this would be one of great weight. As soon as practicable, I would organize classes of those who give promise of becoming suitable teachers, place them under the instruction of the very best teachers you have. I would not have the idea very prominent before the minds of these classes, that they are fitting to become teachers,—perhaps it would not be best to say anything about it to them for some time; but the teacher ought to understand it, to feel the full weight of the charge,—to make it his constant desire to instruct these properly, and his earnest prayer, to lead them to Christ and to holiness. No judicious means ought to be omitted to lead them to God. The teacher should feel that not a single exertion should be relaxed so long as there is one who is not converted to God. The Superintendent should feel this; and the teachers at their prayer-meetings should make them the subjects of fervent prayer. These classes should be selected with care, formed on right principles, led by an even hand, and most thoroughly and judiciously instructed. In order to do this, the Superintendent ought to bear in mind unceasingly, that *his* school must be a model. He must try to be, and to have his teachers, and the whole school, just what he would wish these scholars to make *their* schools, when they come to have the care of schools. · He must indulge himself in no habits which they may not safely follow. For example, I know one Superintendent who as regularly sleeps during the sermon, as the sermon is preached. I doubt whether he has heard a sermon for years. And yet, when he comes to take the head of the school, he feels that every word which *he* says, must be attended to, and would feel that a scholar ought almost to be sent from school, who should sleep during one of his exhortations! I know of another, who uses tobacco in such profusion, that his person is slovenly almost to loathing, and his breath is positively annoying. Can such men feel that they are setting examples which the teachers and the school may safely follow? What an exhibition would a Sabbath School make, should they all sleep soundly through every sermon? It may be said that this is an infirmity, and that such men cannot avoid sleeping in the house of God,—the habit is too strong. I reply, that if for twenty or

even ten years, they have been inducing habits,
which, if followed by all, would destroy all effects of
the Gospel, and even public worship itself, it is time
for them to begin to form better habits; and if they
will not do that, I have no hesitation in saying, it is
time for them to leave superintending the Sabbath
School. Some Superintendents have a lightness
about their conversation and manner, which seem
wholly incompatible with a deep sense of responsibility; or a foppery about their dress which indicates
great thought and care about their beautiful persons, and which cannot be imitated by the school
without ruining it.

It will not be necessary to specify all the little
things which must be avoided by the Superintendent.
Let him constantly feel that his is to be a Model
School for the imitation of all those whom he is endeavoring to qualify to become teachers, and he will
be likely to walk circumspectly.

5. *It is a part of the Superintendent's duties to
form plans by which the older scholars shall be kept
in the school.*

It is a great mistake running through all classes
of this country and of this age, to suppose that the
mind can be matured and educated quick, and while
it is young. Our young men must be educated and
all ripe for active life by the time they have completed their teens; and our girls, almost by the time
they have entered them. Hence the Sabbath School

First method of doing this.

has been considered a sort of nursery, for the benefit
of children; and as soon as scholars have become
mature, so that they can begin fully to reap the advantages of the system, they are taken away, or
they take themselves away. As a general thing,
the scholar who has arrived at the age at which he
feels that he is too old to belong to the Sabbath
school, would receive more good by the next year's
instructions, than by any four or five of the previous
years. The Superintendent will find it somewhat
difficult to alter this fashion; but he should strive to
do it; and he can do very much, even if he cannot
do all that he would wish. I will suggest a few
hints as to the manner in which it may be done.

(a.) *Make the impression that it is dishonorable to
leave the school without a regular written dismission from the Superintendent.*

Let this impression once be made, and the character thus acquired will be worth much in after life. I
have known of several young men coming from Europe
to this country, who have found their certificates of
having been regular members of the Sabbath School,
a number of years, worth more to them than all the
other papers which they brought. Such a certificate
gives confidence, that the character of the bearer is
based upon a valuable foundation. Now, if you are in
the habit of giving a correct certificate when the pupil
leaves the school, and can make the impression that it
is really valuable, you will find the scholars more will-

ing to continue in the school; and if it be disreputa-
ble to leave without such a certificate, few will be
willing to lose what they have been so long in acquiring. In order to effect the object aimed at,
every Superintendent will see the necessity of not
receiving scholars, except in very extraordinary circumstances, from other schools, without a regular
written dismission.

(b.) *Do not let the older scholars get in advance
of the teachers.*

Some teachers are absolutely stationary; they acquire no new thoughts, or if they do, they do not retain them long enough to make them of any use.
They read little, think less, and soon have their
stock of thoughts exhausted. The scholars are sure
to know the depth of their teacher. They will be
inquisitive, quick, bright, and it may be, will go beyond him. As soon as the pupil has arrived at that
point, he will be uneasy,—his duties will become
irksome, and he will wish to leave the school. The
remedy is obvious. Teaching must be provided,
which is sufficiently advanced to meet the wants of
every class, and of every individual. This is a point
at which the Superintendent ought carefully to look;
and perhaps he will find that the uneasiness and
restlessness of the scholars have been blamed, when
the fault is not wholly theirs.

(c.) *Be careful to keep the library filled with books*

suited to the advanced age and improvement of your oldest scholars.

This is one of the best bonds to keep the scholars with you, and one on which you may usually rely with certainty. Books of a high character should be selected, kept in such order as to be inviting; and I am not sure that it would not be wise to have a library separate and distinct for the sole use of the older scholars. I once made the experiment of forming a library for young men and young ladies separate from the Sabbath School. There were shortly several hundred volumes gathered, and they were probably of much greater use than the same number of books are to a Sabbath School in the ordinary way.

(d.) *Labor and pray for the conversion of the older scholars, if not already converted.*

This will give them the spirit of little children. As soon as a scholar is converted to God, he feels that the Sabbath School is more precious than ever before. His pride will not take him from it, for his pride is subdued, and his feelings will lead him to stay. This is the great thing to be attained. Once bring these learners into the fold of Christ, and they will then continue in the school, will improve rapidly, will add a blessing to the school, and you will have the pleasure of seeing them sitting at the feet of Jesus, like a young church, fitting to meet temptation, to do his will, and to receive his rewards.

(e.) *When the time arrives, when the scholars can be more benefited by going into the Bible classes under the care of the Pastor of the church, by all means encourage them to do it.*

This supposes that every Pastor has a male and a female Bible class, which ought to be the case, extraordinaries excepted. These classes will lie at the foundation of the church, and of all that is good among you. I am aware that it is sometimes the case that the Superintendent and teachers are unwilling to transfer their precious charge ; and they feel as a Pastor feels, when his flock is passing out of his hands into those of others. It is human nature, *to wish to keep all the ground which we have ever occupied.* This renders dismissed ministers sometimes unpleasant parishioners,—it makes churches unwilling to colonize and plant new churches, and it makes Sabbath School teachers sometimes clash with the true interests of the cause of religion. Remember that though this is human nature, it is human nature fallen, and the principle is a selfish one.

I have now mentioned, briefly, the duties of the Superintendent. I need not again go over the whole ground in describing the traits of character which he needs, and which he needs assiduously to cultivate. A few words will be sufficient to sum up the most prominent points of character needed.

1 *Age and experience ;*—In order to have a knowledge of the human heart,—a deep knowledge of

his own heart,—the habit of close self-examination,—
in order to have the confidence of the teachers, the
community, and the scholars;—in order to speak and
pray in public acceptably, and appropriately;—and
in order to have that weight accompany his advice,
directions, and instructions, which can be obtained
only by a character known, and tried, and approved.

2. *Devotedness to religion;*—that he may be a
man of prayer, by which alone wisdom that is profitable to direct can be obtained;—that he may be
unwearied in his attempts to aid the teachers, that
he may thoroughly understand the lesson himself, and
communicate it with a simple and sincere desire to
save the soul.

3. *Evenness of temper;*—that the school may feel
that the hand which holds the helm, never varies,—
that the teachers may find their intercourse pleasant, and may go to him as to a friend, without ever
expecting to be wounded by irritability;—that parents
may find it pleasant to go to the school, and witness
the improvement of their children,—that strangers
may find a courteous reception, and their visit be rendered profitable. Self-government is invaluable,—
indispensable to the Superintendent.

4. *Great promptness of character;*—that the
school may be opened and closed with great exact-
ness, that no exercises may be long and tedious, that
the teachers and school may know what to depend

7

upon,—that they may know that no changes will take place without great deliberation and thought.

5. *Growing humility*,—otherwise, his station, the deference exacted and paid, and the · influence exerted, will make him a Diotrephes. He must cultivate piety in his own heart, and become like the angels who are ministers to worms of the dust, and are good ministers in proportion as they are humble. True exaltation and greatness consist in great humility.

6. *An example in all that is good;*—he should be fervent, simple, unaffected in prayer, increasing in a knowledge of the Bible, prompt, liberal, noble in charity, untiring in labors, warm in Christian intercourse, growing in all the Christian graces, and living for the salvation of the earth.

Such should be the SUPERINTENDENT of the Sabbath School.

CHAPTER III.

In the enumeration of the qualities desirable in a Sabbath School teacher, it is not to be supposed that every teacher will possess them all in due proportion. Few characters are perfectly symmetrical; and where there are great excellencies, there are usually great defects. The latter must be overlooked for the sake of the former. The success of men in doing good to the souls of men, from the apostle down to the distributor of tracts, depends greatly upon the state of the heart. Indeed, without a right state of heart, all other qualities will for the most part be useless. I begin to describe the Sabbath School teacher, then, by saying, that

1. *He should be a devotedly pious man.*

The office of a teacher is, and must be, one of self-denial; the labor necessary to acquire the lesson to be taught, to understand the best way of communicating truth, the stupidity, restlessness, listlessness, and trying appearance of the class from week to week, the want of government at home, and the utter indifference of most of the parents, the return of the same routine of duties, the obscurity of the station, the amount of labor bestowed unknown and unappreciated, and the entire loss of so much labor, all unite to make the office of a teacher a drudgery and a burden. I cannot express my own views on this point better than to give an extract of a letter addressed to me by a Superintendent,—a lady,—and one of great experience and character. " My own opinion is, that the Sabbath School teacher sustains the same relation to the children of his charge, that a Pastor does to his flock. He is emphatically the spiritual guide of the little ones committed to him, and his responsibility as touching the eternal interests of the six or eight deathless souls who cluster around him on the Sabbath, seems to me to be precisely that which the Pastor sustains to the same number who sit under *his* ministry, and receive from him the bread of life. If children are blessed with pious parents, who not only teach them to read the word of God, but are wont to enforce it with their admonitions and prayers, why place them, during the sacred hours of the Sabbath, under the care of one who cannot be expected, with a heart overflowing with earnest desires for their salvation, to point them to a crucified Savior ? If, on the contrary, the neglected one is from a family where the holy name of God never

falls upon his ear, except from a profane and intemperate father, and where no praying mother com-
mends this child to God, (and alas! how many such
are found in our schools!) is the class of the teacher
who has never felt the love of Jesus, the refuge for
this ignorant and wretched child? I have often, as a
Superintendent, in my experience, had my feelings
severely tried on this very point, although of late
years no teachers have been admitted to the school
with which I am connected, except such as entertain
the hope that they are the children of God. A child
is introduced into the school, perhaps well known to
be greatly neglected at home. My anxious eye is
invariably turned to the seat occupied,—not by the
cold, uninterested teacher, even though a professor
of religion,—but by the devoted, praying teacher,
who constantly pours into the ear, and presses home
upon the hearts of her pupils, the truths of God's
holy word. If no vacancy is found in such a class, I
feel that almost a *wrong* is inflicted upon the
child who is committed to the charge of one who
feels but little for the priceless gems she is forming
for eternity. I can well recollect, a few years
since, an aged and holy mother in Israel entered
our school, leading by the hand two little grand-
children. As I went forward to meet her, she took
my hand, and addressing me in a familiar manner, with a solemnity of countenance, and an im-
pressiveness of voice I can never forget, she said,

7 *

' these are my grand-children ; *remember* that you take care of their souls.   I commit them to you.'   I felt constrained to take these to the class of a teacher whom I knew to be faithful, and to repeat the solemn admonition I had received.   It may be possible, and there probably are cases, where it would be more desirable, than to leave them without a Sabbath School, to place children who have no religious instruction, under the charge of those who do not possess true piety, but who are competent to teach them to read the word of God.   In desolate portions of our country where Christians are few in number, such teachers, under the direction of a devoted Superintendent, who as far as possible will endeavor to make up this deficiency, by giving special religious instruction himself, may be better than none ; but where large churches in our cities and villages contain great numbers of the followers of Christ, every method should be used to impress upon their hearts the importance of fulfilling the injunction of our blessed Master, " feed my lambs."

" I know it is said that teachers in great numbers have been converted in the Sabbath School, and therefore, we should admit those to be teachers who have not piety, for the sake of doing them good.   But I ask, what is the great, absorbing design of the institution of Sabbath Schools ?   Is it not to train up the rising generation for God ?   If this be its first and commanding object, then clearly our duty is to make every thing bear upon securing this great end. A teacher is now and then converted; but how many children may have passed from under his care unwarned and unholy into eternity; or, led astray by his example, others may have entered upon the busy concerns of life with hearts unsubdued by the grace of God! The providence of God may have taken from one a beloved father, and his heart softened by afflictions, and under the influence of the Holy Spirit, he may be just upon the point of submitting to the blessed Savior. He goes to the Sabbath School, but his teacher is not watching with eager solicitude to see the tear of penitence, and to lead the burdened sinner to the foot of the cross. The inquiry which was ready to break from his lips, is driven back, by the look of indifference from his unconscious teacher. The blind cannot lead the blind. A Superintendent, under such circumstances, if faithful, will not fail to do *his* duty; but I am persuaded that no Superintendent can gain that influence over the children of the School which each individual teacher may possess over his class. Those who have had most experience cannot have failed to observe the strong hold which teachers have upon the hearts of the children of their class; and how astonishing is the influence exerted over them by their faithfulness or unfaithfulness. I will mention one fact to illustrate this point. On the distant shores of China lives and labors a youthful missionary, who, I think, was but twenty-one years

of age, when h left a happy home, to go and fulfil
the dying command of his Master, ' go preach the
Gospel to every creature under heaven.' He was
nurtured in our Sabbath School from his earliest boyhood; and when of sufficient age, filled with much
zeal and faithfulness, for several years, the responsible office of teacher. On the evening preceding his
departure from us, at our accustomed weekly meeting
of teachers, when taking his leave, he made this remark, " Do not be discouraged in your work. I am
indebted to my faithful Sabbath School teacher for
the first desires which were kindled in my bosom, and
my final determination to be a missionary of the
cross." It is not certainly for us to say what other
way the providence of God might have opened to lead
to the same result, had this lovely youth been placed
under the care of a teacher possessing a different
spirit; but this seems certain, that this teacher, who
had in charge the training of the future missionary,
will find him a bright gem in the crown of his rejoicing."

I know I shall be pardoned for this long extract
of a letter so judicious, and so much to the point.

Let the question be plainly asked—*what* is to be
taught in our Sabbath Schools? And the answer is
plain,—the way of salvation. Each child is to be
trained up so far as is possible, for the service of God.
Need the question be discussed, who are to be the
guides, as a general rule, to lead the child to the

Lamb of God? It certainly is a work which none but a pious heart can appreciate,—it is to be done by means which none but a heart taught of God can understand and use,—and it requires a continuance of virtues which none but a renewed heart can exercise. I am confident I speak the language of thousands when I say, that as a parent seeking the best, the eternal welfare of my children, I should not,—could not, commit such interests into hands which were not guided by a pious heart. My own feelings have done more to convince me, and to enlighten me on this point, than pages of argument.

We want more than the professor of religion for our Sabbath School;—we want *holiness*—that holiness which, in times that try men's souls, would give up all, and go even to the stake, with the song of life upon the tongue;—that holiness which in these times, can resist the temptations of Mammon, the bewitching allurements of the world,—which are almost as trying to piety as persecutions and the stake,—and which can live for God and his glory.

What, then, do I say to those who are already engaged in teaching the Sabbath School, but who have no evidence that they have been born of God? Shall they at once leave their seats, their classes, and retire? I reply, no: but I say to such, just as I would say to ministers of the Gospel, who should confess that they have never felt the power of religion on their own hearts;—shall they leave the pulpit, and

cease to preach—because they are blind leaders of
the blind? I say to such,—no! brethren, no! You
have ordination-vows upon you. You have put your
hand to the plough; you may not look back;—but
you ought not again to go into that pulpit with an
unholy heart. You ought this hour to go before God,
and with a broken heart and a contrite spirit, to confess your sins, ask for pardon, and sin no more. I do
not ask you to stop preaching because you have an
unholy heart; but I *do* ask you no longer to be so
basely ungrateful as to cherish such a heart. Just
so I say to the unconverted teacher in the Sabbath
School; you do wrong,—you profess to teach the
child what you do not understand,—you try to make
him love that which you do not love yourself; you
profess by the art of teaching, to show the child that
his soul is the great object of life, when you are indifferent and stupid about your own. This is wrong
every way. Would the child pray? Your example
is against him. Would he work out his own salvation with fear and trembling? Your example shows
him that it is not necessary. Would he weep in secret places over his sins, and a hard heart? He is
afraid to tell his feelings to you, knowing that you
are a stranger to them.

2. *The second qualification of a good teacher will
cover the extensive ground of* GOOD HABITS.

This may seem at first view to embrace the whole
of personal character. Perhaps it does. I shall not

st. p to analyze, but at once proceed to mention the habits desirable in a Sabbath School teacher.

(a.) *Perseverance in whatever you undertake.*

No one ought to enlist in this cause without having first well counted the cost; and having once enrolled yourself as a teacher, let there be no turning back. Some are never willing to walk the same path that other people do,—they must strike out something new, and will persevere so long as they feel that they have a new road, and that it will not lead, ultimately, into that which is occupied by other people. Others will set out with great zeal for a time, and it seems as if they were to do something great; but their zeal soon cools, and their courage relaxes. Like some of the beautifully equipped soldiers, who have never known real, hard service, they at the first call of the bugle move off to admiration; but a few miles destroys all their courage, and even their arms seem too burdensome. We do not want soldiers for parade-days, who can show a nice uniform, and who can manœuvre to admiration when on parade, but who cannot endure a long march, and who are worn out by a single campaign of hard service. Remember that you came into the business voluntarily,—of your own choice; and if there were reasons why you should commence these duties, there are many more why you should continue in them. You feel like shrinking away, at times, and can say, 'O that I had the wings of a dove, then would I fly away and be at rest.' You see no fruits of your labors, and you feel discouraged! You cannot persevere! Let me tell you that if we might fall back when we meet with discouragements, then would most of the ministers of the Gospel take off the harness, and retire from their anxieties and responsibilities. I venture to say, there is not a minister in the land who prays for faithfulness, and who weeps over his own deficiencies, that does not at times wish, to retire and leave the work, were it not that he is bound by conscience. You find that the retired, but repeated labors of the school-room are fatiguing,—that you are cut off from many hours of reading, meditation, and even devotion,—that you cannot often go and see your friends abroad, because your class cannot well be left; that you cannot spare time to get your lessons, and besides all this, you do not see that you do any good! I reply, that the children whom you instruct may be young, may be ignorant, may be spoiled by bad example at home,—yours may be the only impressions about religion they ever receive; they are soon to be a part of the nation, and will help to form its character;—and above all, they have immortal souls to be saved or lost. Would you not condemn a minister of Christ who should turn back, and give up his profession because he met with discouragements? Would you not blame a missionary of the cross, who left his field and came home with his hands hanging down, and his heart failing him, crying out, 'that he met with difficulties, and could not persevere?' You do not persevere,—and you chill the hearts and freeze the zeal of all who are engaged with you. You cease to persevere, and perhaps your class is scattered,—perhaps others become discouraged, and your example may, for a time, destroy the school. You desert a work which God has most abundantly blessed,—by which he has raised up multitudes of new friends, and by which thousands have been led to heaven ;— you abandon the work, too, at a day when we need a thousand active, devoted men, to every one whom we now have. Stand, then, at your post, and in your lot. Do not attempt too much at once. Do not be fickle, and change often. I admire the spirit of Mr. Charles, one of the most successful teachers in Wales, —a man of a noble spirit. "My maxim has been for many years past," says he, "*to aim at great things, but if I cannot accomplish great things, to do what I can, and be thankful for the least success,* and still follow on without being discouraged at the day of small things, or by unexpected reverses. For years I have laid it down as a maxim to guide me, *never to give up a place in despair of success. If one way does not succeed, new means must be tried ; and if I see no increase this year, perhaps I may the next.* I almost wish to blot the word *impossible* from my vocabulary, and obliterate it from the minds of my brethren." You must not expect to see the mind of each scholar shoot up, and mature at once,—

R

to see old habits at once thrown off, the effects of a bad training at once counteracted. It will require time, and persevering labor. "We cannot and we do not expect that the human marble, (to borrow the figure of an old philosopher,) is to leap out upon us, self-formed, and self-wrought, from the quarry. But it requires the force and the art of the chisel, to fashion it into all those shapes of grace and beauty which it ought to wear." Teachers are moral sculptors, and must be contented to labor long and faithfully to fit these models of all that is good, for the various niches of society. One single teacher in the school who has genuine perseverance, will do more for that school than a score of fickle, changeable, and easily-discouraged teachers. Who can help admiring the following specimen of this quality? "I knew a pious young man who was sustaining himself at a literary institution by the labors of his own hands, and almost as a matter of course, the true energies of Christianity began to develop themselves. His feelings became much affected by the spiritual condition of a populous neighborhood, which had never enjoyed religious privileges, and consequently did not appreciate them. He visited the families of that neighborhood from house to house, and endeavored to open a religious meeting among them. They would permit no such thing. Not discouraged, this young man turned to the children, and went round and invited them, one by one, to meet him on Sunday-mornings in a Sunday School. Several children acceded to the proposal, and then he again went round to find a room for them to meet in; but every door was closed against him. He told the children to meet him under a shady tree upon a grassy bank; and thither they came, and he prayed with them, and taught them to study the word of God, and the children were delighted with their Sunday School. So it went on from week to week, with increasing interest, and increasing numbers, till one Lord's day opened with a cold storm of rain. The teacher repaired to his tree at the usual time, supposing some few children might be there; and there indeed he found almost his whole school; wet and cold, it is true, but they had warm hearts in their bosoms, and how could they forego the enjoyments of their beloved Sunday School for a single morning? The teacher took off his hat and prayed as usual for the blessedness of God upon the exercises, and began to teach, when a man in the place told him that for *that* time he might take the children into his stable. The teacher turned to the children and said: 'This man offers us the use of his stable, and it was in a stable that Jesus Christ took shelter when he was a little child. Let us go.' This is what I mean by *the energies of Christianity.*"

2. *The second habit to be mentioned is that of* PUNCTUALITY.

The teacher should constantly bear in mind that the great thing which he wishes to accomplish is to

form proper habits in his class. These form the character; for as has been quaintly remarked, " man is
only a bundle of habits." The remark of Robert
Hall is a weighty one—that " if we look upon the
usual course of our feelings, we shall find that we
are more influenced by the frequent recurrence of
objects, than by their weight and importance ; and
that *habit* has more force in forming our character
than opinions have." In all the instructions given to
teachers, this habit is insisted on ; and yet I fear it is
not sufficiently felt. " A requisite," writes one of my
most valued correspondents, " which all will agree to
be indispensable in a Sunday School teacher, is
punctuality. No one *can* be a good *teacher* who is
not a punctual one. Every thing valuable in a class
depends, under God, upon this. In my experience I
have never seen a blessing follow the labors of a
teacher who failed in this particular. It is always sufficient ground to believe that a teacher
does not love his work, if he be found absent from
his post, when his fellow-laborers are pleading for the
blessing of God upon their labors. As a certain consequence of his delinquency, the children become
dilatory in their attendance. I have long since made
up my mind that the duty of the Superintendent in
such cases is to enforce the rules of the School, however great the trial may be to his own, or to the
feelings of others. When the interests of the school
are thus at stake, he is not at liberty to choose his

course. The path of duty is always that of safety, though it may lead through trial. I do not value the labors of any teacher who is unwilling to step out of his path of ease or convenience, in order to fulfil the responsibilities which he has voluntarily assumed in his Master's vineyard."

Teachers err here, frequently, through want of consideration. Suppose a school consists of one hundred and fifty scholars, and the teachers twenty-five. Suppose several teachers come so late that the Superintendent must delay opening the school for five minutes. This seems a short time to wait. Take the one hundred and seventy-five which compose the school and multiply it by five, and you have eight hundred and seventy-five minutes lost. Suppose this take place once on every Sabbath; the loss for one year is seven hundred and fifty-eight hours; and suppose the same set of teachers continue this for five years, it would be three thousand seven hundred and ninety hours. If, now, we suppose the habit to be by them perpetuated in the school, and transmitted down, and, above all, be woven into the habits of the hundreds of pupils, and become a part of their character, no arithmetic can compute the evils of such a habit.

You come late this morning to your class. The results are, that your scholars are disappointed; they take their seats, see the school opened, and feel lonely, having no teacher. The Superintendent feels at a loss what to do. He sees the lambs without a guide. He waits as long as he dares to do. He goes round the house to find somebody whom he may lay hands on and press into the service. Finding none, he has to come back, and take the class, and unite it, most reluctantly on all sides, with some other class. The whole school is disturbed by the process. He kindly says, he " presumes the teacher is sick." This is done, and soon you come hurrying in, with that quick, noisy step, which always indicates a consciousness of being too late. The class must again be disunited and taken to their own seats, while the school is again disturbed, and the mortified Superintendent sees that you are any thing but sick. Let me assure you that you have attracted notice,—shown that you were of some importance,—but you have lowered yourself in the estimation of every one in the house. A want of punctuality amounts to robbery. 'A short time since at a village in the neighborhood of London, a committee of eight ladies, who managed the concerns of an institution which had been formed for the relief of the neighboring poor, agreed to meet on a certain day, at twelve o'clock precisely. Seven of them attended punctually at the appointed hour, the eighth did not arrive till a quarter of an hour after. She came in according to the usual mode, with " I am very sorry to be behind in the appointed time, but really the time slipped away without my being sensible of it; I hope you goodness will excuse it." A Quaker lady replied, " had thyself only lost a quarter of an hour, it would have been merely thy own concern; but in this case, the quarter must be multipled by eight, as we each lost a quarter, so there have been two hours of useful time sacrificed by thy want of punctuality."'

The following description of a teacher who lacked the quality of punctuality, though longer than I could wish, is yet so graphic, that I may not withhold it.

" About this time a new teacher offered his services, who was deemed in every respect qualified to instruct this class; he possessed good natural understanding, a well-cultivated mind, and, in some respects he was industrious and persevering. He rose early, except occasionally on Sabbath mornings, when he though it prudent to indulge himself a little. Sundays were the only days when he ever left home without private prayer for a blessing on the concerns of the day. Indeed, he found no time: as it was, he generally went late to the school, and on more than one occasion, he came in just in time to hear a stranger address the children on the importance of always being early and punctually at school. When he thus lost an hour in the morning, he felt somewhat displeased with himself, and nothing seemed to go right all day. The children soon acquired the habit of coming late; perhaps they did not wish to hurt the feelings of their teacher by being in their places an hour before him. However this may have been,

from his indifferent manner, one scholar after another
strayed away altogether; as his class diminished, the
Superintendent continued to fill it up with new scholars Sunday after Sunday. The Superintendent soon
found that he might as well turn the scholars out of
school, for it amounted to the same thing; and he
found it necessary to urge upon this teacher the importance of complying with a rule of the school,
which made it the duty of the teachers to visit the
absentees, and report the cause. Indeed the teacher
soon began to feel ashamed of his reduced class; perhaps he was fearful it might be thought by some that
he did not possess natural ability to interest and instruct the class; and he determined that he would
inquire after the absentees. About the middle of the
week he found leisure, but then recollected that his
roll-book was locked up in the school-room; and by
the time he found it convenient to see the Superintendent and obtain a list of the names, it was Saturday afternoon.

"It proved to be an exceedingly unpleasant day,
but he was determined to do something before another
Sabbath; and off he went with a list of absentees
sufficient to have formed a large class, with hardly
time to call upon half the number.

"He had considerable difficulty to find where many
lived; some had removed, and one or two had some
time since tried some other Sunday School, which
they liked much better. He inquired at one place

for Mr. J., and found no such person. When the mother of the boy appeared, he informed her that Joseph had not been at the school the last two Sundays. Joseph being there, said he was at school on Sunday afternoon week; and the teacher just recollected that he *himself* was absent that afternoon, and could not contradict the child; and after saying a few words on the importance of regular attendance, he went his way.

" The next house at which he called, he saw the father of George, and told him that his son had not been to school for a few Sundays past.

" No," said the father, " he has not been for five weeks. Previous to sending him to the Sunday School, he stayed in the house and read, or went to church with his mother. As we knew much good had been received in Sunday Schools, and many of our rich neighbors sent their children, we were persuaded to send George, and we had him ready every Sunday, and thought that he attended the school regularly; but last Sabbath he came running home, followed by a friend of mine, who informed me that George spent every Sunday with a crowd of bad boys near his house, and they had just broken his parlor window. And now, as I cannot be certain that he will do any better, I shall keep him in the house."

" At the next place the teacher knocked very gently at the door, for he had lost some confidence in himself. He did not knock again, or wait long, for

he had no time to lose; and perhaps quieted his conscience with the thought, " well, I have called, and
if no one comes, it is not my fault;" and away he
went, without ever looking back.

" We shall only mention one more call which he
had some difficulty in making, not knowing exactly
who to ask for. Here he saw the mother of a boy
who had been in his class;—introduced himself as the
Sunday School teacher, and inquired about her son
James, who had been absent from the class. She
looked sorrowful, and said she believed " James was
better off,—she hoped he was in heaven."

" What! is James really dead?"

" Yes," said his mother, " he died of a fever from
taking a severe cold one Sunday, in the street: he
was ill just thirteen days on Thursday week last."

" When the teacher recollected himself a little, he
said, " he could not have thought it so long a time
since James was at school"—inquired " whether he
thought he was going to die, and what were his
views." The mother replied that as he became
worse, he was very much alarmed at the thought of
death—talked about the Sunday School, and longed
to see the teacher he *used* to have, and wished me
often to read the Bible to him; and when he became
very ill, and near his end, seemed resigned to die.
We asked him if we should send for *you*, and he did
not seem to desire it. He said, " the Sunday School
teacher we have now has never been here, and may

be he would not like to come," and then he held up his poor, thin arms, and said, "I don't think he'd hardly recollect me, I've fell away so much."

"James died without seeing his teacher; and his poor mother entertained the hope that he was happy, because—he once loved the Sunday School—was desirous of hearing the Bible read, when he could not do any thing else,—and appeared willing to die, when he found he could not live. This teacher!—he seldom thought of James while he lived, but he never forgot him when he was dead!"

I will add here, that a teacher can never obtain implicit and unhesitating *obedience* in his class, unless he is a man punctual in every respect: and to be a successful teacher, he *must* have unyielding discipline over his scholars. This, if properly obtained, will greatly increase the respect, the esteem and affection of his class. If a teacher cannot succeed in securing the obedience of a scholar, the way is hedged up for doing any good to that individual. I think the remark is as true with regard to the Sabbath School class, as to the family-circle. Every thing goes wrong where children are disobedient and undisciplined. The point which the teacher will have to urge the hardest, probably will be, the *habit* of punctuality,—in getting the lesson, in reciting it, and in being present when the school is opened. And let every teacher understand that he can never

secure this habit to his class, unless he has it in per
fection himself.

3. *The third habit which I would mention, is that
of constantly improving the mind with a view to
teaching your class.*

One thing which makes all teaching so weari-
some, is the great effort made at the moment of
giving instruction to create thought, illustration, and
materials by which to excite and keep up an interest.
You may just as well plunge into business, and expect
to create capital to meet your engagements from
day to day, as to expect to do this. You must lay
up materials beforehand, and be in the habit of
doing so. And here, too, unless I am careful, I shall
send you off on a wrong track. I do not mean that
you must sit down and read Rollin's ancient history,
or the voyages and travels of the day, for the *sake*
of finding something by which you may interest your
class; but I mean, that when you read a book,—
when you meet a stranger, when you hear an interesting conversation, save all that you can. It will
all be of use in your instructions. Make it an object
to cultivate your *memory*; for without a good memory you cannot long be an interesting teacher. Mon-
taigne could write books on philosophy, and was a
man of great learning; but he neglected his memory,
till he could not call his own servants by name, and
could remember nothing which was not written down
in his memorandum-book. Such a man, though he

might embody the learning of his age, would never be fit to teach a class in the Sabbath School. See every thing at which you look;—hear every thing to which you listen; and, like the bee, have the habit of gathering honey, even if it be but little, from every flower with which you meet. Every fragment of knowledge, every illustration of truth, every delightful impression which you receive, will aid you as a teacher. Aim to improve from week to week in your manner of teaching. Do not hurry children over the ground faster than they understand every thing as they advance. Some will take long steps, and expect the child to follow and take steps equally long. Some will try new schemes,—find they cannot always be original, and soon fall back into the old course. Others will find that when the time for teaching comes they have no materials on hand, and so they resolve, in despair, to resign. Now you should neither resign, nor yet plod on in the same old, dull way. Make it your business to discover the different dispositions of your class, see what their habits are,—how they came by their habits, what have been the defects in their education, and study by what means you can counteract and correct those habits and defects. This will put your own mind and ingenuity to work. The teacher must seek for *self-improvement*, if he would do good in the Sabbath School. There are but three thoughts on this subject which I would suggest at the present time.

1. Lay your plans to improve the mind by studying a little every day. This portion of time may be short,—probably will be—owing to your business; but let it be improved. Do not say, ' I will study two hours,—or one hour,'—but that you will daily spend at least twenty or thirty minutes in the cultivation of your mind. Have a particular half-hour selected, and do not let any thing shove you over it. Let it be the time of day when nothing *can* cheat you out of it. One-fourth part of an hour every day, diligently and wisely improved in self-cultivation, will help a man to grow in wisdom.

2. Let this season of self-improvement be devoted to the most judicious reading. The mind of ages is on the pages of books, laid up—and a little digging will give you gold. Original thinkers are the minds with which you should come in contact. Do not try to read much—too many pages,—but make every thought your own—so completely your own, that you can retain it through life. You will, of course, use your influence to have your Sabbath School Library contain books of a high order.

3. Acquire the habit of reflection. Without so doing, your observations, your readings, your facts, your conversations, will all be useless. Who would often go to a store to make purchases, where the goods were thrown in, scattered, heaped up, hardware and crockery together, oil and linen, muslins and groceries, essences and tobacco,—all *there* indeed, but no one

thing at hand, and no power of saying where the thing wanted may be found? Make your own mind the laboratory into which materials are gathered, and where they are analyzed and reduced to their proper elements. And do not be discouraged. Cold wishes will not discipline your mind; cold wishes will not add to the furniture with which they are adorned; but once acquire the habit of making self-improvement, and you will shortly be surprised at your advancement,—at the ease with which you advance, and at the pleasures connected with the process. Teachers will complain that they cannot interest their scholars; or that the scholars leave them as soon as they reach a certain point; but if they will faithfully improve themselves,—acquire the *habit* of doing it, they will not feel these discouragements. You can hardly be too careful in cultivating a habit of close attention. It is a great thing to be able to read the human heart, or in common language, understand human nature. This can be obtained only by close and careful observation. You will wish to create a desire for thorough study,—by which every thing may be *understood* as the child proceeds. How can you do it? You will wish to create a strong love of books, and a desire to read. This will be an immense blessing to the child. How can you accomplish this? You will need to know how much good or hurt a single exhortation, or even a single word may do, if timely or untimely used. An incident in the life of Mrs. Hemans will illustrate this point. As a child, Mrs. Hemans was an object of admiration, and almost devotion, for her extreme beauty; her complexion was remarkably brilliant; her hair long, curling, and golden. Who can tell how little or how much impression passing words, carelessly spoken, may make upon one so sensitive? One lady incautiously observed in her hearing, " I know that child is not made for happiness ; her color comes and goes too fast !" She never forgot this remark, and would mention it, *as having caused her much pain at the time it was spoken.*

The teacher should understand, and understand it well, that there is scarcely any thing so painful to the human mind in its undisciplined state, as *thinking.* To overcome this repugnance, and to teach the child so that he will love to think, is perfection in the art of teaching. Said a prisoner, in one of our new State Prisons, where a chaplain regularly preached and taught them from the Bible.—" You do not understand it. [He was comparing the old prison, which he preferred, to the new.] *There,* by day and night, it was hale fellows, well met; and *here,* the last thing at night is prayer, then retirement, where we see no one and speak to no one during the evening ; then go to bed, but cannot go to sleep; but *think, think.* If we get to sleep, and awake in the night, we see no one, and hear no one, but THINK, THINK. When morning comes, and we go out, the first thing is prayer. We see our fellows, but say nothing; and at night, again, after prayer, we go alone, and THINK, THINK."

3. *The third habit to be cultivated is patient labor.*

The remark is too trite to be dwelt upon, that nothing of value can be obtained in this life, without labor. You need, not merely the power to compel yourself at times to sit down to patient labor and drudgery, but you need the *habit*, so that it may be a thing of course. You need it in the weekly duty of improving your mind, and in getting the lesson to be taught. You need it when you meet the class and endeavor to instruct them. You need patience in your intercourse with your fellow-teachers, and in the thousand, little, nameless trials and vexations incident to and inseparable from the duties which return upon you every week. You will not be surprised either, if you find mental labor and patient habits of labor somewhat irksome to yourself at times; but every regular return and performance of any duty will render it less irksome, till it becomes a positive pleasure. The very penances of the darkened Catholic, we are informed, if regularly performed, at stated, periodical times, soon become a part of the devotee's happiness, and he is lost without them. This power of habit is one of the greatest aids to good men in all their efforts at self-discipline or usefulness.

9 *

4. *Cultivate the habit of watchfulness over yourself.*

We can see many imperfections in others,—even a mote in the eye. We should remember that others are as quick to see them in us; and that children, of all others, are quick and good judges of character You have not a single habit, good or bad, with which your class will long be unacquainted. If you are quick and irritable, they will be quick to see it, and what is far worse, will be long in losing the bad impressions which they receive. I can truly say, that no impressions of my own childhood remain so vivid and so deep, as those received during two winters, while under the instructions of an irritable teacher. He never struck me,—he never inflicted any pain upon my body, and yet I shall carry to the grave those deep, unpleasant associations and feelings which his irritable temper created. And this will be found to be the testimony of not a few. By all means, command yourself, and keep the current of your passions quiet and even. The Quaker who said that he was naturally quick and passionate, but who cured himself entirely by always speaking in a low tone,— as he who could command the tones of his voice, could command his passions,—had not a little of genuine philosophy in his theory. You will always find that irritable men speak loud; and on the contrary, when you hear a man who is a loud talker, you instinctively associate his voice with a quick and

passionate disposition. Your own character will communicate itself to your class. If you are light and
trifling, they will be so; if you are talkative, they
will talk much and think little; if you are irregular,
they will be; if you forget your promises, they will
forget theirs.

You should watch over yourself also, because your
usefulness depends upon the opinion which children
entertain of you. They cannot respect a man who
is wanting in a proper degree of gravity; who is not
far above them in knowledge in general, and in a
knowledge of the lesson in particular; and who is
not consistent and exemplary in all his deportment.
Never forget that you meet the children on the *Sabbath*, and that yours is the work peculiar to that
sacred day. Let all your influence be hallowed.
The eyes of the school are all upon you; and not
only your own class, but the whole school, watch and
weigh your character; and you aid in giving a
coloring to the whole school. The parents of the
children too, are watching you,—some praying for
you,—that you may be able to lead their beloved
child to God and to holiness; others looking to see if
there be really any thing in religion above a mere
form. Of this they judge partly by seeing you, and
still more by seeing the character which you are
giving to their child. You will have some children
more amiable than others; watch yourself that you
do not feel, and still more, that you do not *show* par-

tiality. This is a delicate part of your duty. It is absolutely impossible to love all alike; but it is a duty not to show partiality in your class. This watchfulness will do more for you than to aid you in teaching and influencing your class. It will help you to be a more perfect Christian,—it will make you every way more happy. No teacher should live without self-examination, and that, too, at stated times. At the best, this is a season none too pleasant: but if you can review the Sabbath, and see that you have had circumspection, and watchfulness over yourself, and have set a guard around your conduct and character, as a Sunday School teacher, you will find that even the hour of self-examination is pleasant. It is always delightful to feel that we are making progress in self-discipline.

5. *The habit of prayer.*

No language can adequately describe the effects of converting one sinner to God,—the effects exhibited in time and in eternity. And the teacher should have nothing lower as his standard than to see every child committed to him converted to God, and trained up to be a devoted Christian. Do you go to your class with less interest than you go to your worldly business? Do you hear the lessons as a task? You may be sure your heart is not in the work; and you do not pray over it. Do you feel cold or indifferent towards the school, or towards any particular pupil in your class? If so, you do not pray for that school or that scholar. You cannot pray for a child without feeling a deep interest in his welfare. Do you labor year after year, without seeing your scholars converted to God? The reason is probably to be found in your want of prayer. Notice the following curious fact. 'A writer says that he witnessed a revival in a Sabbath School of which he was once a member. It was principally confined to those between the ages of seven, and twenty. A large number professed an interest in Christ. But all were of one sex, all were *girls.* Although some of the *boys* were considerably impressed, yet not a single individual of them was known to have been converted. One after another of the little girls gave her heart to the Redeemer,— while the boys, members of the same families,—their brothers, lived on in sin, the enemies of God. What does this mean? How is this to be accounted for? Does not the following fact explain the mystery? The teachers of the little girls came apparently from their closets, from the very presence, the audience-chamber of the Most High. Their hearts seemed glowing with love for their Savior, burdened with a sense of the worth of the soul, and the immense responsibility which rested upon them. They warned and entreated their scholars on the Sabbath, and repeated their instructions during the week. A rich blessing followed,—*a blessing proportioned to the fidelity of the teachers.'*

No one can discipline his own heart, and grow in

Christian character, without prayer. No one can accomplish any thing, either good or great, without it. You should be a man of prayer for yourself, your class, the school, and for the world. You will be in no danger of over-estimating the effects of the *habit* of daily prayer upon your own character. I look at it not merely as a means of drawing down blessings upon your labors, but as a thing of inestimable value to yourself. Seasons of temptation,—of luke-warmness,—of backsliding, will come,—the love of many will wax cold,—the light within your own heart will burn dim,—and nothing but the *habit* of daily prayer will make you safe. Peter, probably, had not been in the habit of prayer before his conversion. His habits were not fixed, and therefore, in the hour of temptation, he sinned;—while Daniel, who, for many years, even from his youth, had been a man of prayer, and had formed *habits* of prayer, withstood temptations incomparably greater than those which overwhelmed Peter.

Let it be most distinctly impressed on the mind, that we never accomplish any thing in religion in which the heart is not deeply engaged; and the heart is never engaged, when the closet is neglected. A teacher never can enjoy teaching, or do good to his class, who is not habitually at the throne of grace at stated periods. The following is invariably the result of the labors of a prayerless teacher. A visiter was sent out to call upon the families represented in the school. In the course of his calls, the following conversation took place between him and a little girl.

"Do you attend Sunday School?"

"Yes, Sir."

"How are you pleased with the school?"

"Not so well as I have been."

"What is the matter?"

"I have a new teacher, and I do not like her so well as my old teacher."

"You will probably become better satisfied after you have become better acquainted with the method of your teacher's instructions."

"I do not believe I shall ever love my new teacher so well as I did my old one."

"Perhaps the fault is in you."

"Perhaps so;—but I *cannot* love her so well as I did the old one."

"What can be the cause of this difference in your feelings?"

"My former teacher took a great deal of interest in me; and while hearing me recite, took great pains to explain every thing in my lesson, so that I could understand it; and after the lesson was ended, she spent the time in reading something to the class which is useful, or in telling us how we ought to live. But my present teacher just hears my lesson, appears distant, seems to have but little interest in the class, and as soon as the lesson is closed, she leaves the class for another part of the house."

Such cases as the above would occur but seldom, if our teachers were habituated to prayer from day to day, and always remembered their class in their prayers.

I return from the *habits* of the teacher, to consider briefly the remaining qualifications which do not come under the general head of habits.

3. *Humility is a most desirable qualification in a teacher.*

The teacher has to deal with the heart; and that is so universally and naturally proud, that it does not love to admit any advances but those of humility. The humble man can always have access to any man's heart; while the proud or vain man is uniformly shut out. In the business of teaching in the Sabbath School, you will need not merely the appearance of humility, but the thing itself, if you would feel happy. Without this grace, you will be in danger of feeling that the Superintendent or the teachers do not do right,—they usurp authority, or they violate rights, or they misuse you; that you do not have your proper place,—the class you have is one of the lowest, poorest in the school,—perhaps the most uninteresting of all. Why should *that* class be given to you? Another teacher is more popular, more noticed, more thought of than you, and pride tells you that you are almost a martyr to injustice. If you are constantly thinking of yourself, wanting praise, unhappy without it, talking about yourself,—

giving hints of your own estimable qualities; if you
use stratagems to obtain praise, such as inquiring
about your faults in order to learn your excellencies,
—if you find yourself constantly consoling yourself
with the thought that you are not appreciated, and
that you are of more consequence than others seem
to think you are;—if you are pained when others
receive praise in your presence, and feel disposed to
detract from their merits, perhaps by speaking dis-
paragingly of them; if you find yourself comparing
yourself with others greatly to your own advantage,
if you feel ready to excuse every fault in yourself, to
palliate and defend,—you lack that humility which
is essential to the comfort, the happiness, and the
usefulness, of the Sabbath School teacher. Let the
sentiment so beautifully and quaintly expressed by
Taylor be engraven on the memory; — "Give
God thanks for every weakness, deformity, and im-
perfection, and accept it as a favor and grace of
God, and an instrument to resist pride and nurse humility; ever remembering, that when God, by giving
thee a crooked back, hath also made thy spirit stoop,
or less vain, thou art more ready to enter the narrow
gate of heaven, than by being straight, and standing
upright, and thinking highly. Thus the Apostles
rejoiced in infirmities, not moral, but natural and ac-
cidental, in their being beaten and whipt like slaves,
in their nakedness and poverty."

4. *Benevolence to the souls of men is an indispen sable requisite to a good Sabbath School teacher.*

No one who has not made the trial can know how many little trials and vexations attend the faithful teacher. He meets with ignorance and stupidity, deplorable, and apparently incurable; with habits perverse and corrupt, which have been woven into all the education of the children ;—with dispositions which seem to have no right side ; and yet he must *love* these children, or he can do them no good. He must love them all, for however unlovely and unamiable the child may be, he will never let the teacher do him any good, till he is sure that he loves him. You must not consider that class as some do, a company but little better than apes, whose mischievous pranks are to be the source of constant misery and vexation. You must have the confidence and the affection of your class, or you can do them no good. In order to this, you must have an unquenchable love for the souls of men,—a love like that of Christ, which many waters cannot quench, nor floods drown. This will lead you to overlook the many little vexations which beset you ; just as a man who is bent on reducing and subduing his farm, for the sake of the gains hereafter to be received, learns to forget the trees, the stones, the roots, and the brush which have to be removed before he can effect the object at which he aims. This love to the souls of men will render you elastic, and yet firm in your labors, easy

Benevolence should be warm.   Contracted feeling natural.

of access to your scholars, and ready to communicate information and hints to your fellow teachers, or to receive it from them. Every hint you will receive with gratitude; and every ray of light which you receive, you will reflect upon the path in which your class are walking, that thereby they may be led to heaven. Any man who is not warmly affected to the souls of men should not be a teacher. You should have so much of this interest that you are led to the duties of your station by the bent of your own inclinations. The zeal should be a true zeal to labor for Jesus Christ,—the oil that feeds the flame should be of heavenly origin, and not the result of an ardent temperament, or a splendid imagination. Your piety should be constant as well as burning. You should know that you are capable of great self-denial, and can be regular in all your habits. You need not possess "the razor's edge, but must have the blade of a well-tempered knife." Divest your character of all sloth, effeminacy, and indulgence.

We are too apt to feel that the object of life is to move in our own little circle, enjoy the full cup of mercies which God bestows, and to creep into heaven at last,—a kind of selfishness which has no example, and no parallel in the lives of Christ and his Apostles, and no countenance in the Bible. We look forward to the millennial day,—believing in the explicit language of prophecy, that 'truth and mercy, the peace and righteousness of our Messiah's kingdom,

whatever temporary checks they may suffer, shall, in
the end, overcome all opposition; and though the
river of God may, for a time, be discolored and pol-
luted, by the pernicious soil over which it rolls its
tide, yet it shall, at last, free itself from every foreign
mixture, and send forth its ten thousand pure streams,
to gladden all the nations of the earth.' Such is our
belief; but so far from feeling that *we* have individually a part to bear in the great work, we lay our
head on the pillow of down, and feel it hard that
any one should even knock at our door and ask for
bread. We want our missionaries to take their lives
in their hands, and go and wear down and die among
the heathen; we want our ministers to be in season
and out of season,—to labor in the study, and bring
no oil into the sanctuary which has not been beaten,
while we lay out work enough for them out of the
pulpit to consume all their time and strength; but
when we come to act for the souls of the young, and
for the conversion of the world in the Sabbath School,
we are apt to feel that a frozen heart, a dead piety,
narrow views and stinted labor, will do. It is not so.
I know the field is comparatively a humble one, and
that ambition would not go there,—for the crown
which she seeks is not there. You may not be able
to train up an Apostle; but you may prevent one
from becoming a Judas. Had Mahomet, when a
child, been placed under the care of a faithful devoted Sabbath School teacher, who can believe he

would ever have been what he *did* become? The
fact is, in the kingdom of Christ, great learning is
not demanded, great and striking and splendid
talents are not necessary, in order to be useful, to
bring souls to Christ, and to win the crown of life,
but *holy, devoted*, disinterested piety is the great
thing needed. This will bring wisdom from above;
this will overcome difficulties, bear up under discouragements, enable us to see the fruit of our labors
here, and to anticipate their reward hereafter. Let
me invite you, as we close this chapter, to unite with
me in the beautiful prayer of a glowing heart. " And
thou, Lord Jesus, afflicted Father of the Christian
name, blessed Martyr of humanity, blameless Pattern,
universal Priest, unerring Teacher, omnipotent King
of truth, of righteousness, and of peace, deign from
thy glorious throne to smile on this weak attempt,
and to accept this poor offering! It is a tribute, for
the life thou hast given, for the blood thou hast shed,
and for the joyous hopes thou hast inspired, to cheer,
and to direct our mortal pilgrimage. Meek Spring
of heavenly Wisdom,—boundless Ocean of universal,
ardent, unprovoked, and undiscouraged charity, pour
thy Spirit into my breast, and into the breasts of all
thy servants whom I here address. Teach them to
interest themselves in this blessed work, as becomes
men, who are distinguished by thy venerable name,
and honored by the ministration of thy glorious Gospel! Baptize us all with the fire of that love which
10 *

is stronger than death! Delightfully oppress our gratitude with the everlasting mountains of thy benefits, until every sentiment of frail mortality be suppressed, —until faith give us the victory over the world,— over life and death,—until love compel us to exclaim, *Yea, doubtless, and I count all things but dross that I may win Christ; and I am willing not only to suffer bonds, but to die for the sake of my Lord Jesus Christ, by whom I am crucified unto the world and the world unto me.*"

CHAPTER IV.

OTHER MEANS OF DOING GOOD BESIDES TEACHING.

It is no dim mark of the wisdom of God, that since he has planted in the human soul a love of variety and a desire of change,—the present never satisfying the heart,—he has made abundant provision in all the departments of life to meet these wants. The employments of life, so wearing upon the spirit, must be checked and broken up every day by sleep, —the cares of life must be laid aside for food and to supply the wants of the body ;—the change of seasons must change the employments, and, in some measure, the dress of every family. From childhood to the grave, provision is made for us to pass through changes almost infinite. The farmer, whose employment is more necessary to the sustenance of the world than any other, would find it drudgery, and life itself a dreary, prolonged misery, were it not for the constant changes in his business. As it is, this constant change, the new objects continually coming

115

up, render his employment one of the most delightful and bewitching possible ; and I doubt not that Washington had more happiness and saw more charms in life while making his experiments, inventing his tools, and managing his farms, than while he occupied the chair of state, the admiration of his country and of the world. This variety, incident and necessary to every kind of business, ought to be regarded as one of those decided marks of the wisdom and goodness of God, which he has devised to keep the mind from being too weary, and the habits of the soul from becoming monotonous, and itself torpid. Is it not an admitted fact, that when a man does but one thing,—such, for example, as grinding the glasses for the lens of a telescope, from sun to sun, and from year to year, from childhood to old age, that such a man is not cheerful, intelligent, or in our sense of the word, happy ? All elasticity of the soul is naturally destroyed by monotonous labor. The more laborious and responsible the duties and 'station, so much greater is the need of variety to relieve the mind and feelings. A minister of the Gospel would wear out shortly, were it not that God has connected variety with his office. Were he to write all the time, he would become exhausted and nervous. Were he to speak all the time, he would either destroy the mind by keeping it keyed up too high, or become insufferably dull. Were he to visit all the time, his mind would be too undisciplined to allow him to be even a

THE SABBATH SCHOOL TEACHER.   117

Useful to the Sabbath School teacher.   First means of doing good,—*visiting*.

tolerable preacher. It is from the fact that these various duties are connected so as to relieve tedium, and to call different powers and sympathies into exercise, that the pastoral office perfects the character of a minister, making all parts more symmetrical and well-proportioned, than any other station in the ministry.

These remarks apply in their full force to the duties of the Sabbath School teacher. His great duty is to instruct his class, but collateral with this, there are other duties equally necessary, and equally important to render his character complete, and the sphere of his usefulness full. They will add equally to his happiness and usefulness. I propose, then, in this chapter, to mention some of the collateral means of doing good, which the teacher has in his power.

1. *A regular system of visiting the families to which the scholars in your class severally belong.*

You have seen friends become cold, distant, and finally break away, and never again become reconciled to each other. You have seen husband and wife change, revile and hate each other, separate, while every year only seemed to render their enmity more intense. The link once broken between husband and wife can seldom be mended. But you do not often see children and parents becoming enemies. Let the child be deformed and diseased, and it does not wean him from the love of his parents; let him become an idiot, and their love will not change; let

him become vile, and they will throw the mantle of
charity over him, and still encircle him in the brightness of hope ; let him leave his home and herd with
the vile, and throw away all that is lovely or valuable, and they will still cling to him.   And even when
he is so degraded that he feeds with the swine in the
field, on the first appearance of his return, however poor and wretched, the father sees him afar off,
and runs to meet him,—to fall on his neck, and to call
him his son.   It is hardly possible to wear out or to
annihilate this heaven-planted love between parent
and child.   And it is the existence of this love which
gives the Sabbath School teacher such power.   In
committing his children to you, the father commits
his highest hopes,—the mother her richest treasure.
It is like a deed by which they commit their all to
you.   Does not the Apostle recognize this principle,
and appeal to it, when he says, that God, who spared
not his only-begotten Son, will with him freely give
us all things ?   By having the children put into your
hands, you have a means of doing good to those parents and to their family, unspeakably great.   You
wish to know the influences, under which, this and that
child has thus far been placed.   A visit to his parents
will help you to understand them.   You wish to have
this and that trait of character corrected.   The
parents either do not see the faults, or know not how
to correct them.   A few hints from you may aid them
greatly.   Perhaps the family are not in the habit of

going to the house of God. You may, by a careful use of your influence, lead them there. They may have notions and impressions concerning your school, or concerning religion, which counteract all that you can do on the Sabbath. A few visits may remove all these impressions. They may be bringing up their children in idleness, ignorance, and sin: and your counsels may alter the whole course of conduct in this respect. You can see their condition, and shortly, can place in their hands a tract, or something of the kind, which will exactly meet the evil which you wish to correct. Knowing the habits of the family, you can aid the child in selecting such books as will be useful at home, and encourage him to read, or to have them read at home. If you can once gain the confidence of the child, the way is open, and it will be easy to gain the confidence of the parents; and when that is gained, it will add to your former influence over the child. A physician once said to me, that he had a patient in whose cure he could make no progress. Every visit found him in a new condition, and with new symptoms. Every medicine prescribed seem to work by a new and unheard-of rule. At length the physician set himself to work to find out the difficulty. It was this: the mother of the patient took it into her head that the prescriptions of the physician were too powerful for the constitution of her child, and in order to counteract their mischievous tendency she gave some powerful nostrum soon after taking the medicine, as an antidote. It is just so with many children. Their parents are constantly neutralizing all that you do on the Sabbath. This evil can be met and removed only by your visiting the family. I would recommend that you visit regularly once a month, every child in your class,—even if your call is but short. It should make no difference with you whether the parents are rich or poor,—high or low. All who are willing to commit their children to you will be glad to see you, and will be grateful for the interest you take in the welfare of their children. In addition to this, you ought to call upon every child who is absent, before the Sabbath following. The child may be sick, and in that case he will be glad to see you. He may have fallen into bad company, and in that case you ought at once to see him. He may have deceived his parents, and in that case they ought to know it. I have never known other than a good school, where the rule was invariably practised, that every child who is absent from the school, shall be visited during the following week. I cannot too strenuously urge its importance. But be careful not to have these calls to inquire after delinquencies, seem like duns, as a creditor calls upon a debtor, when the visit is disagreeable to both parties. Let there be so much of *heart* in all your intercourse with parents, that they shall see that you seek only the real welfare of their child. If possible, always have something on your mind interesting to communicate, and let all your conversation, if practicable, be in the presence of the children. After one or two visits, you will never feel at a loss how to make your visit interesting. For the convenience of these visits, the Superintendent ought to have regard to the propriety of having the same class dwell in the same part of the parish, as nearly as possible.

Unless you are really conscientious in all that you do, you will be in danger of neglecting this system of visiting under the plea that you have not *time*. In nine cases out of ten, this plea will not be received by the Great Head of the church. A Superintendent, speaking of his school, says, " visiting, in many instances, is faithfully attended to; but in a few instances, almost entirely neglected. One teacher, who is an apprentice, and has to labor till nine o'clock every evening, manages to visit nine scholars a week, —while others, who are not half so much confined, plead that they have no time to do so. Need I say he has a full and interesting class? Oh! that there were more whose hearts were as much in the work! We should no longer hear of empty seats and drooping schools." Were *all* our teachers equally prompt and faithful, what a spectacle would our schools present! But does each, on an average, afford one such teacher?

On making these visits, the first thing desirable, is to get the good-will of the parents. This you will

11

invariably do, if you are kind and courteous, if you are mild, and above all, if you are sincere, and without guile. In these visits, from time to time, you will give such hints as will aid the parents in co-operating with you for the good of their child. I would respectfully, but earnestly urge the parents to visit the school. If you can get them to come and see the school once in three or four months, you will find that such visits will increase their interest in the school more than any thing else which you can do. They will see the system,—see the children happy,—see all the teachers interested and laboring for their good. It will do the children good; for every child loves the approbation of his parents, and their manifestation of interest in his welfare will ever stimulate him to greater effort. The highest motive which a child can have, before his heart is renewed by the Spirit of God, to do well, is the approbation of his parents. Some of those parents whom you thus invite to see the school, are praying people; and they will pray more fervently for you in consequence of every such visit; some of them have never attended to the subject of religion, and they will here see it in active operation. The teachers, the scholars, the parents, will all be benefited by such visits of the parents. One of the most admirable features in the Sabbath School system is that it gives the teacher such supervision over the moral education of each scholar; and through the child, opens such a wide field for influence upon the family in which the child lives. Let no pressure of business, no calls of pleasure, no pleadings for ease, lead you to neglect this most important part of your duties and privileges.

2. *Making a proper use of the Library.*

There seem to me to be three points in regard to the Library of a Sabbath School, which ought briefly to be noticed : viz. *its necessity,—materials of which it is composed,—and the best method of using it.* Upon each of these points I feel bound to say a few words.

1. *The necessity of a Library.*

Sabbath Schools have been established without Libraries, and by proper effort, may do good; but they soon drag heavily, and droop. Others have very poor Libraries, and the teachers cannot see the need of having them made good and complete. Let me tell you what a good Library, properly managed, will generally do.

(a.) *It will create a taste for reading.*

You go into some families, and the parents will tell you that their children " do not love books,—do not take to books,—or do not take to learning :" in other words, their children have no taste for books. The parents think it is a kind of destiny. Their children are doomed to be comparatively ignorant, while some families which they can name, are growing up fond of books. Now all the destiny there is about this, is, that the children do not have suitable books. Any

child and every child will love books, if you will put
suitable books into its hands *before it leaves the cra-*
dle. But many families have no such books,—feel as
if it was money thrown away to buy them. The
child sees nothing but the big Bible, perhaps a volume
of Sermons, an old Geography, or a few Newspapers,
—these constitute the library of the house, and is it
any wonder that there is no taste for reading? Any
wonder that every association connected with a book,
is gloomy, and almost painful? Now the Library of
the Sabbath School meets this very difficulty;—it
furnishes reading suited to the child's capacity,—
deepens the impression by cuts and pictures,—and
creates, gradually, in him, a confidence that even *he*
can master the contents of a book; and when this is
once done, the child has acquired a taste for reading.
This acquisition, I hardly need say, will be a treasure
to him. The happiness, the respectability, and I had
almost said, the salvation of a child, are near being
insured, when once he has acquired a decided taste
for reading. Every Library should be selected with
this in view.

(b.) *It will supply those with books who otherwise*
would never have them.

I speak not of those destitute parts of the world,
such as new settlements, and nations emerging from
heathenism, where a book is a rarity;—but of our
most favored portions of country. Every parish and
ever- school will contain families too poor, or too

ignorant, or too parsimonious, to procure books for their children. Thousands and thousands are now reading the books of the Sabbath School, who would otherwise be entirely destitute. A Library owned by a Sabbath School, answers almost as good a purpose as having each family own it;—and in cases where filth and ignorance prevail, even better. It carries light to all,—quenches the thirst of all, and goes where nothing else can go.

(c.) *A Library occupies the vacant hours of children.*

I have already said so much on the importance of *habits*, that I am almost afraid to use the word again; and yet when the question comes, what shall be done with the leisure moments, and fragments of time, which the children of every family have, I cannot but again allude to it, and say that the habit of reading during this leisure is unspeakably important. Put suitable books, attractive books, into the hands of children, and they will, insensibly to themselves, form the habit of occupying these seasons with reading. These habits will abide through life, and will be an increasing blessing.

(d.) *A Library will create taste and draw out genius.*

All who remember their childhood,—and who does not remember it?—can look back and see that this or that bias was given to their character,—this and that lasting impression was made by such and such

11 *

books which they read. A few years ago, and the
reading for children was of the most preposterous
kind, the most unreal scenes, the most foolish stories,
the most frightful inventions were the companions of
the nursery. These made impressions which lasted
through life. Thanks be to God, this rubbish and
trash is passing away. Minds of the first order are
now engaged in preparing books for the young.
Genius feels honored, in being allowed to cater for
the mind, destined to be immortal, when it com-
mences its existence. And though we have accounts
of ministers, and missionaries who have been raised
up in the Sabbath School, yet I do not believe these
are all who have become great and good by means
of this institution. And I believe there are minds
forming there, and taste creating there, and genius
growing there, which will hereafter wield the pen,
and pour out the thought which will affect the earth.
It is not to be a long time before the taste, the literature, and the genius of the earth, will be, to a great
degree, nurtured in the Sabbath School. The Libraries will help to do the work.

(c.) *A Library will refine and elevate the intercourse between parents and children, and between
the children themselves.*

Much that is foolish, and much that is vulgar, in
the intercourse between families, and between children, arises from the vacuity of the mind. They
have no ideas—nothing to talk about. Not so when

Will carry reproofs where needed. Sixth use,—attach scholars to the school.

that family have access to a Library, and once acquire the habit of reading. The conversation among children is soon perceived to be more refined; the intercourse between the parents and the children is gradually softened, more gentle, and more amiable. There is a tendency in books to refine and soften character, which is irresistible. A vulgar man, either in words or in thoughts, cannot be a man who reads. How many hints will parents receive from these books which they will gradually incorporate into their system of family management! how many rebukes will they receive, without the mortification usually connected with reproofs!—how many impressions will they receive, which will gradually but certainly modify their character! And how many impressions —for it must be remembered that it is *impressions* which form the character of children,—will children receive from these books, which will make them more kind and dutiful at home—more docile and modest abroad—more free from that boisterous impudence which is so common an attendant upon a bad education! Every family-circle into which the books of the Sabbath School Library are admitted, will be softened and refined. Of this, from what I have seen, I have not a doubt.

(f.) *The Library will attach the scholars to the school.*

Every human mind wants something towards which it can look forward. If the child has nothing else to

do, but to go and recite his lesson and hear the remarks of his teacher, he will soon become weary
But he looks forward. At the close of the next Sabbath, he will receive a new book. It is his property
—entrusted solely to him for a whole fortnight. The
trust is pleasant. The prospect of pleasure to be
derived from reading is cheering; the curiosity
awakened as to the book which he will receive, is a
stimulus. But in addition to this, he knows that his
parents are delighted with the books,—his home is
rendered more pleasant,—new books will be added
every year, and shortly, he will have a larger book,
and then a larger, till he has read them all, and is
master of all they contain. These pleasures, these
hopes, this stimulus, will hold the child to the Sabbath School, year after year, till the great design
of the system has been realized in his case.

(g.) *The Library will do good where nothing else
can.*

You know of a family in which profaneness, for
example, is indulged; you cannot yourself reprove it
successfully; you cannot send the tract which will
meet the case. Suspicion would awake. But you
can aid the child to select, and encourage him to read
aloud at home, the book which will be a mirror in
which that family may see their likeness. So of in-
temperance, or of any other known sin. There are
books prepared to meet all these cases; and they are
generally so well aimed that they will hit the game.

Many a family have been drawn to the house of
God, and have become permanent worshippers in
consequence of the arrows which they received from
these books. The child with the sling and the stone
from the brook, has been made to do what a sword
could not. The heart arrays itself, whenever you
reprove it,—the pride rises up whenever you try to
persuade men to do directly the contrary to what
they are doing; but when the pages of a little book
speak, this pride and vanity are not aroused. The
conscience can awake and speak, because the passions do not raise their stormy voice and drown her
admonitions.

(h.) *The Library is a powerful means of converting the soul, and building it up in holiness.*

There are, probably, but few families which do
not contain more or less, who have no evidence of
having passed from death unto life; and there are
few families in which the books of the Sabbath
School Library are not read. By this means, old
and deep impressions have frequently been revived;
—new convictions have been awakened—new fears
created, till the soul has arisen, like the prodigal, and
gone to its Father for bread. If these books do not
directly lead the soul to God, they frequently do it
by leading to the house of God, or to a conversation
with some faithful friend, such as the teacher, or to
the word of God and prayer, till it is finally brought
into the fold of Christ. I suppose half a volume

might now be written, containing authentic accounts
of the good done to the souls of men, by means of
Libraries, and doubtless the day of Judgment will
reveal thousands more. But in the waste places of
Zion, where the sound of the " church-going bell" is
never heard, how has the aching heart of the
widowed mother been made to rejoice, when her
smiling boy returned through the little foot-path of
the forest from the distant school, bringing the book
which some sanctified, gifted mind has penned, and
which will aid her in growing in holiness, and in
guiding her babes to the Lamb of God! Her child
shall receive impressions from these books, which will
make him a staff and a comfort in the evening of
her days,—and these books will leave impressions
on the minds of all the family which will abide
forever.

These, in short, are some of the most obvious
benefits of the Sabbath School Library, which, in
my view, render it absolutely indispensable to the
success of the school. Of course, the more complete
and perfect it is, the better it is adapted to the ends
contemplated.

I proceed—

2. *To speak of the selection, or the materials of
which the Library should be composed.*

Great care should be exercised in the selection of
a Library; for a book, like a companion, may make
deep impressions on the child, and give him a bias

which can never be changed. Formerly it was very difficult to get books, which, to any great extent answered the purposes of a Juvenile Library, and men frequently undertook the selection who were wholly ignorant of their duties. I once knew a Judge, who, on being elected to the presidency of a Sabbath School Society, and feeling that his station required him to be a kind of patron, actually purchased and presented to the school some dozen or two of Cummings's largest Geography, as the foundation of the Library. Books are now so multiplied, that the greatest difficulty seems to be, to make the best selection. Some are almost destitute of character; others are too indefinite; and others still, are above the comprehension of children. Two or three hints seem desirable here.

(a.) *A Library should be steadily increased.*

This is usually done once every year; and it ought to be done by the subscription or contribution of the whole congregation with which the school is connected. Great pains should be taken to give every family an opportunity to contribute,—and for these reasons,—first, the larger the increase the more valuable will the Library become, and the greater will be its good influence upon the school, and upon the whole community. All are partakers of its benefits, and all should be urged to aid in its increase; second, the teachers are much encouraged and aided by an increase of good books. They are almost *sure* to find some book which will encourage and benefit them; and thirdly, in proportion as a congregation contribute for the library, in that proportion will they take an interest in the books, will read them, will be careful to see that their children are regularly at school, in order to draw out books. At the return of every year, be sure, then, to make as large a collection as possible to add to the Library. Get the new books as they are published, keep up with the times, and the school will feel the effects of the measure. Do not be afraid of asking the church and congregation for money. There is no way in which they can possibly invest money by which they will be able to receive so great returns.

(b.) *A book is none the less valuable for being old.*

There is a feeling in many, and I fear it is an increasing one, that all books must be considered ephemeral. Like almanacs, they are good for this year, and then they are to be laid aside. This feeling arises, in part, from the peculiar state of things in this country, and is, perhaps, peculiar to this land. Every thing here is changing,—a year alters the face of every thing; and we are in danger of thinking that principles, and truths, and thought, must all change and pass away. In some Libraries, consequently, you can hardly get a book read which has been on hand more than a year. What is added this year, is current; but nothing else is fit to read. This impression or feeling should at once be corrected. A good book will be equally valuable, (with rare exceptions,) as long as the English language is used. Such books as came from the pens of Doddridge, Baxter, Edwards, and Richmond, can never decrease in value, or interest. Who will ever hope to surpass the Pilgrim's Progress? When will the time come when " Little Henry and his Bearer," and " the Dairyman's Daughter," will not draw tears from the eyes of the reader? In selecting a Library, do not feel, that because a book was written before you were born, it is therefore destitute of interest or wisdom. Do not say to the child, " here now is a beautiful new book, just written, and one which will delight you greatly," while you say to another, as you hand him one of the most valuable books ever penned, " I am sorry I have not a *new* book for you, but they are all out; you must take this *old* one now, and I will try next time to get you a new and an interesting work." Truth is imperishable; and she gains nothing by coming out every few years in a new dress. And it seems to me that the teacher would be careful about making the impression that nothing can be valuable unless it be new, if he would only consider the mischiefs resulting from it. There is, of course, a freshness about a new book which communicates itself in a degree to the reader; but let the child be taught that a great and a good thought is something that must live eternally, wherever he finds it, and that those who lived many years ago, dug as deep, o say the least, as any writers of our day, and you

12

will not be troubled by the constant demand for new books.   In other words, the Library will become a thing not to be worn out, and every good book will become a permanent blessing.

What shall be said of works of fiction,—shall they be excluded from the Sabbath School?

A very important and a very difficult question to answer,—and difficult, like all questions of the kind, because there is no great and permanent principle on which to rest the judgment.   My reply is, that the question must be answered by the particular character of each book, and it can be answered in no other way.   If you say that fiction ought in all cases to be excluded, then I ask what you say to the story of Nathan to David, of the story of the good Samaritan by Christ, of the Pilgrim's Progress by Bunyan,—of Parley the Porter by Hannah More, and a multitude of similar works?   Who would wish to exclude such fictions as these?   If, on the other hand, you decide that fiction may be allowed, you throw open the door to such works as Dunallan, Lady of the Manor by Mrs. Sherwood, and all the religious novels, as they are called, which the times have created.   Great complaint has already been made that the books of the Sabbath School Libraries contain too much fiction; that the child glances over the pages merely for the sake of the story, without getting or trying to get the instruction designed to be conveyed.   I am fully satisfied from watching children, that there are some grounds for this complaint, but a little care on the part of parents and teachers will remedy the evil. Any book has too much of fiction about it, when the instruction is so much covered up that the story only dwells upon the memory. But I shall be asked, is it not better to read fiction, and books of fiction for the sake of the story, than not to read at all? Possibly it may be so; but that is not the question with us. We have not now to determine whether we had better have *improper* books, or *none at all;* but to choose between proper and improper books. A book for children and youth may have no fiction, and yet it may be so written that it will be sure to be read. I am glad to see that those who are preparing books for Sabbath Schools, and who are catering for the mind of the young, are beginning to take the right ground on this subject. Story will never be excluded from the world, nor from the religious part of the world; but it should be so written as never to be mistaken for truth,—and as the philosophy of our love for story, is, that it presents human nature in some new position above that of poor every-day human nature, the less we use it in training up our Sabbath Schools, the better. It is impossible to make it acceptable, unless you describe men and children as what they *should* be, rather than what they really are.

A word or two on the biographies of children which are so abundant. While I fully believe in the early conversion of children, and think I have seen many such conversions, I have never yet seen one that I should have dared to publish, had the child been taken away. They certainly do make wrong impressions, and I have no doubt, that through the undesigned partialities of parental fondness, the child is often drawn in more beautiful colors than justice allows. For example, you seldom read of one of these children, who had not a " large, speaking eye, and beautiful, curly hair;" and it was with great point that two children, in different parts of our country, asked the two following questions,—" do all good children die?" and, "do all the good little girls that die have beautiful curly hair?" I was once at the house of a friend, who said he had just received a visit from a gentleman and lady and their child, and was grieved to see that child *very uncommonly ill-behaved, and disobedient to its parents.* Judge of my surprise a few months after, to read a biography of that child, in which it was described as a paragon of all that is excellent,—as having been most dutiful and pious for a year or two,—all of which was accompanied with a steel-engraved likeness, showing the " beautiful head of curly hair." I do not say that the child was not really a convert to Christ. I believe it was. But I as fully believe that if an impartial stranger had drawn up the memoir, much, if not all, that now interests, would be gone. This is true of much that is given in the shape of biography of children. The little reader is led to feel that all good children must die while children, and that none but very beautiful children become good. The following is the testimony of a child nine years of age. " She was very little acquainted with religious story books; in fact her mind had imbibed a love for the Holy Scriptures, which rendered such auxiliaries quite unnecessary; at six years old she read the Scriptures with references, and devoted to that all her leisure moments. She kept a Bible always under her pillow, that she might read it in the morning before she dressed; and when her parents happened to spend an evening from home, she always requested to have a candle in the parlor for the purpose of reading in preference to playing in the nursery with her brother and sister. A Christian friend brought her one day, " Janeway's Token for Children,"—a beautiful collection of narratives, detailing the happy deaths and extraordinary experience of very young children. She had not read long, when she laid down the book with a look of some perplexity, and sat still, evidently deeply engaged in thinking: her mother at length inquired how she liked the new book ? She answered, " I like it, and yet I don't like it." When asked to explain, she said it was very interesting indeed, and very useful to *parents* to read, because it would encourage them to begin religious instruction early; "but I don't think it fit for children." " Why so ?" her mother inquired; she said she " thought it calculated to teach

12 *

children to talk like parrots, and say fine things which they did not feel. I know I will not read it any longer, for fear I would soon not know whether I was thinking my own thoughts, or only trying to persuade myself that *I was one of the wonderful little children.*"

While, then, I would neither condemn nor exclude biographies of children from the Library, I would beg those who write them, to do it with care; and those who put them into the hands of the child, to be care-ful to make the impression that the *imitation* of the feelings and character described, is not at all desirable.

There are, at this day, a multitude of minds cater-ing for the literature of our Sabbath Schools, and no books are probably more eagerly published. But I think there is also, at the same time, a growing anxiety arising in the minds of parents, teachers, and pastors, in regard to the character of the issues ; that the feel-ing is wide and strong, that the desire for story books, and it may be, the mutual competition, has led to a multiplicity of books, little and great, which are so entirely or so nearly *fiction*, that they are received for the sake of the story ; that they are so destitute of deep thought and solemn truth, that many mothers forbid them to come into their houses, because they deem their influence decidedly unhealthy. It may be that my reader will say, " Physician, heal thyself." I am by no means sure that the stricture would be wholly unjust. At any rate, this fear must be recognized, when there is a shrinking from taking any one catalogue and selecting from it ; and when libraries are actually discarded from the schools of some of our best and most respectable churches, because of the impression that great and fundamental doctrines are wholly left out, or so emasculated as to have neither point nor force, it is time to examine the subject. We cannot make men without proper aliment ; and what I am especially anxious for at this time, is, that all who prepare books for Sabbath Schools, especially those societies whose great object is to create and issue such a literature, should most carefully weigh this subject. It will be a disastrous result to have our most judicious churches banish libraries from their schools in order to get rid of fiction. A collection of butterflies may be beautiful, but we cannot with it instruct in the great principles of anatomy.

3. *The best method of using the Library, in order to make it useful.*

So far as the duties of the Librarian are concerned — and they are so important that he should

be excused from all other duties, they should be executed with great dispatch, promptness, accuracy, and
silence.   Were I a Librarian, I should unhesitatingly
adopt the plan invented in Albany, and now used
there, and in the city of Boston.   For simplicity, dispatch, silence and economy of the time of teachers, I
have seen nothing equal to this.*

In using books, children commit two errors.   They
do not fully and thoroughly understand the book
which they return, and they are anxious to take out
large books,—those which are above their comprehension.   To remedy these, is the duty of the teacher.
And so far as his time and circumstances will permit, it would be most desirable for him to be acquainted with the books, and have a short examina
tion of each scholar as he returns his book.   Does he
understand the general scope of the book ?   Does he
understand all the words used in it ?   Does he understand its moral bearings—and in any measure
feel them ?   Perhaps the book was designed to show
the effects of falsehood.   Does he see and feel the
truths ?   By this examination, you can aid him in
fixing, deepening impressions upon his heart and conscience.   You can give variety to your instructions ;—
you can throw light and thought into the mind
through new channels.   By all means advise with
and for your class, as to the books which they had

* See Sunday School Journal, November 4, 1835.

better read, not permitting them to take those which are above their comprehension, and not permitting them to take them faster than they read and understand. Encourage the children to read the books to their parents; and if they can give you a good account of the influence of the book in the family, do not be backward in manifesting your approbation. The teacher will need to use the books himself,— not merely for his own benefit, but as an example to his class. Give them an account of what you read, as a specimen of what you want them to do.

There is a principle in human nature, to which I wish here to make a brief allusion. The reader can probably remember how, when a child, he listened to his mother or father as he took him up on his knee and told him the simple stories of the Bible, such as the murder of Abel, the flood, the story of Joseph, of Moses, Samuel, of David, and of Christ. How interesting! And my reader will remember too, that when he became able to read those stories for himself, how much more he was interested than if he had never heard any thing about them before! The reason is, we love to have our knowledge of any particular thing increased; we derive more pleasure in getting a new thought or new light upon what we have already obtained some knowledge, than we do in getting the same thought or light upon a subject of which we know nothing. I need not stop to analyze the feeling. Perhaps it may be traced back to

pride,—as there is undoubtedly a pain in first con-
templating a subject of which we are *entirely* ignorant. I throw out this hint that the teacher may
seize upon it, and make it of some use,—nay, it may
be made of great use. If in your power, give the
child some account of the book before he reads it,—
of the subject of which it treats. Is not this nature?
Does not the mother tell her child the name, the residence, and something of the character and habits
of the visiter whom she expects, and in whom she
wishes to interest her child? Do you not enjoy a
book more, about which you have heard remarks,
and of which you have obtained some little knowledge previously to reading? Bear it in mind, then,
that our interest in any thing is increased, when we
are conscious that we already know something about
that subject. In talking with children, allow to them
all the knowledge which they do possess, and let
them feel that all that they obtain is only an addition to their stock. I must turn from the Library to
one or two other points.

The teacher will find it very beneficial now and
then to invite his class to his house. These interviews may be rather more social than on the Sabbath, but still, I would have them maintain the character of religious meetings. They should in no sense
be considered in the light of a reward. Their object
should be the increase of the teacher's means of
doing good, of gaining their confidence and good will

Answer to this question.

The question has sometimes been asked me by teachers, why they may not take their class home, and instruct them by themselves; that it would free them from interruptions, and they could advance faster and more pleasantly. My reply is, three-fold; first, that though it might be for the good of your particular class, yet it would *not* be for the good of the whole school. All teachers are not qualified to take this independent course,—they need the influence and stimulus of others, that they may move along with the rest. Secondly, that the teacher is never to ask what would be most *pleasant*, but what is most useful. All experiments in education have been tried, from that of having a tutor or half a dozen tutors shut up with a single child, to that of having a thousand pupils brought together at the university. The result is, that the mind is best educated in contact with other minds; it is stimulated, quickened, cheered, and strengthened. I cannot doubt but an hundred scholars brought together and properly taught, will do better than the same number divided into ten classes, and taught separately. Thirdly, that the checks and interruptions in the school-room are a part of the mental and moral discipline of the school, —such as they must meet with at every step through life, and such as they should be trained to expect from childhood. The teacher, then, who feels like withdrawing his class, and feels that it would be more pleasant to be separated from the school, will recollect that in doing it, he must, to a very great extent, set aside the interests of the school.

The last hint which I wish to give in this chapter is, that the teacher should try to make it a part of his means of usefulness to increase the usefulness and influence of his Pastor.

It is easy for the teachers to ruin the influence of the Pastor upon the Sabbath School; and I am sorry to say that I know of a few instances in which they have effectually done this. The Pastor is shut out, as if the school were altogether in other hands, and as if there were danger of his usurping power, were it possible. By a refined, but sure process, he is cut off from all sympathy with the school. When he goes in, he is treated like a stranger, and the consequence is, he does not often go there. Just the reverse of this should be the course pursued. This school is his flock, and the teachers are his helpers in instructing and feeding that flock. You should, therefore, be very careful not to destroy, or weaken the sympathy between your Pastor and the school. It need not be done, and it never *will* be done, unless by design. You must remember that he is preaching for your mind, and the mind of the most intelligent and gifted in the congregation. Instead, therefore, of finding fault, and complaining that he does not adapt every sermon to the capacity of children, you must take the thoughts of that discourse, and in simple language give them to your class. Instead of standing off, and feeling that you occupy one field and your minister another, encourage him to visit the school as often as he possibly can,—to examine your classes, and to talk to and with the children. Make him acquainted with the particular traits of character which you discover in different individuals, that he may know how to drop a word now and then, which will be " as a nail in a sure place." Strive to make the children love, and respect the office of the minister,—not for the sake of the poor " dust and ashes" which now fills it, but for the sake of having the admonitions, the instructions and the prayers of the minister fall with more weight. In another place, I shall speak of *his* duties; but I cannot forbear to urge upon the teachers the necessity of making your minister happy in your circle, happy in your school, and happy in your confidence and love. It will all be returned to you; for while there is no man who more needs your respect and confidence and love, than your minister, there is no heart which will more quickly appreciate these, nor more quickly and warmly reciprocate them. He relies upon his teachers more than on any others,—perhaps all others, for aid, sympathy, and love; let him never be chilled, by finding he is leaning upon a reed which will pierce his very heart with sorrows.

13

CHAPTER V.

THE teacher who enters upon the duties of his station for the first time, is often, if not usually at a loss what and how to do. He knows in general, that a particular lesson is to be taught, but he has no way of coming at it. He feels his wants, but can neither describe nor supply them. How much would he value a friend who had been over all the ground, and felt his way out through the dark, who could now give him just the information needed! Sometimes it is a great relief even to have a friend aid him in the examination of a single lesson. Let me endeavor to give you some hints which will, I trust, aid you to stand on that firm ground, on which you can help yourself.

1. *Make the Bible your constant study.*

The Bible is the great store-house of light and knowledge on spiritual subjects. Other books are the adders and the scaffolding; this is the temple of

116

truth. The rules which many give for the study of the Bible seem to me, too frequently to overlook one grand characteristic of the word of God ;—viz., that as it required supernatural aid to write it, so it does also to understand it. The Spirit which dictated it, is necessary to understand it; and the Bible cannot be understood, and its true spirit apprehended, except by the mind which is led and sanctified by the Spirit of God. You must have the aid of this Spirit, or you open the word of God in vain. The letter killeth : the spirit only maketh alive. In all your attempts, then, to understand the Bible, be sure to invoke the aid of heaven. Ask, that in God's light, you may see light. Some look upon the Bible as a garden of spices, in which you may walk, and at your leisure pluck the flowers, and gather the fruits of the Eden of God. But this does not accord with my experience. I have found it more like a mine, in which you must dig and labor,—the wealth of which is not to be obtained without labor; a mine, rich in gold and precious things, but it must be wrought day and night in order to produce them. You must have times and rules marked out, in which and by which you will dig this mine, remembering, that all that you bring out will be your own, and will be invaluable to you as a teacher.

In studying the Bible with a view to teach, you have a great advantage over other teachers of religion. A minister of the Gospel has to meet hearers

148   THE SABBATH SCHOOL TEACHER.

Great advantage possessed by the teacher.   One grand end in the Bible.

who are, not unlikely, full of their own opinions, full
of pride of intellect, full of prejudices, and full of
the creations of their own imaginations: they come
to hear, demanding that their taste be pleased and
gratified, that their preconceived opinions be met,
their strong points enforced, their criticisms all
allowed, and after all these demands are met, if perfectly convenient to apply some little part to themselves, they will do it.   Consequently, the preacher
has to arm himself at all points, prepare himself to
meet objections in every possible shape, whether
clothed in language, or only conceived in thoughts.
Not so with the Sabbath School teacher.   He has to
fit himself only to teach *truth*,—not to meet error,
in its ten thousand shapes and forms.   He need not
study to see what a portion of the Bible may possibly
be *made* to mean, but what it does mean; not what
a perverted taste and a corrupted heart may make
it mean, but simply, what is its meaning.   It is never
well, nor is it necessary for him to make any other
inquiry, nor to make any suggestions, except the real
and true import of the lesson under consideration.
Do not get the children in the habit of feeling wise
to pry and enquire and cavil and conjecture about
new meanings.   This is not teaching: it is spoiling
through vain philosophy.   Keep it ever in your mind,
also, that the Bible has one grand end, and only
one;—viz., the single purpose of recovering men
'rom the ruins of sin, by the death and mediation of

This great aim to be kept in mind.   Look at the Bible as a whole.

the Son of God. From this purpose it never wanders. All the emblems and figures look to this. To this all the prophets point, and stand like so many stars, ushering in the king of day. There is no book, no history, no chapter or portion of the Bible, that does not keep this great end in view. This is the key that unlocks all the dealings of God, all that mystery which lay hid *in God* alone, till the incarnation of Jesus Christ. The question is not, what is the simple meaning of each portion, were it a separated revelation from God; but what does it mean as a part of that great system of truth which opens the character of God, as dealing with a race of sinners, whom he is reconciling to himself, by a method new and astonishing in the eyes of the universe. I dwell upon this the more, because I have seen teachers too frequently conning over a lesson, which was to them dry, and almost unmeaning, but which would have been full of interest on the plan now suggested. " No scripture is of private interpretation :" i. e. as I understand it, the different parts of the Bible are not to be interpreted standing alone, but in connexion with other parts, and with reference to the whole. If you take one ray of the rainbow and call it light, you may say that light is red, or green, or orange; but if you look at each ray in connexion with all the rest, you will say that light is not one of these, but consists in the combination of the whole. Most of the parables will teach error, unless you keep this in

13 *

view; and always bear in mind that a parable is not explained by " crumbling it in pieces," but by keeping it together and examining it as a whole.   Do not be afraid of knowing too much about the Bible,— of making it too exclusively the great school-master which is to fit you to instruct your class.*

2. *Strive to acquire great and comprehensive views of the character and government of God.*

All that pertains to the character of God is elevating, ennobling, enlightening, and purifying to the soul.   It is about him and his government that you are to instruct.   The picture which you form in the young mind of his character, and the impressions you give of his government, will probably abide through life, and shape the destiny of the soul in eternity. Suppose you are a skilful mechanic.   You have a large establishment, furnaces for casting, engines for working all manner of iron and brass.   The design of the establishment is to manufacture steam-engines. You have no workmen, but are now about to introduce a number whom you have to instruct.   Some are to do the castings;—some to make the small wheels;—some the nuts and screws;—some to polish, &c.   You wish to teach them to do every part with great perfection.   The question now is, ought

---

* The hints given in Chap. IX. of the Student's Manual on the *Manner of studying the Bible*, contain all that my experience suggests at present.

you not to have a perfect and a clear understanding of all this machinery *as a whole?* Ought you not to know where every wheel is to go,—how it is to play, what power to sustain? Must you not know what relations each part bears to the other parts, and to the whole? This must be so. And you are not fit to superintend such a shop, unless you have all this comprehensive knowledge. Suppose one workman insists that *his* wheel is the most important, and that upon it all depends. Another says *his* wheel is of no consequence, and it may be left out, or poorly made. Another insists that the great balance-wheel is of no kind of use but to consume power to keep it in motion. Are these correct? Do you not need a knowledge of the whole, so that at a single glance you may know the relative importance of each part?

Now the great mistake of errorists and bigoted people, is, that all have some particular wheel at which they work, and insist upon it that this wheel is the most important in the whole engine, if, indeed, it do not constitute the engine itself! It were easy to give illustrations; but I fear they would be so plain that they would create sensitiveness, and thus defeat the very object which I have in view. We grant that every wheel is essential, and may not be left out; but it must be obvious to all, that some are very small, and it is as unwise to say that they are the whole machine, as it would be to insist that they may be entirely left out.

The teacher ought to know who wrote the Bible,—the character which the Holy Spirit made use of in writing each part,—the circumstances which modified this or that character and event. He should know how and why a particular part of the revelation of God came to be given *when* it was given. He should understand that the word of God is not a collection of little histories, of dark and figurative prophesyings, of gatherings of poetry, and scraps and hints concerning the character of God. He must look at it as a whole,—understand it as a whole; and while he must of necessity take it in portions to teach the class, just as the machinist would put one wheel into the hands of one man, he himself must be able to understand where that portion belongs, and what part of the revelation of God it occupies.

One of my valued correspondents writes, and urges me to prepare a course of simple lessons which shall give the child a bird's-eye view of the whole subject of revelation,—holding up Christ as the Alpha and the Omega, " of whom wrote all the prophets,—of whom the types, and shadows, and ceremonies of the Mosaic economy spoke,—that this grand, controlling, amazing subject, may be earnestly and mildly placed before the children's attention, in a simple and unique manner." But can such a bird's-eye view be given to the child, when our teachers, for the most part, are wholly ignorant of it themselves? Such a course of lessons would do great good; and I hope some able pen will present it shortly; but the point which I *now* wish to press is, that the teachers should have these wide, comprehensive views; and they may rest assured that they will be continually walking in the dark, unless they do have them. Such views will always add to your own comfort while teaching, while reading any particular portion of the Bible. Every part will seem to harmonize with other parts, and illustrate them. Every ray of light will aid you, not merely in seeing what you are now studying, but will be equally useful for all other parts. There is a fulness, an apparent greatness and richness about the preaching and the prayers of some ministers, which add a charm to their instructions: perhaps it may be attributed rather to the kind of study here recommended, than to any one thing besides. These enlarged views cannot be acquired at once,—they cannot be obtained without meditation and thought, and frequent comparisons of the word of God with itself; but they *can* be obtained by every teacher. Let them not shrink from study, from meditation, from thought. They *cannot* be fitted to teach the word of God without these. They will be superficial, lean, cold or hot, according to their feelings.

3. *Obtain* CLEAR *and* DEFINITE *views of all you intend to teach.*

Set it down as almost invariably true, that the mind which conceives clearly, can make any other mind see and feel its conceptions. Some men are called *deep* men; but it is generally, as Robert Hall says, 'because when they dive so deep, they bring up nothing but mud.' When you hear a man talk, or when you follow his pen, and find yourself puzzled to know what he means, and when you hear him frequently begging "not to be misunderstood," you may be sure he is foggy in his own mind. A clear mind is under no apprehension of being misunderstood. It cannot well be misunderstood. If you cannot clearly see the thought which you wish to convey to the child, do not make the attempt to convey it. The child will at once be puzzled, and though he cannot tell what the difficulty is, he will *feel* it. It will therefore be best to study your lesson in the manner, and in the order, in which you propose to teach it. You will then be going over the ground in the same path, and will be more likely to see it clearly. Every thought should be so plain in your own mind, that you have no fear of not being able to make the child understand it.

You will find it of immense advantage also, to have accurate knowledge of dates, and places. You ought to be perfectly at home in the Geography of the Bible. Felix Neff tells us that he found that when he came to introduce some simple maps among his people who are scattered up and down the Alps, it gave them a more definite idea of places than they had before. They felt more interest in reading the Bible, more interest in sending the Gospel to the

Illustrated by case of Melchizedec.

places pointed out on the maps; and that it put a new face on things among them. This is good philosophy. The human mind demands to know dates, and places; and God has adapted his revelation to this demand, by giving it at particular times, in definite places, and has thus put it into our power to locate all that is described in his book. There is scarcely any part of the Bible which is not rendered more interesting by definite knowledge of the Geography of the country. Let any one, for example, open the Psalms and read, 'as the hills are round about Jerusalem, so the Lord is about those that fear him,' and then let him look at the map of Jerusalem, and see the clustering hills all round it, defending it from storms, from winds, and from war, and he will see the beauty and force of the comparison. Take a plain case. How often has the sneer of Tom Paine about the parentage of Melchizedec been repeated! And the Christian, when gravely asked to point out who his parents were, has found himself in a kind of maze, almost wondering what kind of a being he must have been—to have been born "without father or mother!" Now if you accustom yourself to obtain clear and definite views of all that you study, all such shadows will be gone. The argument of the Apostle is this: The priesthood of Aaron was not designed to be permanent; Christ was predicted to be a Priest, after the order of Melchizedec, and not after the order of Aaron. Now we know nothing about the genealogy of Melchizedec, not even who his parents were, —(not meaning that he had none!) of course, if Christ was to resemble him, he also would spring from some other tribe than that of Levi,—since his priesthood would continue forever. Nothing can be more simple, and definite, and clear.

4. *In preparing yourself to teach, be sure to get illustrations which shall be clear and interesting.*

This is one great perfection of all teaching. It makes the subject clear, it impresses it on the memory where it abides, and it leaves pleasant associations in the mind. This was Christ's method of teaching. He took the lily, the grass, the tree, the sower, the net, any thing and every thing on which the eye rested, and pressed it into the service of illustrating. adorning, and enforcing truth. Almost every event will aid you, and every paper you read, and every day you live, will add to your stock. The anxious and attentive teacher will seize upon any event, and make it aid him in his work. I give you an example.' A teacher was trying to show a little girl that she did not love God. The child could not see it, or would not admit it. The subject was apparently dropped, and suffered to fade from the memory of the child. After conversing with others on other points. asking here and there a question, the teacher again turned to the child.

"Maria, how long has your Father been gone?"

"Seven months last week, on Thursday."

Example,—dialogue with a child.

" Do you know the reason, now, why you mentioned the very day, Thursday ?

" Yes,—because he said he would try to be at
home in just nine months to a day,—that's one reason ; and the other,—because it seems so long since
he went."

" Does he write often ?"

" He writes to mother every week, and to Sarah
and me once every month. We have seven long
letters of our own."

" Do you know when to expect your letter ?"

" Oh ! yes,—the last Thursday in every month, and
Sarah and I always run to the top of Janner's hill to
watch the stage, and sometimes wait there an hour
or two before we see it come in sight. And when it
does come, then we hurry off to the Post-Office, and
hurry Mrs. Meigs for the letter, and then run all the
way home to have mother read it aloud. Oh ! we
are so glad !"

" I should think by what you say that you are very
fond of your father."

" Indeed we are, Miss B. ; and when father comes
home, because he will come in the eastern stage, and
in the night, we are going to sit up till almost midnight to see him. It will be a great time with us all !"

" Maria, I am glad to see that you love your father
He is worthy of your love. You have answered my
questions very frankly. Will you answer me one
more as frankly ?"

14

" Yes—I—will."

" Well, can you not now see that you do not love
God? He writes letters to you in this book ; you do
not feel so eager to read them as you do those from
your earthly father. He offers to meet you and converse with you. Instead of sitting up till midnight to
meet him, is it not a task for you to meet him in
prayer at all? You say your father has been gone
seven months, and you want him to come back. God
has been absent from you, my dear child, much longer ;
do you feel as anxious to have him return and to see
his face? You know, too, that God is more worthy
and deserving of love than any human father,—has
done, and is doing thousands of times more for you,
and offers to do a thousand times more for you than
any human being can. *Do* you love him accordingly?
Do you now say, Maria, that you love God?"

" Oh! no, Miss B.," said the child, with her eyes
streaming with tears.

All great principles of religion ought to be illus
trated as far as is practicable by examples from
Scripture. This was Christ's method. He taught
the sovereignty of God so clearly, that " they were
filled with indignation ;" and how did he do it? By
telling his hearers that in the days of Elisha there
were many lepers in *Israel ;* but God, in his sovereignty, left them all, and healed none, except Naaman
the Syrian. There were many suffering widows in
Israel during the famine, but God in his sovereignty

relieved none, except one poor woman in a distant
heathen village! All the teaching in the world could
not make this plainer; and every illustration of
Scripture gives the child the habit of inquiring what
great principle the various examples and incidents of
the Bible are designed to illustrate. As an example
of this kind of teaching, I cannot but recommend you
to read the beautiful account of his little daughter,
who died at the age of four and a half years, which
Thomas Scott gives, in a few pages inserted at the close
of the Memoir of his Life. " On my return home one
evening, my wife told me that her daughter had be-
haved very ill, and been so rebellious and obstinate,
that she had been constrained to correct her. In consequence I took her between my knees and began to
talk to her. I told her she had often heard that she
was a sinner against God; that sin was breaking the
commandments of God; that he had commanded her
to honor and obey her father and mother: but that
she had disobeyed her mother, and thus sinned against
God, and made him angry at her,—far more angry
than her mother had been; that she had also often
heard that she must have a new heart or disposition; that if her heart or disposition were not wicked,
she would not thus want a new one; but that her
obstinate, rebellious conduct to her mother, (with
some other instances which I mentioned,) showed that
her heart was wicked; that she therefore wanted
both forgiveness of sins, and a new heart, without

which she could not be happy in another world after death. I went on to talk with her, in language suited to her age, concerning the love, and mercy, and grace of Christ, in a manner which I cannot particularly describe; but my heart was much engaged, and *out of the abundance of my heart my mouth spoke ;* and I concluded with pressing it upon her constantly to pray to Jesus Christ to forgive her sins ; to give her a new heart, and not to let her die till he had indeed done so.

I have good ground to believe that from that time to her death, no day passed in which she did not, alone, more than once, and with apparent earnestness, pray to Jesus Christ to this effect ; adding petitions for her father, mother, and brothers, and for her nurse,—to whom she was much attached. At times we overheard her in her little room to which she used to retire; and on some occasions her prayers were accompanied with sobs and tears. Once she was guilty of an untruth; and I reasoned and expostulated with her on the wickedness of lying. I almost seem now to hear her subsequent confessions in her retirements,—her cries for forgiveness,—her prayers for a new and a better heart, and that " she might not die before her new heart came." In short, there was every thing in miniature, which I ever witnessed or read of in an adult penitent; and certainly there were fruits meet for repentance,—for nothing reprehensible afterward occurred in her conduct."

One great use of familiar illustrations, in addition to that of explaining a principle, is, that they aid you in enforcing truth upon the conscience. The youngest child will be careful not to take any truth home to his own conscience any further than it is pressed there by his teacher; and the teacher will not do this with any effect, if he do not first apply it to his own conscience. Children think and talk in figures and in natural illustrations. The parents of some children in Wales, on one stormy sabbath, were gone to their place of worship, and the children, all under eight years of age, were left alone. They spent their time in what they there call, an Infant's prayer-meeting. Among other simple expressions made use of in their little prayers, was the prayer that " God Almighty would rock them in his own cradle." I have known teachers aided in enforcing the truths contained in their lessons by a selection of one or more of the anecdotes of Whitecross' Pleasing Expositor.

5. *Remember that the teacher must study to furnish new thoughts, as well as enforce impressions already received.*

The process of acquiring new thoughts, and of storing the mind with new materials, will be tedious, or pleasant, according to your habits and circumstances. Application of the mind under any circum-

14 *

stances is no easy matter; but under some, it is pe culiarly unpleasant. To show clearly what I mean, let me briefly state a few marks of difference between Sabbath School teachers who live in the city, and those who live in the country; for all who have noticed the difference, must have seen that it is very striking.

The mind in the city is awake, susceptible, and ready to receive any impression which is desired; but the waves roll on, and the next tide washes it all away. The river runs so rapidly, that it cannot be salted. The mind will receive, but will not retain impressions. In the country, there is nothing to efface impressions; but the difficulty is, to make them. The mind seems to receive impressions most slowly, when the most calm. In the city, we are in danger of carrying our business-habits into every thing, religion as well as other things. We take up religion, teaching, doing good, just as we go to the bank, when the hour is come. It is no self-denial to do the business pertaining to religion. In the country, the danger is of not doing it at all. In the city, we are in danger of doing every thing superficially,—of making our feelings the standard of duty; in the country, we are in danger of sleeping away life for the want of feeling. In the city, we are in danger of acting too hastily—in the country, of not acting at all, or at least, not soon enough. In the city, we trust, that our Christian character will stand the test of the

Inference from this comparison.

Judgment, because we do so many good things; in the country, we trust it will stand the test, because we do so few things that are bad. In the city, we seize upon floating information, and make men and passing events our books; in the country, we read and think more, but are a great while in coming to results. In the city, we go by the fashions, the public voice, and the opinions of others; in the country, we go by self-interest, and are little affected by what is passing without ourselves. In the one case, the fire seems to kindle quick, but wants kindling often; in the other, it burns longer, but is harder to kindle. If in the city we think less, it is true, we think quicker, and we are somewhat excusable for not having thoughts abide, because there is so much to efface them; if in the country, we think more, it is partly owing to the fact, that the mind must turn to itself for employment and amusement. In the one case, the teacher will need to go to books for ideas and thoughts, and will need to study longer for new thoughts; in the other, he will need to go often to books, to give him correct views, definite views, and to recal thoughts and impressions which are constantly fading away. In the one case, imagination, sprightliness will be in danger of being neglected; in the other, clear and definite views will be wanting. Whether, therefore, the teacher has the habits of the city or of the country, he will have deficiencies which nothing but the obtaining new thoughts from books will supply.

Some teachers fill the heads of their classes with words, instead of thoughts. In every lesson, which you study with a view of teaching, you will need to ask yourself, what have I, and what have the children under my care to do with this passage? How am I to explain this and that expression? How illustrate this and that truth contained in the lesson? What new thoughts,—thoughts which I wish them to remember as long as they live, shall I communicate in connexion with this lesson? How shall I gain the attention at the very beginning of the school, so that I can keep it, and deepen it through the exercise? What *one* point in this lesson can I illustrate and enforce in a way that will reach the conscience, fix itself upon the memory, become moulded into the character, and abide through life? Probably it will be wiser to attempt to fasten *one* single point in the lesson upon the minds of all your class, than to attempt more. One nail may be driven home. If you attempt more, you drive them wrong. If we try to enforce too many thoughts on the mind at once, they will, as Rowland Hill says, ' *batter* upon the mind,' without entering it,—a mistake into which many teachers fall, and one which is, as it were, necessary, from their not making it an object to acquire new thoughts, and to bring them to bear on a single point.

The great difficulty with which we meet in preparing ourselves to instruct children, is, that we find
it difficult to conceive of things and describe things
in simplicity, without being abstract.   All have
noticed how eagerly a child will read Bunyan's Pilgrim's Progress. The reason is, that it is all addressed
to the eye and the senses.   You can *see* the sinner
under conviction; you can *hear* his groans and com-
plaints; you can *watch* his progress, trials and difficulties.   There is no other possible way in which the
experience of the converted sinner could have been
given, which would have been so interesting, and so
useful.   Ask a child if he knows what *whiteness* is?
He tells you no.   Ask him if he knows what a white
wall, or white paper is, and he knows at once.   Ask
him what *redness* is.   He cannot tell you.   But
speak of a red cloud, or a red rose, and he understands you.   Talk about *hardness*, and he cannot understand you.   Talk about hard wood, a hard hand,
or a hard apple, and he understands it all.   The Old
Testament, in the infancy of the world, when there
was comparatively no reading and no writing, used
to address men through the senses, and in this way
alone.   If God would speak, he came down in the
shape of a man,—he called from the burning bush.
Would he teach his perpetual presence?   He hung
over Israel in the cloud and in the pillar of fire.
Would he teach that he is a king, and ruler, he has
the tabernacle or tent pitched as the palace of the

invisible King, and appoints the High Priest to be the officer who alone might come and receive the commands of the king. Men were then children, and all the Old Testament teaches them in this way. We must follow this method in teaching children. They cannot conceive of any thing abstractly. The fifteenth chapter of Luke is a most beautiful specimen of teaching through the senses. I once saw a preacher trying to teach the children that *the soul would live after they were dead.* They listened, but evidently did not understand it. He was too abstract. Snatching his watch from his pocket he says, "James, what is this I hold in my hand?"

"A watch, sir;"—"a little clock," says another.

"Do you all see it?"

"Yes, Sir."

"How do you know it is a watch?"

"It ticks, Sir."

"Very well, can any of you hear it tick? All listen now." After a pause—"Yes, Sir, we hear it." He then took off the case, and held the case in one hand, and the watch in the other.

"Now, children, which is the watch?—you see there are two which look *like* watches?"

"The littlest one—in your right hand, Sir."

"Very well; but how do you know that this is the watch?"

"Because it ticks."

"Very well again; now I will lay the case aside,—

put it away there down in my hat. Now let us see if you can hear the watch tick ?"

" Yes, Sir, we hear it"—exclaimed several voices.

" Well, the watch can tick, and go, and keep time you see, when the case is taken off and put away in my hat. The watch goes just as well. So it is with you, children. Your body is nothing but the case; the soul is inside. The case,—the body may be taken off and buried up in the ground, and the soul will live and think, just as well as this watch will go, as you see, when the case is off."

This made it plain, and even the youngest went home and told his mother that his " little thought would tick after he was dead."

Many can make no impression upon the mind of the child because they are so *general* in their descriptions. In preparing yourself to teach, be careful to get the mind filled with particular and minute parts of all you undertake to describe. Suppose you wish to teach your class, ' that what they now learn, and all that they now see, and feel, and do, will abide with them through life.' You wish to illustrate, to enforce, and make them remember this particular thought. You do it by telling a simple story, and you tell it as minutely as possible, something in this way.

' Children, you know that lions and tigers, and such wild creatures live far off in the great woods. Men sometimes go after them, and when they find a young lion, or a young tiger,—not much bigger than a cat, they catch them, and shut them up in a cage made of iron wire, and when they are grown up, they carry them round in carts to show them. Well, a number of years ago, a large red lion, with long hair on his neck, called the mane, and with bright, fiery eyes, was brought along in a great iron cage, to show. The cage was iron,—so that he need not break out and kill people. It was taken out of the cart, and put in the middle of a great barn on the floor. A great many men and children went to see the lion. Some wanted to see him eat, some wanted to hear him roar, and some wanted to see him strike his sides with his long tail; and some wanted to see the man who kept him, put his hand in his mouth. At last an old negro man came. He was a tall, old man, with white, woolly hair, and he carried a great cane in his hand. When he came, he walked slowly, and softly, and came up and looked at the lion. After looking a moment, he began to cry. The tears ran down his large, black face; and then he began to sing, and jump, and dance all round the barn! People thought he must be crazy. But after he had danced awhile in this way, he began to cry again. Now what do you think made him feel so? Can any of you guess? I will tell you.—Lions live in Africa,—a place which is a great way off from us. There are plenty of woods there, and the lions live in them. This poor old negro was born in Africa; and when he was a young man, some wicked people came and caught him and brought him away from his home and his friends, and sold him as a slave. He had never gone back,—never seen any of his friends. He had not seen a lion since he came from Africa; and now when he came to see one, it made him think of his home,—his home, where he used to see lions when a boy! It made him think of his boyhood, and called up his parents and friends to his mind, and it seemed to carry him back to his own home of child-hood. These thoughts made him jump and cry and act so! Do you not now see, children, how that what you do, and say, and learn *now,* while you are children, will be remembered as long as you live? This is what makes me so anxious to teach you good things. Now I want you all to remember this story of the lion, and the old gray-headed negro; and re-member too why I told it to you,—to show you that what we learn when we are children, will be re-membered when we are old people, if we should live so long. Don't forget it.'

I may be thought to be tediously minute; but those for whom I write will not be unwilling that I illustrate my thoughts by examples, when I am urging them to do the same to their classes. Almost any simple story will answer your purpose,—always supposing it to be *true.*

6. *The teacher must provide himself with some helps to aid him in preparing to teach.*

Most schools use Questions of some kind or other,

15

and in the present state of Sabbath School teach:ng, I have no doubt that this is wise. But this of itself cannot make a good teacher. He should have a Bible with References,—which he should feel is to be the great interpreter, in connexion with a Concordance, so far as obtaining a knowledge of the Bible is concerned. In addition to this, he will find other helps, such as maps, diagrams, Geographies, Natural History, Antiquities of the Bible, and the like, of great use. Were I to select a commentary, I should decidedly place HENRY first on the list. For obtaining interesting and rich views of the Scriptures, I think it decidedly the best in the English language. No man can read it daily, without becoming wiser and better. To the teacher, it is almost invaluable. I recollect when I first commenced the ministry and was teaching a Bible class, I rode on horse-back through deep mud, eight miles to get Henry, long enough to examine one single chapter, and thought myself abundantly compensated for time and trouble. For a single book, I know of nothing so useful to the teacher as "The Encyclopædia of Religious Knowledge,"—a book of nearly thirteen hundred pages, and as a whole, of great and permanent value. It contains what would cost ten times its own price, if the separate books, containing all its information were to be purchased. Let me beg of the teacher to read some,—even if it be but little, every day. No man can live, and forget as much as every man must, and keep up with the times, without reading and filling up the mind. We love a modest man. We have confidence in such men. The reason is, that they are usually modest in consequence of reading, comparing their views with others, and obtaining knowledge which is the result of experience;—while a man who does not read, is in danger of throwing out half-formed notions, crude opinions, and theories which are based upon a false philosophy. A man who does not read, can have no confidence in himself any longer than he is associated with minds similar to his own. Besides all this, a mind that is not improved by reading will soon have used up all it possesses; and when the man finds that his stock is completely exhausted, he is in danger of retiring in discontent, and mourning over the stupidity and degeneracy of the times. The reading of which I am speaking, has direct reference to the lessons to be taught. That reading is always the most valuable which has an immediate end directly in view.

7. *The teachers' meeting should be punctually attended, and made useful in preparing to teach.*

Since a kind providence has placed me in the ministry, there has been no part of my congregation in which I have taken a deeper interest than the Sabbath School. If I have in any measure been useful to it,—and God has been pleased to bless it abundantly in converting its members,—it has been principally through the teachers. Our method has been

this.   We had a long room fitted up, and a table in
the shape of a T, capable of holding fifty teachers.
At the head of this table I have been accustomed to
meet my teachers once every week.   The Superintendent always sat at my right hand.   On this table
were laid Reference-Bibles, maps, dictionaries, &c.,
as each one chose to bring,—always having a good
Map of Palestine present.   I have then requested the
teacher nearest me to read a verse of the lesson;
asked him questions, and talked with him about it,
just as if in a parlor.   If he could not readily answer
the question, I say, " can any of the teachers answer
this question?"   Any one answers, who pleases.   Or
if he gives an answer not quite satisfactory, or not
quite full enough, I ask, ' has any teacher a different
opinion,' or, ' would any teacher add any thing to
this answer?'   Sometimes these questions lead us into
long and deeply interesting conversations; for after I
have put the questions relating to each verse, all
have permission to question me.   And at the end of
the lesson, I ask, ' has any teacher any question to
ask, which has not been satisfactorily answered?'   I
have met hundreds of teachers in these meetings,
have never seen a meeting which was not deeply interesting, have never seen any thing occur which was
painful, disrespectful, or otherwise than pleasant.   I
can truly say, that some of the brightest hours of my
life have been spent with teachers in the Teachers'
Meeting.   I have never seen any disagreement among

themselves. Each one should come to these meetings
endeavouring to bring a teachable, kind spirit; to
bring his share of intellectual food which is to make
up the feast, and to feel that he is doing all that he
can to make the meeting profitable and interesting.
A lesson *talked* over in this way will be taught with
great pleasure and profit. I have sometimes been
delighted with the illustrations which they have
brought in; and sometimes have felt that I was aiding them when they ask, " how, Sir, would you illustrate this and that truth contained in this lesson, to a
child of six years?" The minister and the teachers
who have been unacquainted with the pleasures of
these meetings, are ignorant of what will always
cheer, encourage, enlighten, and warm the heart.

8. *Prayer is indispensable to him who would acquire knowledge in order to be a teacher.*

Were the question to be asked how you could make
even fine linen whiter, the answer undoubtedly would
be, wash it in pure water; and the purer the water,
the whiter would be the linen. So if you would
have the mind clear, and pure, there is nothing like
washing it in the pure waters of life. It needs daily
and constant washing, too, for sin daily defiles it.
Nothing will purify the mind like bringing it into
contact with God in prayer; nothing will render it
clear like this,—nothing will enlarge and strengthen
it like this. It is the testimony of all such men as
Payson, that they succeeded in obtaining knowledge

15 *

vastly more rapidly, in consequence of communing with God in prayer.

There is another thought which should not be left out of mind. The Scriptures were given by the inspiration of the Holy Spirit. He is their author. In order, then, to understand them aright, you must go to the same Spirit for light and teaching. He can guide into all truth, and make you wise to lead others to salvation. Your own comfort as a Christian must droop and die, your hopes become faint and darkened, your faith weak and unproductive, and your love to the souls of men will wax cold indeed, unless you keep your heart warm at the throne of grace. I do entreat my reader never to attempt to get a lesson,— never to go to the teachers' meeting,—never to go to your class, unless you have first earnestly sought the blessing of God upon your soul in secret prayer. All meetings of teachers should be opened and closed with prayer. All attempts to do good must be founded on prayer. Were I to say what I deem the greatest deficiency among teachers,—among Christians,— among all who are engaged in building up the kingdom of Jesus Christ, I should say, the *want of an habitual spirit of prayer*. The mouth that speaks in God's name in the pulpit,—the hand that holds the pen which writes for the good of others,—the lips that pour instruction into the mind of the child,—all, all need to be daily sanctified by prayer. This would shield us in the hour of temptation; this would sus-

Conclusion.

tain us when the horizon looks dark and gloomy,—
this would strengthen us when the heart feels ignorant and desponding,—and this would give us the arm
of Omnipotence for our aid, the wisdom of the Infinite One for our light, and the sweet communion of
the blessed Spirit to aid, guide, and reward us.   The
seed sown in the freshness of the morning, and that
which is scattered in the dews of evening, would alike
take root, and bring forth fruit, thirty, sixty, and an
hundred fold.

CHAPTER VI.

COMMUNICATING RELIGIOUS INSTRUCTION.

No one can feel the responsibility of making the first, the deepest impressions, on an immortal spirit on the subject of religion, without great anxiety. It is difficult to know when we are in the right way; still more difficult to know that we do as well as we are able. The few hints, which, in this Chapter, I propose to throw out in regard to the best method of communicating religious instruction, will be, I fear, as far from being satisfactory to the reader as they are to myself: that they will be more unsatisfactory, I have no fear.

Do not begin the work of teaching with a radical mistake; viz. *that it requires very uncommon talents to teach children.*

There are many most valuable men both in our churches and in the ministry, who never make any attempts at teaching children, because they think they have no faculty for it;—that this is a gift of nature which has been denied them, and therefore they can never exercise it. So far is this from being the case, that I believe it to be no more the gift of nature than the talent to express your thoughts to adults. By attention and long practice you can communicate your thoughts to old, or middle-aged people; and by practice you can just as well communicate them to children. And yet how often do we hear the thought expressed, that it requires "*a peculiar talent*" to teach children! What a dearth of teachers in most of our Sabbath Schools, because the impression is so general, that but few have this "peculiar talent!" How many, too, would at once leave their classes, and retire from the field,—could their places possibly be filled,—because they have not this talent! And how many just drag along, year after year, in the school, not expecting, not trying to do much, because they have not this "peculiar talent!" We find some men, by peculiar circumstances, becoming painters, musicians, and artists. The taste that made them so, is thought to be a peculiar gift of nature. Sometimes we call it hereditary, as, for example, when the child of a musician is taught music, and hears music only from his cradle, and grows up fond of music, we call it an hereditary taste; whereas, had this child as early and as assiduously been taught the use of the pencil, he might have had an hereditary taste for painting. Till within a short time, it was supposed that none could be taught to sing except a few gifted ones who were highly favored by nature. It is now found that by taking children early, as great a proportion can be taught music, as can be taught to speak correctly. Scarcely such a thing is known as a blind child who is not a musician,—showing most conclusively, that this power is no special gift of nature. The power of interesting children is one that can be cultivated to almost any extent; and what at first *seems* exceedingly difficult, is, in fact, far from being so. The power of arresting the attention, and of interesting a class, will not come to you as a matter of course, without laborious efforts on your part; but you need not have a fear, if you have the ordinary powers of men, but you can attain to excellence in this department.

I am not without fears lest I weary my reader by the exhortation, *be simple—be simple*, in your teaching. How often have I listened to the teacher who was almost out of patience as he said, ' can you not understand this?—it is very plain!' Now it *is* plain to you, but what is so easy for you to comprehend, may be very difficult for the child to understand. I have no doubt you will, with pleasure, read the following paragraph from the memoir of Henry Obookiah,—one of the most interesting youths ever converted to Christianity. " When he began to read in words of one or two syllables in the spelling-book, there were certain sounds which he found it very difficult to articulate. This was true especially of syllables that contained the letter R : a letter which occasioned him more trouble than all others. In pronouncing it, he uniformly gave it the sound of L. At every different reading an attempt was made to correct the pronunciation. The language generally used on such occasions was, " *try, Obookiah, it is very easy.*" This was often repeated. But it was soon perceived that whenever these words were used they excited a smile. And as patience began to be tried by many unsuccessful attempts, and the words to be used more in earnest, he was observed to turn away his face for the purpose of concealment, and seemed much diverted. As he was unable to express his thoughts except by acts, no explanation was made, and none demanded. The reason was scarcely perceived. But as the attempts to correct the error were at last successful, the circumstance was soon forgotten. A short time after this, long enough, however, for Obookiah to have made some improvement in speaking the English, his instructor was spending an evening pleasantly with him, in making inquiries concerning some of the habits and practices of his own country. Among other things, Obookiah mentioned the manner in which his countrymen *drank from a spring* when out upon their hunting excursions. The cup which they used was their hands. It was made by clasping them together, and so adjusting the thumbs, and bending the hands, as to form a vessel which would contain a considerable quantity. Of this he gave an example. After

preparing his hands, he was able, from the pliable-
ness of his arms, to raise them entirely to his mouth,
without turning them at all from their horizontal
position. The experiment was attempted by his
instructor; but he found that before his hands were
raised half the distance to his mouth, they were so
much inverted, that their contents would have been
principally lost. He repeated the trial until he began
to be discouraged; when Obookiah, who had been
much amused with his efforts, with a very expressive
countenance, said to him, "*try, Mr. D., it is very
easy!*" The former mystery was now unravelled,
and an important lesson taught with respect to the
ease or difficulty, with which things are done by us
that are or are not natural to us,—or *to which we
have or have not been, from early life, accustomed.*"

This is a very important point. We forget how
and when *we* have obtained our knowledge, and are
in danger of speaking to children just as a Professor
in College would address his class. Whereas, we
should always recollect, that what is so easy to us, is
new, if not incomprehensible, to the child. I once
made the experiment with a little boy, of trying to
make him understand every thing which I taught
him. At the close of every sentence and explanation
I would ask him if he understood it? He soon got
so used to it, that he would stop me and say, "*I no
stand;*" and I was surprised to see how often his
open, ingenuous countenance would say, "*I no stand.*"

THE SABBATH SCHOOL TEACHER. 181

Children's views.   Three modes to be used.

Just make the experiment any way you please, and
you will be surprised at the result. I recollect having a long conversation with a little girl on the nature
and society of heaven,—the characters, employments
there, and the like. After a protracted and very interesting conversation, by which I supposed she had
obtained correct impressions, I was thrown "all
aback," as sailors say, by her asking in the most art-
less manner, " *whether her new white frock would do
for her to wear there !*"

The teaching in the class may be divided into
three *modes,* each of which should be used for the
sake of variety : *explanatory,* by which the truths
and facts in the lesson, including the words, shall be
made plain ; *catechetical,* by which, by means of
question and answer, the teacher obtains a correct
knowledge how the lesson is understood, wherein
misconceived, or misapplied ; and *exhortatory,* or the
application, by which the lesson is applied to the
conscience of the child, being so brought home to his
own bosom, that he cannot escape its force. These
should all be used, as times and circumstances seem
to demand. By the mere mention of them, the
teacher sees that in the order of nature, variety of
manner is provided. Sometimes in the first of these,
you will need to go into the second mode, and hold a
long conversation with the class, before you can get
them to understand you. For example, the teacher
meets with the word *Justice* in the Question-book.

16

and asks a little girl what it means. She hesitates, thinks a moment, and says she cannot tell. " I will try to make it plain to you. Suppose it to be a rule in the school that the child who told a falsehood should never again be received into the school, and that each teacher was to see this rule carried into practice. Suppose two of my scholars should be guilty of the sin of falsehood, and I should send one away, and leave the other here, because I loved her ;—would this be justice ?"

" No."

" Suppose one of these guilty children were my own little sister, whom I loved very much, and therefore I let her stay, while I sent others away,—would this be justice ?"

" No."

" Well, then, you see that justice is treating *all persons* precisely as they deserve, without following our own feelings in the case. But I will make this still plainer. I have a book in my hand which contains a short story, and which makes the word justice very plain. Shall I *read* it, or *tell* it to you without reading ?"

' We would rather have you *tell* it to us"—

' True, that is pleasanter ; but I want to teach you how to hear books read, and to learn to read them, and therefore *justice* requires me to read it. If I wish to teach you to understand books, and to go to them yourselves, should I be doing *justly* towards you, always to tell you every thing without reading any thing ?"

" No, no ;—we will hear it read."

" Very well, now see how much of it you can understand.—I will read."

" A striking instance of the stern and impartial administration of justice, is afforded in the history of one of the kings of Acalhuacan, a province which composed a part of the Mexican empire. There was a law which forbid, on pain of death, the speaking of indecent words in the royal palace. One of the sons of this king, for whom he had felt a more particular attachment than for any of the rest, on account of his disposition and virtues, violated this law. The words made use of by the young prince were rather the effect of youthful indiscretion, than of any bad intention. The king was informed of it, and understanding that the word had been spoken by the prince in the presence of his tutors, he sent to examine them. They, being afraid of experiencing some punishment if they concealed the truth, confessed it openly, but at the same time endeavored to exculpate the prince by saying that he did not know the person to whom he spoke, nor that the language was improper. Notwithstanding all this, he ordered the young prince to be arrested immediately, and the very same day pronounced sentence of death upon him. The whole court was astonished at the rigor of the king, and interfered with their prayers and

184   THE SABBATH SCHOOL TEACHER.

The king's son executed as an example of justice.   Variety to be studied.

tears in behalf of the prince ; but no remonstrances could move the inflexible mind of the king. ' My son,' said he, ' has violated the law. If I pardon him, it will be said the laws are not binding on every one. I will let my subjects know, that no one will be pardoned a transgression, as I do not even pardon the son whom I dearly love." The punishment was accordingly executed. The king shut himself up for forty days in a hall, without letting himself be seen by any one. He vented his grief in secret, and to conceal from his sight every thing that might recal his sorrow, he caused the door of his son's apartment to be closed up by a wall. He showed his subjects that although he was incapable of repressing the feelings of a father, and sealing up the fountains of his grief, yet he would never permit them to overcome his zeal for the laws, and the most rigid impartiality in their execution."

" You have now heard the story, children. If the king seems cruel to you in this thing, you must remember that he was a poor heathen without the Bible to instruct him, and that he aimed at doing *justice.* The law, perhaps, was too severe, but it was executed with justice. And hereafter, whenever you see or hear any thing about justice, you will at once know what it means."

By all means study *variety* in giving instruction to children. This is a very important point, and one which may not be neglected. Where the class is

The little girls in Wales.

large enough, sometimes it will be well to vary the lesson so far as to give a topic, or a doctrine, and request them to bring the proof-texts on the next Sabbath. This will occupy their spare moments during the week, and give the teacher an admirable opportunity to enter into close conversations, applying the truths to the conscience. I have before me several letters from one who had been a Superintendent of a Sabbath School in Wales for many years. Speaking on this point, he says, ' Jane and Ann Whicher were two of my dear Sunday School children, the one twelve, and the other thirteen. They had an idle, dissolute father, and a feeble, afflicted mother, and they, by their work of platting straw, supported them. One lesson was to prove that ' God hears and answers prayer.' I always encouraged the children to put marks on the margins of their Bibles, opposite the texts of Scripture to which their particular attention had been called. I was surprised to see the number of bits of paper put into their books on the succeeding Sabbath, and the great number of pencil marks all over their books. After expressing my pleasure at their selection of texts, I inquired how it was that they found so many? 'Oh! Sir,' replied the youngest, ' we searched from Genesis to Revelation.' 'How do you find time to do it, while your work keeps you so fully occupied?' ' Why, Sir, we keep our Bibles open, and look at our work, and then on the Bible.' I paid them a visit during the suc-

16 *

ceeding week, and found them at their work of platting with their Bibles open before them.   Their poor
mother wept, while she described how great a blessing they were to her.   Both of them afterwards became members of our church.'

2. *The teacher who would convey religious in-*
struction properly, must have right views as to the
moral character of children.

Were you to call in a physician to see your child,
you would wish him to have right views of the constitution of your child.   He might say, ' this young
lady has a slow fever, and a bad cough, but I think
slight remedies will cure her.   She ought to see
cheerful company, attend parties of pleasure, and
treat herself as if nothing was the matter.'   ' But,
Sir,' you reply, ' the mother and the grand-mother
of this child died of consumption.   They were taken
just as she was.   From her childhood she has seemed
predisposed to this disease, and I am fearful that a
disease which in some sense seems hereditary, may
soon leave me childless.'   ' Oh! no, Sir, I have no
belief in hereditary diseases, and I shall treat her
as if well, only giving a few simple things, and think
she will throw off what seem to be only the effects
of a cold.'   I ask my reader if such a physician is
the man to whom he would entrust the life of a beloved child?   I hope to be excused if I introduce
here the simple account of a child's views in regard
to heaven.   I introduce it, not for the purpose of ex

hibiting the child, but the views of the parent on one of the most important points ever presented to the human mind.

"I was roused from the multitude of my thoughts upon a sick bed, by the innocent prattle of a little boy, whose childish soliloquy seemed to accord strangely with my own speculations. He is a thoughtful, but happy child, of three and a half years old, *whose innocent feelings seem to rise as naturally and affectionately to heaven*, as to the friends he loves here. I shall give exactly his own sentiments in his own language. He had found a *dead fly* upon the window, and laid it upon his little fat palm, and was looking down upon it with a beautiful expression of childish hope and sorrow. 'Poor fly,' said he, 'you shall not lie here, and burn all up in the sun, if you are dead. I will take you, and when the bell tolls I will carry you to the burying-ground, and I will say, here is a poor fly wants to be buried up; and they will take you and put you away down in the ground. But it won't hurt you, little fly; for you will go to heaven, and be very happy there, with the pretty flowers, and you will never die again. And when I go to heaven, and my mother goes to heaven, we shall see you again, little fly!' And he raised his blue eyes half filled with tears, to my face, and said, '*won't the little fly go to heaven?*' I could not check the beautiful sympathy and the kindly affections of his heart. And he loves now to

188   THE SABBATH SCHOOL TEACHER.

The mistake a deep one.   Remarks on this example.

tel. of the beautiful little flowers and pretty birds he shall see in that world of love and happiness, to which he is ready to go when his parents and brothers can accompany him."

There is much that is very beautiful in all this; and shall I not be excused too, if I say there is much also that is wrong? Does not the description of the human heart, " whose innocent feelings seem to rise as naturally and affectionately to heaven, as to the friends he loves here," partake more of poetry than of truth? Take that child and strip him of his delightful home, and place him in the situation of thousands of poor children in our great cities, and let a stranger be called to instruct him, and will his innocent feelings rise naturally to heaven? Or is he not a sinner,—will he not sin all his life, even when surrounded with God's mercies,—and would he not sin, even if angels were to become his teachers and guides? We know he would. The best teaching, the holiest example will be so far from making him holy, that if he should grow up wild, thoughtless, wicked, and awfully depraved, though it would wring many hearts with anguish, yet it would not be an anomaly in the world. Talk about a child's feelings rising naturally to heaven, when you have so far neglected his education that he knows not why a fly is not as immortal as himself! About his being willing to go to heaven whenever his parents and brothers are ready to accompany him! Why, all the

idea he has of heaven, is his own home, with the
family-circle, and the addition of some beautiful
flowers! He would be just as ready to accompany
his parents and friends to the world of woe, if requested to do so. He can form no idea of heaven,
different from his own home. I do not complain of
the flow of this "beautiful sympathy;" nor of the
love of the parent which recorded it; but I do protest against teachers undertaking the great work of
leading children to God, before they have Scriptural
views of the real state of the human heart. The
Bible recognizes none who are by nature holy;—but
on the contrary, by nature all are children of wrath,
—all need regeneration, and the sanctifying influences
of the Holy Ghost. The preacher who does not keep
the line marked and distinct, who does not divide his
hearers into two classes only,—the holy, and the unholy, will not be likely to wield the sword of the
spirit with power,—and I see not how he can feel
that he is faithful to the stewardship committed to
him.

I would not have the Sabbath School teacher feel
that the children gathered around him are high-
handed sinners,—but little better than fallen spirits,—
that they are to be treated harshly, or scolded into
holiness; no such thing; but I would have him understand before he begins the work, that he is about
to deal with depraved hearts;—hearts that will not
naturally rise to heaven, nor will they cherish and

love the light of the Gospel as you pour it into their
hearts. The heart of man is depraved. The earliest
workings of the soul show that sin is there. You
cannot find the time when the soul rises naturally to
God in grateful worship and love; and while you will
be careful to let your religion appear as sincere, as
amiable, as pleasant, as you can, never forget that
you are teaching a company of sinners. Go on this
principle in preparing to teach; go on this principle
in communicating instruction. Instruct them as sinners; feel for them as sinners, pray for them as sinners. If you go on any other principle, you will stop
short of the great point aimed at,—the renewing of
the heart by the Holy Spirit. Go on any other principle, and you will soon become discouraged; that
tree which you have so assiduously and so carefully
watered, does not bring forth the fruits of holiness.
It is owing, in a great measure, to our keeping this
line between converted and unconverted men so distinct and clear, that this land has been so abundantly
blessed with frequent and powerful revivals of religion.

3. *The teacher must gain the confidence and affection of his class, in order to communicate religious instruction.*

The great Apostle of the Gentiles understood this
well: "We were gentle among you, even as a nurse
cherisheth her children: so being affectionately desirous of you, we were willing to impart unto you,

not the Gospel of God only, but also our own souls, because ye were dear unto us." You cannot reach the heart of a child unless he feels that you are a warm, personal friend. You must meet him with the smile of love, rather than in the sternness of authority. He must be controlled; but feel that the bonds of friendship are around him. He must feel that without fee, or reward, without any selfish aims, you are laboring for his best good. After you have once obtained the confidence of a child, he will scarcely attempt to conceal from you his thoughts, or the emotions of his heart. In order to gain and retain the confidence of your class, let there be no lightness of conduct, no trifling, no laughing, no undue familiarity. This is not necessary. Be careful too, not to wound the feelings of the child by smiling at his ignorance or mistakes. " The teacher," says one who has had great experience, " should have great command over his risibilities. I have often had replies to questions put to poor, ignorant boys, almost irresistibly ludicrous. In one instance there was something so exceedingly ludicrous, that I lost self-command and laughed heartily. I at once saw that I had lowered myself in the estimation of my pupils. I was letting myself down to a level with them. I had laughed in God's house, on his day, and in his presence, when sixty immortal souls were influenced by my conduct. I have too frequently seen teachers guilty of similar conduct." No child *intends* to give a ludicrous answer to your question, and if it strikes you in that light and you laugh at him, you injure his feelings, and leave a sting which will not be soon extracted.

Besides, you will be very careful not to do any thing to diminish confidence in the child, because you wish to draw him out in conversation. Without this, you cannot reach his mind, cannot determine how much mind he has, how far it has been cultivated, or what instruction and influence it now needs. If the child fears lest what he says will strike his teacher as ludicrous, or that he will throw the least ridicule upon his answers, his heart will be frozen, and the fountain of his sympathies will be dried up. Who cannot recal times in his own childhood, when he has been ridiculed, perhaps by those whom he esteemed his best friends, when his feelings received wounds which can never be forgotten while life remains?

Be careful, so far as possible, not to doubt the veracity and the good intentions of the child. Nothing will so soon check, and kill the growth of confidence and love between the child and yourself, as imputing things to him in the name of crimes, when he is innocent. I once knew a fatherless child have his veracity doubted by one who ought to have known better. All he could say to prove his innocence was turned against him, and he was treated as if no proof of innocence would be satisfactory. The child

Example.   Beware of being partial.

colored, sobbed, and retired; but ten thousand kind-
nesses, and ten thousand good opinions, afterwards
could never erase the cruel wound from his bosom
The affections, the love, the confidence, were never
regained, though probably the person who thus cut
them away, forgot it in a few months, if not in a few
days. The teacher will find his own heart a good
instructor in this matter. Every thing should be
avoided which will tend to prevent drawing each
child out into familiar and frequent conversations.

If I mistake not, the teacher will be in danger of
showing something which resembles partiality. There
will be some who are more prompt, more ready, more
attentive, more obedient, more affectionate, than
others. They show more interest in the lessons, and
exert themselves to make their teacher feel happy.
It will be impossible for the teacher not to *feel* a
partiality for such scholars. But let him be careful
not to *show* it. If you let the quick and the ready,
answer nearly all the questions that are asked, you
discourage, and you are in danger of disgusting the
rest. Children are quick to discover partialities, and
keen to feel them. Every one, without exception, has some one or more good traits of character,
though there may be many that are bad, counteract-
ing them. Try to discover what good qualities each
child has,—draw them out, and strengthen them.
This will give you a new and a deeper interest in his
welfare; and this interest thus created in your own

17

bosom, will soon gain his confidence and love. Many Sabbath School children already feel that their teacher is by far the best friend they have on earth, and the one to whom they would go when the heart was enduring its greatest troubles.

You must have the confidence of your class, not in your moral honesty and disinterestedness merely, but also in your intellectual competency for your station. It is sometimes thought that an incompetent teacher will do for a class of very small, or very ignorant scholars. This is not so. An incompetent teacher is never in his place in a Sabbath School. Who needs the proof, that the very best men whom the church raises up, are needed to go as missionaries among the heathen? And yet the heathen are mere children in knowledge. But the work of reaching and enlightening the mind debased, sunken, darkened, and enfeebled by sin, cannot be done by unskilful men; and I believe our best teachers ought to be placed over the classes which are the lowest and the most difficult to raise.

So much depends upon the confidence and affection of your class, that on newly entering upon the duties of teaching, you should make it the first object to secure them. Before these be gained, you can do nothing to any good purpose. Seek, then, to know the habits, the disposition, the whole character of every child committed to you. Visit him when he is sick; visit him at his home. Show him that you are

interested in him, in his parents, in all that can concern him.   No heart can resist kindness; and when
you have the confidence and the love of your pupils,
God has then given you an influence, which, in most
cases, may be the means of leading them to the
Lamb of God.   These plants are delicate, and the
soil in which they are to grow may be very unpro-
pitious; but still, with proper care, you can cause
them to take root and grow.

4. *To teach with success, you must have the power
of gaining and keeping the attention.*

The minds of children are so taken up with the
trifles of the world, that it is difficult to gain and fix
the attention.   But a greater difficulty arises from
the fact that their minds are undisciplined, and they
are unaccustomed to confine their thoughts to any
particular point for any length of time.   The teacher
is in great danger of feeling disappointed and discouraged at this stage, if he be not well prepared to
meet difficulties.   You prepare the mind to give a
good exposition of the lesson, or you charge the soul
with a solemn exhortation, and in the midst of it,
you see one looking out of the window, or hearkening
to the recitations of the next class, or perhaps endeavouring to make sport for one across the room.
Or you find that patience is exhausted, and they
are listless, uninterested, and stupid, while you
are speaking.   Make up your mind to meet all this,
and much more also.   Remember that your ingenuity

will be more taxed by gaining and keeping attention than by all other things. The great secret of success consists in having your own mind deeply interested in your subject. You never know a speaker before any audience fail of fixing attention, when it is very apparent that he is deeply interested in what he is saying. As far as possible, be ready to connect some interesting instruction with all your conversations, and with the answers to all the questions put to you. A teacher is engaged in the historical parts of the Bible. He comes to a place where unclean birds are forbidden to the Jews. The Pelican, the Eagle, and the Swan, are among them. He goes into the reasons why certain creatures were forbidden to the Jews for food, the amount of which is, that in their food, dress, and habits, God made it .as difficult as possible for them to associate with the heathen by whom they were surrounded. He also adds something of the natural history of these birds as their names occur. The class, if they are somewhat advanced, will ask questions.

" How long will the swan live ?"

" It is not known. A goose has been known to live an hundred years, and from the firmer texture of the flesh of the swan, that would probably live longer."

" Does the swan sing ?"

" No, I believe not. The ancients used to suppose it did; but it is now understood that it utters only a kind of shrill hiss, or whistle."

" But I have read of the dying song of the swan, and have just been learning some beautiful poetry about it. Is it not true, that the swan ever sings so ?"

" I wish, Caroline, you would slowly repeat the poetry about it, and I will then tell you how true it is."

" I will try."

> " What is that, Mother?
>   The swan, my love ;
> He is floating down from his native grove,
> No loved one now, no nestling nigh ;
> He is floating down by himself to die :
> Death darkens his eye, and unplumes his wings,
> Yet the sweetest song is the last he sings !
> Live so, my love, that when death shall come,
> Swan-like and sweet, it may waft thee home !"

" That *is* beautiful indeed, and the instruction in the last two lines is very good. But poetry need not always be truth. It instructs by using fables. This is one of the fables of the ancients. But I can tell you about a death which is equally beautiful, and *it is all true.* Shall I tell it to you ?"

" O yes, we all want to hear it."

" You have all heard of Swartz. A little book containing his life is in the Library. He died at the age of seventy-two, having been a missionary forty-eight years in India. He calculated sometime before his death, that two thousand had been savingly converted from heathenism by his means. He acquired

17 *

such a character among the heathen, that when among barbarous and lawless robbers, he was suffered to pass through contending parties of them unmolested, and unsuspected. They said, *let him alone—let him pass—he is a man of God.* A tyrant, named Hyder Ally, while he refused to enter into a certain treaty with others, said, *send me Swartz; send me the Christian missionary, for him only can I trust.* The people had been so cruelly treated that they left their lands, and refused to raise any thing. All they had raised had been seized and taken away. The whole country would soon have been in a famine. The heathen ruler promised justice, and tried to induce them to go back to their farms; but all in vain. They would not believe him. *Mr. Swartz then wrote to them, making the same promises.* All immediately came back. Seven thousand men returned to their land in one day. Such was the man.

" When he came to die, he was lying apparently lifeless, when Gericke, a worthy fellow-laborer from the same country, who imagined that the immortal spirit had actually taken its flight, began to chant over his remains, a stanza of the favorite hymn which they used to sing together, and soothe each other in his life-time. The verses were sung through without a motion, or a sign of sympathy or life from the still form before him; but when the last clause was over, the voice which was supposed to be hushed in death, took up the second stanza of the same hymn,

—completed it with a distinct and sweet utterance,—
and then was hushed,—and was heard no more. The
soul rose with the last strain!"

" Is not this more touching and beautiful than even
the poetry about the dying swan? I hope you will
all remember it, and whenever you read of the swan
you will recollect this story, and recollect how sweetly
death comes to a good man, who has faithfully served
Jesus Christ. We must now, children, go on with
the lesson."

Such a digression is not, in my opinion, lost, were
there nothing but the association of the swan and
the death of Swartz formed in the memory. But
there is more; for the teacher will have no more
difficulty that day to gain and hold the attention of
his class.

Sometimes it will be well to tell all your class to
commit a certain hymn, or a certain portion of Scripture to memory, in addition to the stated lesson. Say
that if they will all commit it thoroughly, you will
tell them the reason why you make the request at
another time, and that when you *do* make the explanation, you think they will not regret having learned
it. By this means, you get something fastened in the
memory,—you awaken curiosity, you draw the attention of all the class towards something which they
hope to have explained hereafter. In this way, you
are sure to gain attention, close, undivided attention,
till that which excited it is finally disposed of. Per-

haps you will feel that the illustration given above, is beyond the comprehension of your class. They are small, and ignorant. You will remember that this illustration is not for your class, but such an one as might be used in fixing the attention of advanced classes. I will, therefore, suppose your class to be very young. They live in the country, scattered up and down the hills and the mountain-side. You are troubled to fix their attention, and are using various means by which to do it. You begin the conversation something in this way.

"Mary, have you learned that hymn which I marked for you?"

"No, not well enough to say."

"But could you not learn one verse?"

"Not well enough to say. I tried, but it was so hard."

"Well, I see how it is. How far do you live from the nearest house, Mary?"

"O that is Mr. Kelsey's! It is more than half a mile."

"Do you never feel lonely when you are left by your mother, when she goes down to the store?"

"O yes, Ma'am, all alone, and I very often go out and swing on the gate and cry, till mother comes home."

"Well I have got a verse of a hymn which just suits your case, Mary. I have but two copies, but if you will all learn it, and say it correctly next Sabbath, I will tell you a story which has something to do with it. But I shall not tell it, unless every one of you has learned it. What do you say,—will you try? Let those hold up their hands who wish to learn it. Very well. Here it is. You must contrive to lend it from one to the other during the week, and *all* must learn it, or I do not tell you the story."

The next Sabbath comes. You meet the little class. They are all there, their faces bright and full of hope. You go through the lesson, and they are all attention. You say nothing about the hymn. But after the lesson is through, one of them puts you in mind of the hymn!

"Oh yes, the hymn! I had not forgotten it, but was waiting to see if you had. Who can say it, and say it correctly?"

You begin, and find that every one says it fluently, and with great ease.

"Well, children, I see that you *can* learn hymns, and I hope Mary will never feel so lonely again, and never say again that she cannot learn whatever I give her."

'Many years ago a German left his country and with his family came into the State of Pennsylvania to live there. He was a poor man, and had a large family. There were no schools there during the week, or on the Sabbath, and no churches. So the poor man used to keep his family at home on the Sabbath, and teach them from God's word,—for he was a very good man. In the year 1754, a dreadful war broke out in Canada between the French and the English. The Indians joined the French, and used to go to Pennsylvania, burn houses, murder the people, and carry off every thing they wanted. They found the dwelling of this poor German family. The man, and his oldest boy, and two little girls named Barbara and Regina were at home, while the wife and one of the boys were gone to carry some grain to the mill a few miles off. The Indians at once killed the man and his son, and took the two little girls, one aged ten and the other nine, and carried them away, along with a great many other weeping children whom they had taken after murdering their parents. It was never known what became of Barbara, the oldest girl; but Regina, with another little girl of two years old, whom Regina had never seen before, were given to an old Indian woman, who was very cruel. Her only son lived with her, and supported her; but he was sometimes gone for several weeks, and then the old woman used to send the little girls to gather roots and herbs in the woods, for the old woman to eat; and when they did not get enough, she used to beat them cruelly. Regina never forgot her good father and mother, and the little girl always kept close to her. She taught the little girl to kneel down under the trees and pray to the Lord Jesus, and to say over with her all the hymns which her parents had taught her. In this state of slavery these children lived for nine long years, till Regina was about nineteen, and her little friend was eleven years old. Their hearts all this time seemed to wish for that which is good. They used to repeat not only the texts of Scripture which Regina could remember, but there was one favorite hymn which they often said over. It was the same hymn which you have just now been saying to me! In the year 1764, the kindness of God brought the English Colonel Bouquet to the place where they were. He conquered the Indians, and made them ask for peace. He granted it, on condition that all the white prisoners and captives should be given him. More than four hundred were brought to the Colonel; and among them, these two girls. They were all poor, wretched looking objects. The Colonel carried them to a town called Carlisle in Pennsylvania, and had it printed in all the newspapers, that all parents who had lost children by the Indians, might come and see if they were among the four hundred poor captives. Poor Regina's sorrowing mother,—a poor widow, among others went to Carlisle to see if she could find her children! But when she got there, she did not and could not know Regina. She had grown up, and looked, and dressed, and spoke like the Indians. The mother went up and down among the captives weeping, but could not find her child. She stood gazing and weeping, when Colonel Bouquet came up and said,

" do you recollect *nothing* by which your child might
be discovered ?" She said, she recollected nothing
but a hymn which she used often to sing to her children, and which is as follows :—

> " Alone, yet not alone am I,
>   Though in this solitude so drear ;
> I feel my Savior always nigh,
>   He comes the weary hour to cheer.
> I am with him and he with me,—
>   E'en here alone I cannot be !"

" The Colonel desired her to sing the hymn as she
used to do. Scarcely had the poor mother sung two
lines of it, when Regina rushed from the crowd, began to sing it also, and threw herself into her
mother's arms. They both wept for joy, and the
Colonel gave the daughter up to her mother. But the
other little girl had no parents. They had probably
been murdered. She clung to Regina, and would
not let her go, and so she was taken home with Regina, though her mother was very poor. Regina began to ask after " the book in which God speaks to
us." But her mother had no Bible,—for the Indians
burned her Bible when they burned her house and
killed her family. Her mother resolved to go to
Philadelphia and buy a Bible ; but her good minister
gave her one, and it was found that Regina could
read it at once.'

" You see, children, why I wished you to learn
that particular hymn.—the same hymn by which

this poor mother and child were restored to each other. I know by your looks that you have understood the story, and hope you will always remember the beautiful hymn, and the story connected with it."

Does my reader say that he cannot illustrate or keep attention awake by a story every Sabbath? Nor do I ask him to do it. I only tell him *how* he certainly can awaken and fix the attention as often as he pleases. Does he say that this is an expensive way of teaching,—that it will cost time and reading and planning and thinking? I reply that you can have nothing valuable without taking pains, and laboring for it. If it requires trouble to fix and keep the attention of your class, you are abundantly repaid for all this, by their decided improvement. As I am certain that I could fill half a volume at once from recollection, with illustrations which might be used to fasten instruction, and to fix the attention, I cannot readily see why teachers might not do it to any desirable extent.

Few have been more successful in teaching children than James Hervey. "On such occasions," says he, "I endeavor to comprehend, not all that may be said, but that only which may be level to their capacities, and is most necessary for them to know. The answer to each question I explain in the most familiar manner possible, in such a manner as a polite hearer might treat with the most sovereign contempt; little similes I use, that are quite low. In

206 THE SABBATH SCHOOL TEACHER.

The great art of teaching.   A faithful teacher.

every explanation I would be short, but repeat it
again and again; tautology in this case is the true
propriety of speaking to our little auditors, and will
be better than all the graces of eloquence."

To sum up all that I would wish to say in thi
chapter, the great art of teaching children and
youth, is to be yourself interested, deeply interested
in what you teach. This will lead you to try various
methods of attaining the great object proposed; it
will lead you to study, to fill the mind with thought.
and to simplify your modes of communicating your
thoughts. It will call forth your ingenuity to contrive
in what ways you can best reach, enlighten, and impress the heart, form habits for this life, and guide the
soul to the next. The following beautiful testimony of
a teacher's faithfulness was found among her papers
after she had gone to the sleep of death. ‘A class
of seven was committed to me for instruction,—of
different ages, from twelve to sixteen, and one was
older than that. Most of them were girls with whom
I had little or no acquaintance, and as I took my
place with them for the first time, I feared I should
not have a very interesting class. However, I resolved to be faithful to my trust when with them,
and in my preparation to meet them; though often
fearful that I fell very far short both in teaching
them, and in commending their case to God in
private.

It has been my habitual practice to press upon

their attention those questions in the lessons which are addressed to the conscience and the heart; and frequently to ask a number more, which the subject seemed to suggest, that, if possible, some valuable and lasting impressions might be made; always requiring every scholar to pay her undivided attention during the whole recitation. Sometimes I was hurt to observe some individual in the class to be gazing about the house in a careless manner; but in general their attention seemed absorbed in the lesson.

'About the middle of summer, one of the oldest members of the class began to be anxious about the salvation of her soul. This concern continued for several weeks, until three more of the class were saying, what shall we do to be saved? These four were all soon brought to rejoice in hope. Two of the others, I soon found, were mourning over their lost state as sinners, while one seemed hardened, and I feared would be left to her own chosen way.

'It was my usual practice to inquire of each individual respecting the state of her mind, after the close of the recitation, in addition to the practical remarks during recitation. Before the time for closing the summer term arrived, I had the happiness of hearing every member of my class express her hope in Christ, and of seeing six of them united with the church. (The seventh united soon after.)

'I could not, should I attempt it, describe what my

feelings were, on meeting my class all rejoicing in the Savior.

'I do not know that my instructions were, in any considerable degree, the means of leading the class to seek religion; this is left to be developed another day. But I felt when I saw them all hoping in the Savior, as if I should like to commit them to the care of some other person, and take another class, that I might still teach sinners.'

CHAPTER VII.

.

INFANT SABBATH SCHOOLS.

BUFFON, in his Natural History, describes the wild Ass which was brought to France, and which was the only one he ever saw. He says it was nearly wild when it arrived, but after great labor and pains to subdue him, they at length got him so tame that a man dared mount him, having two additional men to hold him by the bridle. He was restive like a vicious horse, and obstinate as a mule; still, Buffon thinks that if he had been accustomed to obedience and tameness from his earliest years, he would be as mild as the tame ass, or the horse, and might be used in their place.

Now the Scriptures describe human nature by saying, that 'man is born like a wild ass's colt!' If this graphic description be correct, then we cannot be too anxious to begin the process of subduing and training, too early. The men who are engaged in catching taking and exhibiting wild beasts, never

18 *   209

think of catching one that is old, or even grown up.
They take them as young as possible, and even then,
find it difficult to manage them. They act on the
soundest principles of wisdom.

The experiment has often been made of taking
young savages, sometimes from the Indians of this
continent, and sometimes from the eastern Isles, and
educating and civilizing them; after expending much
money and pains-taking, we have almost uniformly
been disappointed by having them return to savage
life, and savage habits. Some years since a young
New Zealander was carried to England, where he
lived many years, was carefully educated, and introduced into the most refined society. When his education was completed, he returned to his home, and
at once returned to the habits, the character, and the
degradations of savage life. This has almost uniformly been the result of attempts to civilize and
educate young savages. And why? On what principle can it be accounted for? I reply, that *the
work was begun too late.* The impressions made
upon early childhood cannot be effaced. You may
take the young savage, and make a palace his home,
and he is like the wild ass's colt; he longs for the
forest, for the lawlessness of savage life. This principle is deep, uniform, unalterable. I cannot describe
it so well as it has been done by a gifted pen; and the
description is so true to nature, and so beautiful, that
I cann't deny the reader the privilege of enjoying

what can never be read, without stirring up the deepest fountains of the soul. I refer to Mrs. Hemans's
exquisite description of the deep impressions which
are made upon early childhood; and though longer
than I could wish, yet I can see no part that may be
omitted. It is a dialogue between a patrician lady,
and a poor boy from the mountains, whom she wishes
to adopt as her son.

LADY. "Why would'st thou leave me, oh! gentle child?
Thy home on the mountain is bleak and wild,
A straw-roofed cabin with lowly wall—
Mine is a fair and pillared hall,
Where many an image of marble gleams,
And the sunshine of pictures forever streams!"

BOY. "Oh! green is the turf where my brothers play,
Through the long bright hours of the summer day;
They find the red-cup moss where they climb,
And they chase the bee o'er the scented thyme;
And the rocks where the heath-flower blooms they know,—
Lady, kind lady, oh! let me go!"

LADY. "Content thee, boy, in my bower to dwell!
Here are sweet sounds which thou lovest well;
Flutes on the air in the stilly noon,
Harps which the wandering breezes tune;
And the silvery wood-note of many a bird,
Whose voice was ne'er in thy mountains heard."

BOY. "My mother sings, at the twilight's fall,
A song of the hills far more sweet than all;

She sings it under our own green tree,
To the babe half slumbering on her knee,—
I dreamt last night of that music low,—
Lady, kind lady, oh ! let me go !"

LADY. " Thy mother hath gone from her cares to rest,
She hath taken the babe on her quiet breast;
Thou would'st meet her footstep, my boy, no more,
Nor hear her song at the cabin door;
Come thou with me to the vineyards nigh,
And we 'll pluck the grapes of the richest dye !"

BOY. " Is my mother gone from her home away ?
But I know that my brothers are there at play !
I know they are gathering the foxglove's bell,
And the long fern-leaves by the sparkling well,
Or they launch their boats where the blue streams flow,—
Lady, kind lady, oh ! .let me go !"

LADY. " Fair child, thy brothers are wanderers now,
They sport no more on the mountain's brow,
They have left the fern by the spring's green side,
And the streams where the fairy barks were tied !
Be thou at peace in thy brighter lot,
For thy cabin-home is a lonely spot !"

BOY. " Are they gone,—all gone from the sunny hill ?
But the bird and the blue-fly rove o'er it still ;
And the red deer bound in their gladness free,
And the heath is bent by the singing bee,
And the waters leap, and the fresh winds blow,—
Lady, sweet lady, oh ! let me go !"

My reader will say, not merely that this is beautiful, but that it is true to nature. The man whose
childhood was spent on the sea-shore, who often at
that period stood on the firm rocks eyeing the storm,
and the heaving of the deep, as the white waves
rolled in upon the rocks, will never forget the impressions. These scenes will haunt him through life, and
often in his dreams will he plant his foot on the very
place, and leap the deep crevices, as he used to
do when a boy. A gentleman was conversing with a
fine young chamois-hunter on the Alps, upon the
dangers to which he exposed himself. The young
man stood upon the edge of the precipice, and drawing up his noble figure, and grasping his rifle still closer,
replied, ' my father and my grand-father both lost
their lives in this business,—they lived in that little
cot where I live. I expect one day to lose my life
in the same way ; but I would not exchange my home
and my situation for that of the richest man on the
wide face of Europe.'

Let any one take two children at the age of seven
years, the one the son of a savage, and the other the
son of a gentleman, and it would be next to impossible, by any training, however skilful, to make their
characters alike. The love of savage life, the impressions of childhood, could never be removed. But
let these boys be educated together, without any dis-
tinction, from the age of two years, and the results
would undoubtedly be widely different. Probably

more is learned, and deeper impressions are made
upon the mind between the ages of eighteen months
and three years, than during the same period of time,
in any subsequent part of life. From the hour that
the child becomes capable of noticing what is passing around him, he receives impressions from example, and circumstance and situation. So powerful,
indeed, are the gradual and unnoticed influences of
these early days, that we not unfrequently see the
indulged and humored infant a petty tyrant before
a year old, at two years of age, a discontented, irritable thing, causing every one but its mother to turn
away from it with disgust. At this period of life, the
child is making observations, forming opinions, and
acquiring habits. Notions, right or wrong, are now
becoming so completely a part of his character, that
they can never be eradicated. He can now be made
so fearful and superstitious, that through life he will
dread to see " the new moon over his left shoulder,"
and will never feel perfectly calm alone and in the
dark. We should not lay the blame on the disposition,
as we are too apt to do, till we are sure that the
glaring defects of character, which are frequently
seen in manhood, are not the results of neglected
education, just as we frequently see a tree, stunted
and dwarfed by a wall, a shade, or a dry soil.

'Education begins with life. The touch first ministers to it; afterwards the sight; and then the hearing. This is our guide in seeking to assist the pro-

gress of Nature. We must begin with present and
tangible things; we must then give absent things a
visible form by picture; and the picture which meets
the eye may lead to the description which finds its
way to the mind only by the ear. The reason why
the earlier instructions of the nursery should be thus
embodied in picture, in story, and in narration, is evident; children cannot understand any thing beyond
them. Every thing is fresh to the mind of a child.
Curiosity is constantly awake, and novelty is constantly feeding it. Objects and incidents which have
no interest for adult life, are sufficient to entrance the
thought of infancy, and fill the heart with bounding,
new-born ecstacy. Many persons in writing for children have evidently forgotten to sympathise with the
period of childhood. They have ceased to remember
with distinct vividness, the times in which men and
women were all kings and queens to them; a house
their world; a garden their paradise, and the merest
trifles were possessed of a mysterious power to agitate
them with anguish or delight. The evil of such writing
for such a period of life, dwells not simply in the bad
taste which it exemplifies. Unnatural in itself, it
produces unnatural and even dangerous consequences.
The mind of infancy, moved by the gentlest impulses,
is over-strained and distorted by the violence of such
premature excitation. Terror is produced instead
of fear, suspicion instead of caution, extravagance
instead of generosity, and morbid sentiment instead of

benevolent principle. These effects, in numerous instances, have been perpetuated through every period
of after-life. The man and the woman have never
been able to recover themselves from the fear and
apprehension, the false sentiment, and injurious excitement, which are considered to be common to
childhood, but which are not proper to it, and which
will only be common to it, as the child is exposed to
injurious treatment, by the absurd tales of the nurse,
or the nursery book.'

The preceding remarks have been made to show,
what ought to be engraven on the heart and memory
of all,—that EDUCATION BEGINS WITH LIFE. Before
we are aware, the foundations of the character are
laid, and no subsequent instruction can remove or
alter them. Linnæus was the son of a poor Swedish
clergyman. His father had a little flower-garden, in
which he cultivated all the flowers which his means
or his taste could select. Into this flower-garden he
introduced his little son from his infancy; and this
little garden undoubtedly created that taste in the
child which afterwards made him the first botanist
and naturalist of his age, if not of his race.

The reader will infer also from what I have said,
that I am in favor of having infant classes attached
to every Sabbath School where it is practicable. I
do not mean that they should be in the same room,
but that each church should endeavor to have such
a school, and for the same great objects for which

First reason.

they have the Sabbath School at all. But with a view to being definite, I will briefly sum up the reasons for such schools.

1. *It will give two or three years of additional culture, both intellectual and moral.*

Very many parents complain that their circumstances prevent their continuing their children at school so long as they could wish; but they seem to forget that they may gain all that they want, and even more, by beginning their education two years earlier. I have often seen children taken from school at sixteen, the parents lamenting that their circumstances would not allow them to continue longer at study; while these parents seem to forget that had they begun sufficiently early, their children might have had what was equivalent to two years more of education; just as I have seen a farmer, whose lot faced the street, exert himself and violate his conscience by removing his fence, and crowding up towards the road; perhaps he would gain half a rod of land, the whole length of his lot; while at the *back-side* of the lot there would be a rod or two overrun with brush and briars, which, if cultivated, would be equally valuable with that in front. How many are solicitous to cultivate the front of the lot, and leave the back to the dominion of briars and thorns! But the plan of having infant classes attached to the Sabbath School, brings the child under moral and intellectual culture at the right time; and if the instruction be judiciously managed, it will place the child in advance of children who do not have it. There can be no question of this. Not that the child can gain as much knowledge which will abide, between two and four years of age, as between sixteen and eighteen; but if his education begins at two, he will at four years, have that discipline of mind by which, at the end of ten years more, he will be as well educated as if he began two years older, and continued his education the same length of time. It is the early discipline of mind, and the early impressions, which are so important in the education of an immortal being.

2. *Such schools lead the child up in nature's own way.*

There is only one possible way by which an infant class can be taught, interested, and kept together; and that is by following the path of nature. Any thing artificial, strained, or labored, will not do here. At a boarding school, or at an academy, you may create artificial character and taste: but in a class of little children, you must be simple, easy, natural, in your instruction. Every one knows how difficult it is to unlearn what is wrong. For example, if, when a child, you learned to spell certain words incorrectly, you know how difficult it is in after years to spell them right. So of pronunciation, or of any other wrong habit. No small part of education is spent in unlearning what is wrong. But begin to teach children in the Infant class on the principles of the Gospel, and in the only way in which at that age you can interest them, and you avoid all this. Education begun in the simple way in which nature teaches, becomes invaluable, because its progress is easy, and rapid. Habits are formed which may be carried through life. Hence,—

3. *Invaluable habits are found in the infant class.*

The most valuable part of education consists in giving the child a command over his own powers of mind. Take, for example, the power of commanding the attention. Some have this power in great perfection, and can at any moment task the mind; others can do it more imperfectly; and others, to a very limited extent. You will frequently find a conscientious man who mourns over his condition. He tells you that in worship, and even in prayer, his attention will wander. He joins in the prayer which is offered, follows a little way, and then, before he is aware, off flies the mind, and he is thinking about something else. Again he brings it back, fixes his attention, and resolves that his mind shall wander no more; the resolution is scarcely made, before he is again gone. It does not alter the case, whether he is in the house of God, at the family altar, or in the closet. He wonders why it is so, and mourns over the state of heart which allows it. Now all this wandering of the mind could be controlled, had the man learned

how to do it in childhood. How many hours of sor
row, how much loss of enjoyment, comfort, and improvement would have been prevented, had he only
learned how to command his attention in early life!

Take another example, that of reasoning. We
are commanded 'always to be ready to give a reason for the hope that is in us.' But how frequently
do you find men who cannot command an argument,
nor answer an objection; not because they are so
ignorant, but because they cannot command their
thoughts and gather up their strength at once. They
can reason, but so slowly that it is of no practical
use; can answer an objection, but not till the cavil-
er has gone away, and gone, believing them unable
to answer him. This is all owing to the want of
the habit of using the powers of the mind from infancy. It will all be prevented by the proper use
of the Infant Sabbath School. No one, who has not
examined the subject with attention, can conceive of
the advantage which a power over the mind, acquired
in very early life, gives to its possessor; and few are
aware how much of this discipline may be very
early obtained. I will adduce an example to the
point. There were two little boys who were twins,
whose names were James and John. They were
just six years old. One day their teacher had been
telling them about God,—how great, and wise, and
good he is. Among other things he said that 'God
was so great, that he filled all heaven.' After their

teacher had left them, they began to talk about what they had heard from their instructor.

"John," said James, "did not our teacher say that God was so great that he filled all heaven?"

"Yes."

"And he said that the heaven of heavens, which is the greatest heaven of all, could not hold him?"

"Yes."

"Well, John, if God is so very great that he fills *all* heaven, I don't see how there will be *room* enough for us, and so we can't go there."

"Come to the window," said John. "Do you see that man yonder coming down the street, and walking this way towards us?"

"Yes."

"Well, James, you can *think* all the way to him, so that your *think* reaches all the way to him."

"Yes."

"Well, then, James, does your *think stop* the man from walking towards us?"

"Why, no."

"Well now, God is just like our *think;* and if our *think* does not stop the man from walking towards us, neither will God stop us from going to heaven. He fills heaven, I suppose, just as your *think* fills all along up the street."

Here then was reasoning, sound, correct, unanswerable reasoning. It was natural too; the first object seen, a man walking, served for an illustration,

19 *

—it is easy, simple, and yet as correct as a learned Professor could have given. But nothing but a very early discipline of mind could have given such power. It is this very discipline which the child acquires in the infant class.

4. *It will be the means in many instances of coun teracting the poison of wrong example and wrong teaching at home.*

The teacher should not accustom himself to suppose that the teaching and example at home must, of course, be wrong. He will find many delightful examples to the contrary. But in very many cases, he will find the child yet so stupid that he has hardly noticed example or instruction,—his mind not yet having been aroused, or else, that so far, he has been educated wrong. In consequence of those influences and circumstances in which you find the child, he would grow up a very imperfect, and perhaps a very undesirable character; but by taking him now, just as his powers begin to develop, and his mind to expand, you may lay the foundations for a character, every way desirable. You may undo, and more than undo all that is done even at home, to lead him to ruin, for this life and the next.

5. *It will be the means of doing good to the fami lies in which the children live.*

You take the child from the nursery. Perhaps his parents have just enough of what looks toward religion, to let him go to the Infant Sabbath School

This indeed is a part of their religion. The child has his memory and thoughts filled with what is good, —with simple precepts from the Bible, or beautiful thoughts which piety has expressed in poetry. He carries these home, he prattles and repeats them all over at home, and the parents every day hear the prattler. They listen to his hymns; he asks them questions, tells what his teacher says at the school, and what God says in his word. Now it is not in the human heart to hear this from a beloved child, and remain unaffected. The little preacher will be heard, and he will throw an arrow too, which, though it goes from a feeble bow, may be made to sink into the heart by the influences of the Holy Spirit. Thus every child becomes a little missionary, and preaches the Gospel in the nursery, in the parlor, and to those who, perhaps, would neither hear nor heed it from any other person.

The prejudices of some parents are easily excited, and the teacher should take great care to allay them as easily and as quickly as possible. As soon as practicable, they should, a few at a time, be invited to visit the school.

'After laboring for about a fortnight, (in a new school at Glasgow,) not a little surprise arose from a diminution in the number of the pupils, the cause of which we were unable to conjecture. A singular incident, however, unravelled the mystery. While busily engaged one morning, a person, apparently

about forty-five years of age, with well-patched garments, and much shrewdness of countenance, came
in, and without uttering a word, took a chair with
the greatest gravity, and looked all around with the
most prying and minute attention.

'As he had violated the rule laid down,* and evidently was not one of those who had been engaged
in establishing the school, I approached him, and
stated, that, as his presence interrupted the children,
I must request him to withdraw; assuring him that,
in a few days more, ample opportunity would be
given the public of observing the effects of what was
then doing. To this he replied, without the movement of a muscle, "I'm thinking, ye ken, there can
be no gude ganging on where people wish to keep
things sae muckle to themsels." I then proceeded to
reason with him on the necessity and propriety of
the regulation, when he answered in the same imper-
turbable style, "Ye'll no hae time to du what ye
expect; for its weel understood what ye're doing, and
ye'll maist sartainly be defaited. I am thinking
ye dinna find sae mony bairns as ye had when ye
first begun." Becoming very impatient, from the increasing disorder of the children, I urged him to retire; when, as he arose, and was on the point of
going, he said, "It's my duty to tell ye, that it's cur-
rently reported in the neebourhood, that ye're teach-

---

* It was agreed that no persons should visit during the first
month.

ing the children the Roman Catholic releegion, and
I am weel satisfied its true, for I've seen for mysel;
and there's the beads ye learn the children to count."
To my great astonishment, the object he pointed out
was the Arithmeticon, which I told him was the instrument which we employed for teaching numbers,
and many other things; and on which I promised, if
he would sit down again, to give him a lesson. He
seated himself accordingly, observed its adaptation
to the purpose with great delight, and stated, at the
close of the explanation, that he was perfectly satisfied, and would do all in his power to bring back the
absentees. He kept his word to the letter, went
round to all the parents himself, and, in consequence,
the whole of them returned."

6. *It will be the means of early developing and
cultivating the conscience.*

No one, probably, can tell how or when, the idea
of God, the grand conception of an omniscient, presiding mind, first reached him. It was too early for
memory to retain. But whenever this idea does become formed in the mind, then conscience can be
called out and cultivated. Of course, this is at a very
early period of life. This is the great work of life.
Some do not use the means to awaken and call conscience into being; others do not assiduously cultivate
and cherish her when developed. Proper teaching
will always create conscience, and give her power,
even though you may not be sensible of it at the

time. " I had taken some pains," says a teacher, " to explain the tenth commandment to the infant school under my care. A few weeks afterwards, I was in company with one of the little girls, who was about five years old. In the course of our conversation we spoke of another child of the same age, that lived very near. " Charlotte," said she, with much animation, " has got a pair of new shoes; they are blue, and *very* handsome." Then pausing a minute, with her eyes fixed on the floor, she added, " *but I must not covet.*" I had some fear that this child did not derive much benefit from the school; but I saw enough in this incident to correct my mistake, to inspire me with new zeal and confidence." Every degree of influence which conscience can obtain over the child in the very morning of its existence, the greater power will he have to resist temptation, the more likely will he be to become a blessing here, and a monument of the grace of God forever in heaven.

Permit me now to mention the MATERIALS with which you can operate in the instruction of an infant class.

There will always be some things which are local, which are peculiar to your school, and peculiar to each individual; but I intend to mention only those which are general, universal, permanent, and upon which you may always rely without a possibility of being deceived.

(a.) *Love of friends.* It is not in the heart of man

to do otherwise than love those who love us. No child will come to your school who does not love his parents, and his nurse, and love them, too, just in proportion as he has been the object of love. You may make use of this principle. You may call the warm affections of the child around you, may gain his confidence, and so obtain his love, that he will put his very heart into your hand to be moulded by you at your pleasure. Strive, then, to make each child your friend,—feel as a friend to him, and he will reciprocate your love. His heart has not been chilled by heartless professions, nor has he yet learned that there may be butter and honey upon the tongue, while there is war in the heart. Let him not learn this lesson from you.

(b.) *Love of imitation* is a natural principle, on which you may rely with certainty.

The mother takes her infant in her arms, and smiles in his face, till he imitates and catches the smile, and returns it. This is probably the first attempt of the child to imitate; but from that moment, he never ceases to imitate, more or less, till he dies. Every one knows how quickly a child will catch the tones used in the nursery, will repeat the stories, or the songs, the words, the looks, and the motions, of those with whom he associates. It is thus that a child is so quickly corrupted, and often ruined by associating with other children who have already been corrupted by others. I have seen a little fellow walk

the paved street with his mouth filled with oaths and
segars, declaring that he did not believe the Bible!
The poor child probably could not even read the
book of God, but was imitating some poor, depraved,
apology for a man. A traveller noticed this love of
imitation even in Africa. 'Resting one day,' says he,
'while our oxen were feeding, I remarked a number
of children around our wagon, humming a tune, to
which they were beating time. Their appearance
instantly suggested the idea of an infant school. I
communicated my idea to Mr. Read, who had acquired some knowledge of the system. We instantly
arranged them to the number of perhaps fifty, to
make the experiment. In the midst of Caffreland,
among some of the most beautiful scenery in the
world, I observed the readiness and enthusiasm with
which the children entered into the spirit of the system, and heard them pronounce the English words
which they had never before heard with all the propriety that might have been expected in an English
school, and saw the eagerness with which the parents
partook of the delight of the children. I could
scarcely believe my own eyes and ears, and could
not help reflecting what a mighty influence these
schools might have in raising that interesting people,
had we only the necessary agents and apparatus."*

---

* See "Early Discipline Illustrated" by WILDERSPIN, the
principal originator of the Infant School System.

A still more interesting instance of the strong ten-dency to imitate, which children possess, will be found in a paragraph from the same writer.

"A very pious and excellent man, who had been in his majesty's service, and had lost part of his right arm, was engaged as master. My opinion was that he would be suitable in every respect; but I was in an error, as the sequel proved. All acquainted with the infant system know that it includes much manual exercise,—such as clapping hands, putting the arms out horizontally, and holding them up perpendicularly —and with these evolutions he was much pleased; but having only one hand, he was compelled to pat with his stump. In consequence of this, every child in the school, to my great surprise, bent his arm and patted with his elbow; when I told them to put their arms out, they still bent one in imitation of him, and twisted the body round to make the shortened arm parallel with the other; and every movement was made in the same way. I bade them not to do so, but in vain; and as great distortion would have re-sulted, I was compelled most reluctantly to dismiss him.—The necessity of this he clearly saw, and, from his delight in the work, greatly deplored.

"I have since seen, from visiting many schools, that any physical defect should prevent the engagement of a person, however desirable in other respects, either as a master or mistress. I know, for instance, a master who had a cast in his eye; and all the young children squinted; and another who had a club-foot, in imitation of whom all the children limped. Should a teacher stutter or stammer, the young children, from the strength of the imitative power, at a very early age, will do so too. Similar effects will arise from any defects of this kind in monitors, and hence children in such circumstances should not be thus advanced."

(c.) You have the *principle of curiosity.*

The whole world is not only new to the child, but it is deeply interesting. He first acquires knowledge, and gratifies his curiosity by his taste, next by the eye, then by feeling, and then by the ear. These are only the avenues through which he seeks to gratify his curiosity. As the life of man here is but a vapor, as he comes into the world entirely ignorant of every thing, it is a wise provision of God, that he shall not only learn as he lives, but that his curiosity shall ever make him awake, and eager to learn. There is no pleasure in ignorance, while every acquisition of knowledge, however small, gives us pleasure. A child will frequently destroy his play-things to see how they are made. More than one child has been sufficiently precocious to break open his rattle-box, to discover what it was that made the noise. It would be a hopeless task to instruct a child, were it not for this principle of curiosity. As it is, the teacher may not only use it, but he may stimulate it, by letting the little learner see that he can obtain knowledge,—

that he can enjoy the pleasure of having his awakened curiosity gratified.   Remember that this principle of curiosity will be gratified; and if not learning what is good, every child will be learning what is evil.

(e.) You have *the principle of confidence* to aid you.

No species of duplicity is more cruel than that which abuses the confidence which the child naturally puts in those who are older than himself.   You may go into the nursery and tell him of ghosts, and fairies, and witches, and he will believe it all.   You may tell him any story, however improbable, and as his experience cannot detect the improbabilities, he will receive it as truth.   You may make promises, and they will be received as good: and it is not till months and years of deception, not till his heart has been wrung with disappointments, that he learns not to give you his implicit confidence.   His confidence is like the fresh rose that opens in your garden in the morning,—as sweetly and as beautifully blooming, as if it were not possible that its very glories should tempt you to pluck it, then neglect it, and then throw it away.   You will make abundant use of the confidence of the children in the Infant class, but you must beware how you abuse it.   Take every proper method to let the child see that you put confidence in him, and he will reciprocate it all.

(e.) You have a *natural conscience* by which to operate.

There seems to be a reverence,—an innate principle of reverence towards God, created in the heart of man, and engraven on his very constitution. When the mind is darkened, misguided, or instructed wrong, this becomes fear and superstition. When it is controlled by the will of a despot, it becomes the iron instrument with which tyranny crushes our race. The despot always seizes hold of this principle, and makes use of it for his own selfish, unholy purposes. You will find this principle in the mind of every child, more or less distinctly developed; and you can and ought to make use of it. You may always take it for granted that the principle of reverence will be found in the heart. You could not create it, were it not so; but as it is, you may use it at once, and always in the great and difficult work of instructing the child. This is the conscience,—a fire which burns beautifully in the morning of life,—whose flame is smothered by the dirt of earth during the days of youth and manhood,—but which, at the close of life, again frequently breaks out, its flame fed by remorse, —showing with what fearful light it will flash upon the soul forever.

These are the materials with which you will begin the work of teaching an infant class on the Sabbath. There are others, such as memory, hope, fear, and the like, but they can all be resolved into those already enumerated.

I proceed to give a few hints on the instruction of an infant class in the Sabbath School.

1. *Do not feel that an extensive apparatus is necessary.*

There are cards, and pictures of almost every thing in nature, prepared for Infant schools. They may all have their use at particular times, and under particular circumstances. But we want to be able to say to any man and to any lady who has a heart to be useful, you need not wait and mourn that you have not all the apparatus prepared for infant schools. You may not get these for years, and may never do it. Are you willing and desirous to go to the work? If so, let there be no delay. Who would think of keeping a steamboat on the stocks, and never launching her and putting her to use, because she has not yet all the paintings, gildings, carvings, awnings, and trappings, with which such vessels are so abundantly decorated,—which add to their expense enormously, and consequently to the expenses of travelling in them? Who would mourn that his steam-engine had not more wheels and cogs, more valves and machinery about it, when every bystander sees, that the very simplicity, is its excellence? The fact is, many an infant school has failed and come to nothing, though burdened with apparatus,—because the teacher relied on these to do the work of sustaining the school; while others, with

20 *

no apparatus, or next to none, have lived and flourished. I once stopped at a hotel which my fellow-passengers greatly admired. The carpets were Brussels, the tables of rich mahogany, we had silver forks with which to eat, and plated candlesticks and wax candles with which to go to bed, servants so numerous as to be annoying. I could not admire it, for I observed that almost all who put up there, put on the airs of rich people, and high-livers at home, and when they left, found their bills such as would not be likely to tempt them to go there again. In every thing that is valuable, or with which we can take comfort, there must be simplicity. I know of several most interesting and valuable Infant Schools, in which the only apparatus is the Bible, and perhaps a few printed hymns.

The reader will be instructed as well as amused on reading the following description of Wilderspin's first attempt at teaching an Infant School.

'As soon as the mothers had left the premises, I attempted to engage the attention of their offspring. I shall never forget the effort! A few, who had been previously at a dame-school, sat quietly; but the rest, missing their parents, crowded about the door. One little fellow, finding he could not open it, set up a loud cry of "Mammy! Mammy!" and in raising this *delightful* sound, all the rest simultaneously joined. My wife, who, though reluctant at first, had determined, on my accepting the situation, to give me her utmost aid, tried, with myself, to calm the tumult; but our efforts were utterly in vain. The paroxysm of sorrow increased instead of subsiding, and so intolerable did it become, that she could endure it no longer, and left the room; and, at length, exhausted by effort, anxiety, and noise, I was compelled to follow her example, leaving my unfortunate pupils in one dense mass, crying, yelling, and kicking against the door!

'I will not attempt to describe my feelings; but, ruminating on what I then considered egregious folly in supposing that any two persons could manage so large a number of infants, I was struck by the sight of a cap of my wife's, adorned with colored ribbon, lying on the table; and observing from the window a clothes-prop, it occurred that I might put the cap upon it, return to the school, and try the effect. The confusion when I entered was tremendous; but on raising the pole surmounted by the cap, all the children, to my great satisfaction, were instantly silent; and when any hapless wight seemed disposed to renew the noise, a few shakes of the prop restored tranquillity, and, perhaps, produced a laugh. The same thing, however, will not do long; the charms of this *wonderful* instrument therefore soon vanished, and there would have been a sad relapse but for the marchings, gambols, and antics, I found it necessary to adopt, and which, at last, brought the hour of twelve, to my greater joy than can easily be conceived. Revolving these circumstances, I felt that

that memorable morning had not passed in vain. I
had, in fact, found the clew. It was now evident
that the senses of the children must be engaged;
that the great secret of training them was to descend
to their level and become a child;—and that the
error had been to expect in infancy what is only the
product of after years.'

The following remarks of a lady who speaks from
experience, are exceedingly judicious. ' I have been
averse to teaching these young children astronomy,
or geography, or botany, and especially mathematics,
partly because it obscures their tender minds with
things too high for them, and partly because it requires too great a number of cards, and too extensive
apparatus. But with the Bible in my hand, I would,
from the first chapter of Genesis, direct their attention to the formation and character of plants, the
creation and use of the heavenly bodies ; and forming
a meridian at the garden of Eden, I would begin to
lead their young minds to trace the successive spread
of mankind over the face of the earth, and thus,
without any conscientious scruples about making my
little pupils too learned, I would " in process of time"
lead them over the whole known world and gather
every astronomical, geographical, and botanical and
scientific hint, which is found in the Scriptures, accompanied with every hallowed improvement which
it sanctions, and upon which the Spirit of God is
promised as an instructor. There are sufficient

materials in the Bible to be a means of laying
the foundation in the infant mind of all that knowledge of the works of God, which, with proper direction, may lead to that knowledge which is life
eternal. Oh! how little sensible we are how un-
mixed our first instruction should be! He who has
said, " My word shall not return unto me void, but
shall accomplish that for which I sent it," will never
let any right use of it fail of a blessing. The minds
of children will receive and return instruction through
this medium with such effect as will frequently make
both teacher and scholar " bow their heads and worship." Thus instructed, these pupils, with a pebble
out of the clear stream of truth, might, in after life,
pierce the armour of those giants of error who defy
the church of the living God, and for whom the
Christian watchmen are now so laboriously arming
themselves to meet these great antagonists.

' I would make the inimitable politeness of Abra-
ham, when he purchased the possession of a burying-
place of the children of Heth, a specimen of what
religion can do in polishing the manners, as well as
improving the heart. From the Bible we learn just
enough refinement of manners as, on the one hand,
raises us above roughness and incivility, and makes
us, on the other, a reproof to the fastidiousness and
insincerity of high life ; and I should expect far more
success in endeavoring to raise human nature from
its native miserableness, than in endeavoring to de

liver it from the pollutions into which polished society commonly so called, had entangled it. It is the happy medium in every thing which the Bible portrays as the path of perfection; and Agur's prayer contains far more, I am persuaded, than we shall ever in this world probably learn from it. It is a part of the two-edged sword of truth.'

Whether more or less use is made of cards and pictures, and things of that kind, it must never be forgotten, that it is the *heart* with which you are to make the deepest, and the most valuable impressions. The eye may aid you, but after all, it is the tones of voice, sweet, clear, patient, upon which success chiefly depends.

2. *Let the teacher cultivate gentleness in himself.*

While the teacher must aim to exert a powerful influence over the children, and the most important too, which they will ever feel, let him remember that he must do this,—he can do this, only by being gentle. You wish to mould the temper to gentleness, to patience and forbearance. The passions are to be repressed and disciplined, the affections, the sympathy, and the tenderness of the soul are to be drawn forth. You neither wish nor expect to take these children and subdue them by the rod; you expect to be able only to lead them. Your own temper and feelings must, then, be under absolute command, and the child must never feel that his teacher has forgotten to be gentle. Let me quote you a passage from

the beautiful pen of Henry Martyn. " I walked,"
says he, " into the village where the boat stopped for
the night, and found the worshippers of Cali by the
sound of their drums and cymbals. I did not speak
to them, on account of their being Bengalees. But
being invited to walk in by the Brahmins, I walked
within the railing, and asked a few questions about
the idol. The Brahmin, who spoke bad Hindostanee,
disputed with great heat, and his tongue ran faster
than I could follow, and the people, who were about
one hundred, shouted applause. But I continued to
ask my questions without making any remarks upon
the answers. I asked, among other things, whether
what I had heard of Vishnu and Brahma were true,
which they confessed. I forbore to press him with
the consequences, which he seemed to feel, and so I
told him what was my belief. The man grew quite
mild and said it was *chula bat*, (good words,) and
asked me seriously at last, what I thought—was idol-
worship true or false ? I felt it a matter of thank-
fulness that I could make known the truth of
God, though but a stammerer, and that I had declared it in the presence of a devil. And this I also
learned, *that the power of gentleness is irresistible.*"

It is very desirable, if not essential to the success
of an Infant Sabbath School, that there be singing.
It gives variety, soothes the feelings, cheers the mind,
awakens the attention, and adds cheerfulness to the
whole business. The teacher should be able to lead

the singing himself, if practicable. If not, some one should be associated with him who can. I may add here, that not unfrequently, if not generally, a lady will manage an infant class better than a gentleman. She has more patience, can descend to the minutiæ better, has more elasticity and versatility, more soft-ness and kindness in look, voice, and manner, and can work through difficulties with ease, in cases where he would either stand still, or burst through at any cost. One of the most interesting Infant schools within my knowledge is taught by the young wife of a clergyman in New England. She spends the whole of the Sabbath afternoon with her little charge. The school contains about one hundred and twenty; and I doubt not she is doing more for the good of the human race than many who wear plumed hats on their heads and swords by their sides.

It is important to remember that at first, and for a long time, there should be no one present except the teacher and the little pupils. It is impossible for a teacher to do justice to the school, if a single adult individual be present. I would by all means insist on this. As a general rule, children ought to be sepa-rated and by themselves as much as possible while receiving instruction.

You will need to be careful that your school is not like a prison. Little children must have motion fre-quently; nature requires it, and you must follow the leadings of nature. At the same time do not cherish constant restlessness,—as if the great object of the school was to keep the children in some kind of motion.

3. *Let the teacher remember that he must cultivate deep and ardent piety, if he would be successful.*

The romance of an Infant School will be soon worn off. It cannot be made a play-thing; it cannot be an exhibition. It is not to be the wonder of visiters, or the astonishment of parents. It is not to be made a mere reciting, or repeating machine. Nothing of this will regenerate the soul, or train it up for the trials of earth or the glories of heaven. It must be the gate of heaven; and the aims of the teacher must be pure, holy, lowly, and yet lofty. He cannot meet the trials, the vexations and the troubles of his station without piety,—deep piety. If there be a station of earth which requires the heart to be warmed and cheered and sustained by love to Jesus Christ, it is this. Redeeming love must be the theme on which the soul never tires. He must be a man of prayer. No one can fill the station without help drawn from the everlasting hills. Prayer must be the morning offering, and prayer the incense of the evening oblation,—and prayer must carry on the work. Oh! if you feel desirous of teaching a class of infants in the Sabbath School, and are not guided to the work by much prayer, I do hope you will weigh the subject well before you go any further. No part of the Sabbath School is so difficult to in-

21

struct and manage as this; and no part is more interesting, more important, or will receive more good
from right instruction, than this. It is a little fountain, but from it several little rills flow, small indeed
now, but one which will swell and grow till each becomes a mighty river.

There may be an infant class or an infant school
in connexion with every Sabbath School in the land.
It ought to be so; and why is it not so? Is it not
because we have considered these little ones too
young? But may not this impression be a mere prejudice? Some thirty years ago our churches thought
that every one must serve the devil till at least
twenty years old; and the consequence was, that it
was a very rare sight to see young men and ladies
under twenty entering the church with the purpose
of living for God. Few young people then professed
to serve God. Was this not a very great mistake?
And shall our churches let Satan still have the very
best part of life with which to take possession of the
soul? No, they must not do it. Let every minister
and every officer in our churches, and every Superintendent at once take up the subject, and resolve
that there shall be such a class or classes connected
with every Sabbath School in the land. Then shall
we have begun at the right period of life, to sow the
seed; and then will our blessed Redeemer gather to
himself a glorious harvest,—for the garners of im
mortality.

CHAPTER VIII.

SINGING IN THE SABBATH SCHOOL.

THE soul seems formed for music. The savage cannot be found so barbarous as not to have some way by which to create musical sounds; and the savage who, for the first time, hears the notes of a well-regulated band, will crouch down upon the ground, entranced by notes so far exceeding any thing of which he has ever before conceived. The band in passing through the street will draw every family to the window; the flute whose soft notes float over the still waters on the summer's evening, will cause the Indian to lift the paddle from the water, and let his canoe drift noiselessly down the stream. And the proudest monarch on earth will kneel and weep during some of the strains of the mighty organ, and the choir as they sing the Messiah.

War has pressed music into his service, and made the heart leap even upon the field of death, by the notes of the bugle, the trumpet and the clarion. The horse and his rider both feel its power, and by it rush into the ranks of death. The charge is made, and man is brought breast to breast, under the united influence of music and the war-shout. What notes, deep, awful, and spirit-stirring, were those which rose over the field of Waterloo, as Death rode through the ranks, on his pale horse? The roar of cannon, the groans of death, and the murderous shout of battle are all softened down by music.

Pleasure has made music her waiting-maid. The ball, the dance, the theatre, would all expire, were it not that music gives her constant presence, and pleads with a voice so sweet, that the world cannot resist it. Any price will be paid for music, if it shall have the quality of being exquisite. The man is now living who annually receives more for the music which he creates on his violin, than would support eighty of our ordained missionaries. A lady who has earned great fame in the theatres in Europe as a singer, has been offered, if she would come to this country at least an equal sum. She declined the offer, and probably no sufficient inducements will be offered to cause her to come, and consequently the music of her voice will never be heard this side of the Atlantic. I mention these facts,—not to find fault, for that is useless, but to show the strong love which we all have for music.

Almost every nation, perhaps all nations, have national airs, by which the love of country is deepened, and a national feeling is created and maintained. The popular air, "Yankee-doodle," will probably create an American feeling as long as our nation exists; and the airs, "God save the king." and "Rule Britannia," will never cease to call the heart of the Briton to his own glorious Isle. The soldier from Switzerland, and from the Highlands of Scotland will weep at the national airs which call their hearts home to the place of their birth and childhood.

It is not a matter of surprise, then, that from the fall of man to the present hour, as we have reason to believe, religion has made great use of music to aid her disciples. It was early taught in the schools of the Prophets, and from them went out through the length and breadth of the land of God's people. Not only so, but God made special provision for its use, in giving to his church those inspired songs which bear the name of David, and which will be sung as long as the church exists on earth. From the days of David down to the third century of the Christian era, music was exceedingly simple, touching, and effective. It was the music of nature, so to speak, and consisted in little else than a refined delivery, superadded to sacred poetry. Music, in the most ancient ages of the world, was the parent of poetry Deborah wrote her wonderfully sublime song, that it might be sung and committed to memory by the army of Barak. The great poem of Homer, it is said, is the daughter of music,—a composition which

21 *

250   THE SABBATH SCHOOL TEACHER.

Homer's influence.   Provision of Providence for music.

has had more influence upon the character of the earth, probably, than any other book in existence, except the Bible. 'From Homer,' says Pope, ' the poets drew their inspiration, the critics their rules, and the philosophers a defence of their opinions; every author was found to use his name, and every profession writ books upon him, till they swelled to libraries. The warriors formed themselves upon his heroes, and the oracles delivered his verses for an swer.'

God has not only created the ear to delight in the melody of sweet sounds, but has created a most wonderful musical instrument for the use of every one. Between the top of the throat and the root of the tongue, he has made an enlargement,—a cavity of two or three inches, and most wonderfully lined it with delicate membranes, ' so stretched that the air passing through them makes a sound as through the reed of a clarionet. This would be a curious instrument, even if it admitted of no variation of sound; but it is furnished with five cartilages, which contract and expand the cavity at pleasure in different ways, so as to give different vibrations, and of course, different tones. In this small space, then, in the throat of every human being, is an instrument with a compass of from two to three octaves, which has the command of every semi-tone, and subdivision of note, swell, trill, &c.; and not necessarily exposed to the imperfections of artificial instruments, but so clear, so rich,

so sweet, when well used, as to be the highest standard of comparison,—in these points, for the flute,
clarionet, piano, and organ.'

Now let any one consider this wonderful provision,
prepared and at hand every where, created by God
himself,—let him remember that the soul is so delighted with music, that the highest and sweetest
emblem by which inspiration could describe heaven,
is that of the ten thousand times ten thousand, angels and men, joined in one mighty choir, before the
throne of God, and all unitedly praising him forever
and ever,—and then say if singing ought not to have
a prominent place in all systems of education?
Especially, ought it not to have a very - prominent
place in the very nursery of the church—the Sabbath School? I cannot but feel that we are very
far behind the proper standard on this subject; and
I plead in behalf of every child, with the earnestness
of one who was himself neglected in childhood in
this particular, and who has in consequence suffered
a loss of enjoyment which no language can describe.
By such neglect we inflict a wrong upon the children,
which is not the less real or cruel, that they do not
now feel and mourn over it.

Till within a short time, it has been an opinion almost universal, that but a few could be taught to
sing ; that the talent for music was a peculiar gift
of nature, entrusted to a favored few. Parents have
decided,—unless, indeed, their child learned to sing

almost by inspiration, that *their* children had no taste for music. The opinion has become so prevalent that but a very small part of our congregations even pretend to sing, or suppose themselves capable. Nor are they capable, at the present time and under the present circumstances; but would it have been so, had proper pains been taken when they were children? How much pains do parents take to teach a child to speak correctly? Had children the opportunity of hearing speaking, and of being taught to speak only as they have opportunity to learn to sing, would any more be able to talk, than are able now to sing? I shall not contend that every child who can be taught to speak, might be taught to sing; but I believe the exceptions would be very rare. Allow me to state a few plain facts.

1. In an Orphan Asylum in Germany containing two hundred children, there are only two certainly, who have not learned to sing, and that too, correctly. These children, of course, are taken early, and probably considerable pains are taken with them; be this so or not, the fact is one of great weight in deciding such a question.

2. In all the common district schools in Germany, singing and music are taught, and every child is as much expected to read and write, and perform music, as to read, write, and recite any other lesson. It is not pretended, indeed, that these are all first-rate singers, or that they go deeply into the science of

music; but that they go far enough to be respectable performers in sacred music.

3. When a gentleman wishes to have his daughter taught music on the piano, the question, in these days, is not asked, ' has the child an ear for music,— can she ever learn music?'—but the question is, can he afford the expense of the instrument and of the tuition; if he can do that, every music-teacher will engage to take care of the rest, and to create a taste, sufficient, at least, to make her a performer who shall be the pride of her parents. This could not be done, if it were true, that the power of being a musician must always be innate.

4. The Puritans of New-England, almost without exception, were accustomed to have singing at their family devotions, in which *all* the members of the family soon learned to take a part. This was so of the Scotch covenanters. They were denominated a ' Psalm-singing generation' in part, because all, old and young, were accustomed to sing.

5. It has been found by the Professors of music of the present day, who have made extensive trials, that they can go into a common school, and take the children as they rise, and teach them *all* to sing. There are, indeed, rare cases of organic defect, just as there are cases in which the eye has been known to mistake red for green,—in which singing cannot be taught. But these are exceptions; but were the season of childhood faithfully improved, few would be

pronounced as unfit to join in the songs of Zion. The right habits, however, must be formed at the right time, which is childhood. Few children fail of being able to sing, whose parents are singers, and who, as a consequence, hear singing from their very infancy. In cases in which an attempt has been made to teach a school to sing, and it has failed, I would suggest whether it has not been in consequence of not having it *very simple*. You may teach a child any thing, even mathematics; but you must begin with what is very simple. The Methodists seldom fail to get all their children to sing their simple music. The following is from the pen of Wesley. " About three o'clock in the afternoon of the Lord's day, April 20, 1788, I met between nine hundred and a thousand of the children belonging to our Sunday Schools in Bolton. I never saw such a sight before. They were all exactly clean, as well as plain in their apparel. All were serious and well-behaved; many, both boys and girls, had as beautiful faces as, I believe, England or Europe can afford. When they all sung together, and *none of them out of tune*, the melody was beyond that of any theatre. And what is best of all, many of them truly fear God, and some rejoice in his salvation. These are a pattern to all the town. And this I must avow, there is not such a set of singers in any of the Methodist congregations in the three kingdoms as in this town. There cannot be; for we have near a hundred such trebles, boys and girls, selected out of our Sunday Schools, and accurately taught, as are not to be found together in any chapel, cathedral, or music room, within the four seas. Besides the spirit with which they sing, and the beauty of many of them so suits the melody, that I defy any to exceed it, except the singing of angels in our father's house."

There are two points to be insisted on in teaching children in the Sabbath School to sing: viz.—that the *vowels* are to be pronounced clearly and distinctly, just as we pronounce them in speaking. If this be overlooked, and the vowels and consonants be run into each other, it will be singing in an unknown tongue. Great pains should be taken to have the enunciation clear and distinct. The other point is, to have them taught to place the emphasis right, so as to have the music correspond with the words. What is the object of singing, except to give the words more power and interest? How can this object be accomplished, except by attention to the emphasis? This suggests another inquiry; viz: what hymns shall be used in our Sabbath Schools? I shall speak with diffidence on this point, because there is a great diversity of opinion and practice, and because I am not perfectly satisfied that any of them are right. In very many schools, perhaps the majority in the land, Hymns are used, selected and arranged on purpose for Sabbath Schools, such as the Union Hymns and the like. The great advantage is thought to be, that in such a selection you can have a great variety

from which to select, and, that they are altered and
rendered simple, and thus adapted to childhood. It
is true, these two objects are gained; but I am not
certain that it is not at too great an expense. By
taking the prepared selection, you have variety,—a
great variety; but, do you not wish to have the child
begin to sing the hymns, and from the book, which is
used in the church, and from which he is to sing all his
life, and thus have his earliest associations connected
and linked in with what he will use in the house of
God? Can any hymn-book,—ought any hymn-book
to be so dear to the associations and the heart, as
that which is used in the house of God on the Sabbath? And then, as to the simplicity of the selected
hymns,—I am aware of all that may be said in their
favor; but let me ask, if their simplicity is not principally effected by altering the most beautiful hymns
in the English language,—such hymns as we have in
all our churches on the Sabbath? The child, in the
Sabbath School, sings a hymn, say the Coronation
hymn, "All hail the power of Jesus' name," as he
finds it in the hymn-book prepared for the School:
he goes to his father's pew, and hears the same hymn
sung just as the author wrote it, without any alteration,—which is he to love, and with which is he to
have the sweetest recollections of life associated?
to my own mind there cannot be a doubt but the
warmest, deepest, tenderest associations of his heart
should be associated with his worship in his father's

pew. Let any one, who has grown up in the use of a hymn as it stands in our church singing-book, and one which he has sung all his life as it reads there, go into the Sabbath School and take up the same hymn altered, and see if he can take any enjoyment in reading it. I would with diffidence ask, too, if we are not under a mistake in supposing that a Sabbath School needs a very great variety and number of hymns? How is it with the Christian,—is he ever tired of singing, " Come holy Spirit, heavenly Dove"? —or its sister song, " Oh! for a closer walk with God"? Do we not prefer in our sweetest meetings to sing over the songs which we know, the tunes which we know, because they recal other and dearer times, and are also pleasant now? In teaching children to sing in the Sabbath School, then, I would offer the following hints; viz.—

1. To use the words of a hymn as it reads in the book used in the church, and which they will probably use through life.

2. To have the selection of hymns very limited, so that the whole school may soon learn them, and have them at their command.

3. To be careful always to have the same tune and the same words used together. There are great advantages in this. Children can learn only by repetition, and tunes and words thus connected, always bring pleasurable associations to the mind.

There are two methods of teaching a Sabbath

22

School to sing; the one is, by introducing the black-board and instructing the children as you would a class of adults by teaching them the notes.   It seems to me that this is objectionable in that it takes much time, it seems to turn the school aside from the appropriate business of instruction, and it takes holy time for what ought to be learned during the week. I would, therefore, prefer to have the school taught to sing by the ear on the Sabbath, a few simple easy tunes, and to have provision made to have them regularly and thoroughly taught on some other day, to sing by note.

If the reader shall feel that the above remarks are not very profound, he may be assured that they are offered with diffidence, and are thrown out more as hints upon a difficult subject, than as a guide. They claim nothing beyond what the common sense of each teacher would suggest.

The question of singing brings up another subject intimately related to it, and one not so easy to dispose of to the satisfaction of all. I mean the question, shall the Sabbath School be divided, the males and females separated, and each sex be under its own Superintendent?   It has been rather a growing fashion of late years, to have two distinct branches, in different rooms, and under two different heads.   The great advantages of the plan seem to be, that the girls are taken away from the corrupting example of the boys,—that the two branches are both more quiet, orderly, more carefully watched, and more faithfully instructed. I am not sure that I shall be altogether popular in what I am going to say; but those who disagree with me, will have good sense enough not to feel my arguments, unless they have weight. There will always be exceptions to general rules, and there will undoubtedly be exceptions to this; but as a general thing, I should prefer to have the school altogether in one room, and under one Superintendent. I will offer my reasons as briefly as possible.

1. In all the general features of Sabbath Schools, throughout the land, we had better have them alike, as far as possible, as simple as possible, and as convenient as possible. It would be next to impossible to have this feature become general. But few churches have more than one place, or can provide more than one, and I should be unwilling to have the impression go abroad, that a Sabbath School may not be perfect with but one room.

2. It seems to be the design of Providence that the sexes shall modify and benefit each other, even from infancy. Those families present the most delightful picture, in which the children are composed of both sexes. If they are all boys, they are rough, noisy, and need something to smooth down their roughness. If they are all girls, they need the buoyancy and strength of character which they acquire from associating with their more stormy brothers. It is so in

the Sabbath School. If you say that the girls
suffer by being placed in the same room with the
boys, I say unhesitatingly that the boys suffer
without them.   They will not be so spirited, so interested, so mild, when taught by themselves.   The
girls may suffer *some* by being in the same school
with the males; but the boys will suffer *very much*
where this is not the case.   I have no need of trying to explain the philosophy of the thing; but every
one knows, that whatever may be the case with the
female sex, *our* sex need the presence of females
from the cradle to the grave, and there is no period
in life, in the formation of our character especially,
when we ought to be deprived of it.

3. By being all in the same room, the Superintendent, the minister, or the stranger, can address them
better.   He will do it with more interest, more animation, and more feeling.   So of the devotional exercises.   Say what you will in commendation of a
lady's powers,—say that she is better qualified to
teach, is quicker, more interesting, more devoted and
holy,—it is all true ;—but after all, she is *not* so well
qualified to talk to a school, to make addresses, and
to lead in prayer, as is the man.   She is not, because
God did not create her for this object.

4. If the argument for separating the schools has
weight, it must rest upon the supposition, that the
habits of the children, their education at home, &c.
have been such, that they would be injured by being

together. If this be so, such a school will need to be governed,—and governed, too, with no weak hand. In such a case, probably, it would require, to say the least, as much of government in each department, as in both, were they united; because, a school composed of both sexes is vastly more easily governed, than the same number of either sex, by themselves. Now is a lady ready to go into a large school,—too rude to be associated with the males,—and govern it as it ought to be governed? Can she do it without sacrificing much of that gentleness and mildness, which woman can never sacrifice without loss?

5. By having the school all in one, the Library is much more accessible to all, more readily managed, and all have equal opportunities to obtain desirable books.

6. The influence upon the teachers is decidedly good, when the schools are both in one. They study the lesson together, they feel the power of sympathy when hearing the lessons, there is more animation, life, and interest. I believe this will be found to be the experience of all who have long been engaged in Sabbath Schools. But in seasons of revival, when the Spirit of God is present, when there are awakenings, and conversions,—when you wish to act upon the whole, to use the principle of sympathy, and have the scholars act upon each other, it is of vast importance that the school be all in one room, under

22 *

one head, one influence, and all led to the same place,—viz., the cross of Jesus Christ.

7. It is desirable to have the schools both united in one for the sake of the singing. It is the order of nature that the voices of males and females be united in singing. Neither can accomplish the ends of singing alone. Perhaps it may be said that the schools might be brought together once a day, at the close of the exercises, and thus all unite in singing. I reply, that this will be any thing rather than simple and easy, unless they are so located that folding doors only shall separate them, which will not be the case in many of our schools. That there are and must be disadvantages in both methods, there can be no doubt. If there are more dangers connected with having all the school in one, there are also more decided advantages. These remarks apply to schools generally; but there is nothing essential to the particular mode of managing them, without which they cannot succeed.

An old gentleman from England gives me the following account of a school which he raised up in that country. I quote it not more for the last sentence, than the whole account. " I commenced my school thirty years ago, all alone, with twelve children. If any were absent or late three succeeding Sabbaths from any other cause than sickness, he was dismissed and another was selected from the numerous applicants, to take his place. When I thought

it best, I raised the number to twenty-four, and
finally to sixty, beyond which I would not go.   As a
teacher I stood alone for seven years, and with great
opposition against the school.   Eight of my first
twelve soon became my Bible-class.   They were
closely attentive during all their examinations, and
they became teachers of their respective classes
under my inspection as their superintendent.   One
of these eight is now a faithful and laborious minister
of the Gospel, and the others were all early in life
members of the church with which I was connected.
Many of these sixty I have seen happy on their sick
and dying beds, though some have gone on hardened
and yet miserable in their iniquity.   I once reproved
a vain young man, a stranger whom I met in a pas-
sage-boat, for profaneness.   There was a solemn
silence in the boat for ten minutes.   Every eye was
fixed on him, noticing the mental perturbation which
was visible through his countenance.   After this he
said, 'Ah! Sir, if I had followed the advice which
you used to give me in the Sabbath School, I should
be a much happier man than I now am.'   After in-
forming me who he was, and giving me his history,
he added, 'And there, Sir, (pointing to a box,) in the
bottom of that box under a napkin, is every book
which you ever gave me, and when by accident I
lift up the cloth, they make me tremble.'

"I have a few times in my life given a musical
lesson as an encouragement and reward to the chil-

264   THE SABBATH SCHOOL TEACHER.

Results of experience.   Duty of teachers who cannot sing.

dren, but it tends to dissipate the mind from the more important work before them, and I do not think that any good was ever produced by it. Teaching without notes is sufficient, and best for a Sabbath School."

As to the number of times singing shall be introduced into the school, each set of teachers will decide for themselves. If the Superintendent can conduct it, he, by all means, should do it; if he cannot, let him be careful to obtain the proper man to do it, and in every practicable way assist and encourage him.

But there will be some teachers who are not singers,—who cannot aid in this exercise; what shall they do? How can they be expected to aid in promoting singing? I ask such if they do not wish they could sing?—if they would grudge any expense if they could, by it, only purchase the power of singing? Do they not regret that no one taught them during their childhood? Let them recollect that the blessing whose loss they so deeply mourn, may now be communicated to the children. Let them spare no efforts to have all the children possess this high enjoyment. No efforts will result in greater effects. Children, when once taught, love to sing. Hardly any thing can add more to the enjoyment of a being, made up of affections and reason, as men are.

One thing more. Some seem to feel that singing God's praises is beneath them; that this part of divine worship may be left to hearts destitute of grace, and to lips never sanctified by prayer. I cannot but protest against this feeling. Let the theatre and the opera be under the control of the wicked,—let the songs of revelry and folly pass through the lips of the profane;—but shall the Christian,—the redeemed sinner, who hopes to sing the praises of redeeming love to all eternity in heaven, shall *he* refuse to sing of that love here on earth? The glorious church in heaven sing God's praises before the universe, and angels join in the songs, even ten thousand times ten thousand,—and shall it be, that Christians are above singing these praises here on earth? Shame, shame to a love so cold a gratitude so dumb!

CHAPTER IX.

How far the Sabbath School should be made a
Missionary Society, or be used to aid the cause of
missions, is an important, but a difficult question to
answer. There are difficulties connected with it,
unseen at the first glance. My own views can be
briefly expressed, though I fear they will not be satisfactory to many whom I respect, and who may differ
from me.

I begin by saying that I do not think it advisable
to organize our Sabbath Schools into regular missionary societies, temperance societies, education societies,
&c. I am acquainted with some schools which have
all these, with the addition of anti-slavery and colo-
nization societies; and if the Christian community
should be further divided into parties, would doubtless have every party represented. It seems to me
that the great object of the Institution is the *Sabbath*

School, and I should tremble to be the one who should turn it, or begin to turn it from its appropriate work. The object is to take children of all ages, conditions, habits, prejudices, and influences, to teach them the word of God, and to form their characters upon that word. There can be but one predominant object before a school,—and the rest must, of course, be subordinate. That predominant object should be to teach the Bible, and to lead the souls of the children to God. It must never be lost sight of. For example, if I am teaching my class to-day, the parable of the ten virgins, I wish no other object to come before the mind. I wish to teach that particular thing, so plainly, so clearly, and so forcibly, that it shall never be forgotten. My work for the day is to do this. Now I cannot do it, if the attention of the school is to be diverted, and if a part of the time they are to act as a missionary, a tract, a temperance, or any other society. Every teacher must feel that his object is nothing less than to see each of his pupils embracing Christ, and growing up in holiness. If a school becomes a missionary society, and takes that character, that object becomes the predominant object, is more thought of, talked of, calculated upon, than any other object. Is this best?

Another thing. A Sabbath School whose great object is to be a missionary society, must be a small one; because comparatively few parents feel an interest in missions. They are not willing that their

children should be different from the rest of the
school, and yet are not willing to aid them in contributing.   The result is, they either keep their children
at home, or send them to some other Sabbath School.
Sabbath Schools can fulfil the great object at which
they aim, in no way so rapidly, surely, and pleasantly,
as by keeping to their great object. By doing this, the
world, the indifferent, the irreligious, and the profane,
will entrust their children to their care. They will do
less to counteract your instructions ; and the only cavil
which the heart of malice can invent is, that you
teach them the Bible. The institution is a broad one.
It is to embrace all denominations,—frequently in the
same school, and it must stand on broad ground.
From this high position I would never have the institution descend. I make these remarks with the more
emphasis, lest those which are to follow shall have
undue influence.

But I would have the spirit of Missions always in
the Sabbath School room. The very employment
of the teachers is that of being domestic missionaries.
They act in character only as they have the missionary spirit. They are laboring for the conversion of
the world, and from this they can never turn aside ;—
this they can never forget. They must, and they
will, then, create more or less of the missionary atmosphere around them. They will, and they ought
to introduce the same spirit into the school,—ever
bearing in mind,, that none but a regenerated heart

can truly and deeply enter into the great work of converting the world to Christ.

How far, then, should the subject be introduced, and what ground should it occupy?

It is evident at the very first view, that only general views, and the great subject of converting the world can be introduced; for if you are to bring in each wheel of the machinery, and try to interest the school in sending missionaries abroad, sending Bibles and tracts, raising up ministers, and feeding the destitute with the bread of life, you have all the time consumed. I reply, then,

1. That the school should be taught on the subject of missions, in connexion with the Bible.

The Bible predicts a day in which the earth shall be converted to God. Prophets, apostles, and martyrs prayed, rejoiced, suffered and died in view of such a day. The church of God at the present time expects it; she prays for it; the Lord's prayer anticipates it;—and the church universal is now beginning to labor for this great object. She will not be disappointed,—the heathen will be given to Christ for his inheritance, and the uttermost parts of the earth for his possession. The school should be taught this from the Bible,—so plainly and clearly, that every child may see that we stand on right ground, and on an immovable position, when we labor and pray for the salvation of the earth. Let them be taught that we do not run without being sent; that we go by command, by direction, by the aid, the countenance, the promises, and the blessing of God. We cannot, shall not be disappointed. The millennial day will come. I feel that it is very important that this light be poured into the mind in early life ; that the child, as he grows up, may understand the great principles of action which govern the church of God,—that he may know how to defend them ;—that his confidence in them may be deep and unshaken, and that his sympathies, as far as possible, may be enlisted. How often such a lesson should be given out, each school will determine for itself. Perhaps once in two months will be sufficiently often. These recitations should always be in connexion with the Bible, and might be classified something in this way.

(*a.*) How does the description of the Bible in regard to the heathen, correspond with their state at the present day ; and how does this state compare with that created by the full light and influence of the Gospel ?

(*b.*) What does the Bible say is the only remedy for the condition of the world ;—and how does this correspond with the experience of men ?

(*c.*) What were the results of the missions in the days of the Apostles, as they went among the heathen ; and how do these results correspond with the effects produced by missionaries in our days ?

(*d.*) What trials attended the preaching of the Gospel among the heathen in the apostolic days, and

what trials in these times? What trials and difficul
ties will always have to be encountered? What
inferences to be drawn in regard to our prayers and
sympathies for those who are engaged in this work?

(e.) What part have children taken in the cause
of religion, as mentioned in the Bible, and what have
they to do in the work now before the church?

(f.) What sacrifices does the Bible require of us
in the work of converting the world to Christ, before
we have done our duty?

Questions like these, to any extent, may be raised,
and all founded on recitations in the Bible. They
will be answered by a complete knowledge of what
the church is doing at the present time for the salvation of the world. This plan, or something like it,
will give the teacher a most admirable opportunity
to contrast the condition of the heathen, and especially
heathen children, with those who have the Gospel;—
to show the superiority and the divinity of the Gospel, and to impress the heart with a sense of obliga-
tion and gratitude. The responsibility of the child
who is born in the land of the Gospel, can be urged
upon him with great force and power. It can, I have
no doubt, be made a powerful auxiliary in leading
the soul to submission, and conversion.

2. The information communicated respecting
modern missions, should be as definite as possible.

" A mission in an unknown country has no local
habitation for the mind to fix upon. It can awaken

only a vague, uninteresting, transient perception : and the church will never enter heartily into a plan for Christianizing all nations, until it becomes acquainted with the geography of the world."

If, for example, you have occasion to give an illustration of the principles of missions,—and there are some most admirable illustrations in it,—from the history of the Greenland Mission, try as far as possible to make the child understand the Geography of the country, the climate, natural features, and all those deep shades of the picture which the hand of nature has put on. Let all the information be of this definite kind. It is impossible for the mind to be interested in any other way. It might be well, too, to have a committee, consisting of a few of the teachers, and as many of the older scholars, to correspond with some one or more missionary stations, to make inquiries respecting their school, their children, and their wants. I have seen a school thrilled by the reading of one such letter from a missionary station. There might be, if thought best, a special meeting of the school to hear the letters read ; and be sure to read the letters sent from the school, as well as the answers received, at the same time. May we not, if we have the true missionary spirit ourselves, do much towards creating and perpetuating a missionary spirit in our Sabbath Schools, and that, too, without an organization so distinct that it shall create prejudices in the minds of worldly people? Shall we not, also, go on the principle, that our children are to become Christians, and ministers, and missionaries, and thus lead them to begin the work of sympathizing with the fallen world from their childhood? I have no doubt but all this can, and might, and ought to be done; and I pray that the spirit which baptized apostles, and all the "sacramental host of God's elect," may baptize the children of our Sabbath Schools.

3. There ought to be a system of contributions for the spreading of the Gospel, introduced into every school.

The object of introducing such a system is three-fold;—to raise money by which to carry on the plans of the church,—very considerable sums, too, might easily be raised in our Sabbath Schools;—to teach the children how to exercise benevolence, and of consequence, to acquire the habit of it, as every exercise will strengthen the habit,—and to teach the child to exercise self-denial in obtaining the money which he contributes. Every thing of this kind should be regular and periodical; and perhaps the plan of having a contribution brought in once every month, will be a good one. As far as possible, encourage the children to give the money which they have earned by some labor or self-denial. Show that you are interested in their little contributions, and encourage them to feel that the smallest sum, given from right motives, is neither overlooked nor forgotten by the great Redeemer. At the same time avoid making the impres-

23 *

sion that giving in this way is piety,—because a child may bring his pennies, and yet carry the heart of a little Pharisee. Avoid, also, casting blame or censure upon a child who does not contribute,—at least till you know the reason. His parents may be too poor,—he may have no parents, or they may be unwilling to furnish the child with money, and he knows not how to earn any himself. I have known children make very great sacrifices to earn money,—others to endure great self-denial to obtain it, in order to contribute; and I have known others whose feelings were cruelly and unnecessarily wounded when they could not contribute. Some teachers who have so far acquired the confidence of the class as to know the real situation and disposition of each one, have hired such children as were unable otherwise to obtain money, to do little jobs for them, for which they have paid them, and thus the contributions of the teacher passed through the hands of his poor scholars.

But every school should have regular, stated seasons of contributing, and an object to which the charity is applied so definite, and so tangible, that they can all see that the little stream of charity which takes its rise in their schools, does, indeed, flow into the great river, and swell its tide, and cause the waters to reach those who are perishing with thirst. As to the precise mode of doing this, every school will choose to have its own way and method. Go on the principle,—it is always safe and sure, never yet

Conclusion.

been known to fail,—that God will never be indebted to his creatures for the smallest gifts to him; he will reward them all, and return the cup full and running over; and while I do not believe that a school or a child can do any thing like purchasing his own salvation with his contributions, I do, at the same time, believe that he is more likely to receive salvation, in consequence of such charity. Let them begin life, as if the service of God was to be the object of life, and see that it is the object of your life; let them feel that in this life, we only begin to enter upon a service so glorious that the angel feels honored in being a servant in its cause,—a service which brings peace of conscience here,—a support which is stronger than hope as we pass from time into eternity, and that it will lead to what more than fills the measure of our hopes, and more than satisfies the highest desires of the soul.

CHAPTER X.

DUTY OF THE CHURCH AND PASTOR TO THE SABBATH SCHOOL.

I BEGIN the remarks which I am about to offer on this subject by taking it for granted that every church will wish to have a Sabbath School under her immediate care, sympathy, and direction, and that she would be glad to know what her duties are, that she may perform them to the best advantage. Every church ought to know when she has performed her duties to the Sabbath School, and I shall esteem it no small happiness if I may be able to lay them plainly before her.

There are certain errors which prevail extensively among our churches in connexion with the cause of Sabbath Schools, — errors which discourage the teacher, and frequently destroy not a little of the good which would otherwise flow from his labors. I wish briefly to specify some of these errors.

272

FIRST ERROR; *that children who go to the Sabbath School do not need so careful instruction at home.*

It is far from being improbable that the day of Judgment will reveal the names of many who with the lips favored Sabbath Schools, and sent their children to them for the very purpose of throwing off the trouble and responsibility of religiously instructing them at home. 'I need not talk with my child on the Sabbath on the subject of religion; I need not try to bring his conscience under the light of the Bible; I need not endeavor to gain his roving attention with the view of fixing his thoughts on God and eternal things;—especially I need not give him the opportunity to say by his looks, " my father, I do not see you bearing this holiness and showing it in your life, though you urge it upon me and profess it yourself;"—I need not take him alone and pray for him. and over him,—because—he goes to the Sabbath School. I am careful to have him go constantly, and he is there instructed in religion. If I also teach him, he will hear so much about religion, that he will be disgusted.' Such is the language of the heart, while the child is turned away from the father's table, and sent to find bread at the hand of strangers. Alas! for such cruelty. God has laid duties upon parents which they can neither throw off, nor delegate to others. The Sabbath School was designed to co-operate with parents, to aid them in training their children up for the service of God on earth, and for the rewards of this service in heaven. It cannot so take the place of parental instruction as to excuse the father or the mother from doing their duty. You can never know, till the light of eternity reveals it, how cruel it is to push the child from the bosom of his parent; and if he lives after that parent is gone, memory can never lead him to the spot,—the chamber in which his parents used to pray with him and teach him. The cultivation of the heart of the child will draw it out with love and reverence. That poor child who has no parents, finds in the Sabbath School a substitute for the kind and tender admonitions of parents; and that child who has parents will find it an additional blessing. But the head of the family is the priest whom God hath placed there to minister to the temporal and spiritual wants of the little congregation, and woe to the family and woe to the church, when the Sabbath School shall supersede the religious instructions of the fire-side. When it shall be left to the teacher in the School to do the work of praying for the children and of instructing them, one of the most glorious ends of the family relation will have been lost sight of, and one of the dearest privileges of the child will be destroyed,—that of being led to God by his own parents.

'Many seem to think that the responsibility is transferred from themselves to the teachers. When their children are committed to the school, their duty seems done. They hope and believe it is well with their children, since they are enjoying Sabbath School instruction,—with what kind of fidelity or appropriateness they are unable to tell. But they indolently conclude, since they patronize the school, and their children are there, all is well. But no parent ought to be satisfied with this. He ought to have a personal acquaintance with this important business. He should be their principal instructor himself.

Let every kind and every reasonable degree of influence be thrown into the Sabbath School, but do not intrust to others the exclusive care of immortal minds. *Burnish these precious jewels with your own hands.* Transfer the responsibility of training them up for God to no mortal. None have a parent's heart to feel,—none a parent's account to render. And none, if they are what they ought to be, can do this work so well.'

SECOND ERROR; *throwing all the responsibility of the school upon the teachers.*

Some churches will do so much as to select and vote for a certain number of men and women to be teachers once a year. Others will not even do as much as this. All is left in the hands of the teachers. If the Pastor, amid all this apathy, is disposed to take hold and lift and aid the teachers, it is very well; but if he is not so disposed, it is just as well. Are the teachers in your school faithful? The church does not know; she only knows that they have all the work to do. Are the teachers qualified? The church does not know; she hardly knows who they are. Do they study the lesson and understand the Bible, or do they come, and yawn over the lesson, impatiently waiting to have the long hour of recitation over? The church does not know. Do the teachers meet and pray together for grace, and patience, and the qualifications which the Holy Spirit only can impart? Do they read,—do they keep up with the times,— are the books in the Library such that they can receive benefit from them? The church does not know. She never attends the meetings of the teachers,— never unites with them in prayer, and has only a general impression as to the popularity of the school. When asked to contribute, she feels that all that she does by way of giving money, is a kind of bounty to the teachers, and not for the benefit of the children, and the families of the whole congregation. This is a criminal course in a church. The interests, the immortal, undying interests of your children ought not thus to be put out of your hands and away from your knowledge. The whole church ought to meet with the teachers, to pray with them, to sympathize with them, and to share their burdens, and their discouragements. There is neither justice, nor mercy, nor the spirit of the Gospel in thus rolling off the burden upon the teachers,—a burden which no set of teachers whom I have ever seen, are competent to bear.

Sometimes a church will send a committee into the Sabbath School to examine it. This is a very little better than nothing; but the whole church ought to be so well acquainted with it, that no committee can add to her information.

THIRD ERROR ; *an inadequate sense of the import-ance of having good teachers.*

When teachers are to be selected, it is frequently the case, that the church look around to see,—not who is qualified,—but who will *do,* taking the lowest possible standard by which to decide the question. One will be selected, not because he is the proper person, but because his father may think it strange if he be omitted; another, because she belongs to a very respectable family, and it would be a pity not to have the influence of such families; and a third, because he seems to sit so loosely upon his seat in this church that it becomes necessary to tie him by making him a teacher, lest he go somewhere else. Can a school be expected to flourish when its teachers are selected on such principles ?

Blessed will that day be, when our young men and our young females shall make it a part of their edu-cation and thoughts while studying, to prepare them-selves to become Sabbath School teachers ;—and when a generation shall rise up who know how to reach the mind of children, because they were taught in the Sabbath School, and thus obtained their qualifications. As things now are, we are wofully

24

deficient in good teachers. I speak this, not to re-
proach, nor to blame any who are teachers. They
shall have great credit for what they are doing; but
I know they are not so vain as not to be sensible that
I am speaking nothing but the plain truth, when I
say that our teachers, as a whole, are far from being
properly qualified. Perhaps most of them have done
the best they could,—we are thankful to them, and
we regret that they are not better furnished. But
why are they not abundantly qualified? I put the
question to every church, why are they not qualified?
And why are first-rate teachers so scarce? I reply,
because the church has never yet felt this subject,
nor attended to it. Heretofore, if a father gave his
son any education, it was to enable him to read, and
write, and keep his accounts, and thus get through
the world. Perhaps he gave education sufficient to
qualify him to teach a district school, or to enter a
store as a clerk. But how few fathers and mothers
have thought and planned and prayed over the education of their child, because they were anxious, that
by this education, that child might be well qualified
to be a Sabbath School teacher! How common to
have a committee selected who must carefully and
thoroughly examine the man who proposes to teach
a day-school, and yet, when the same children, who
compose this week-day school, are gathered into the
Sabbath School, and are to be instructed in the great
concerns of religion, they may fall into the hands of

any who may happen to be willing to take them. They may be Christians or not, they may be such as the child could not be entrusted with in a school on other days, or not. Is this right? No, no, it is not. Teachers must be raised up in the bosom of the church. They ought to be pious, holy, devoted, patient, untiring, disinterested men. And the church can never do her duty to the Sabbath School, till she prays over this subject, makes it one object in the education of her sons and her daughters, to qualify them to become teachers in the Sabbath School.

FOURTH ERROR : *that of having inadequate views of the aid which a family receive from the Sabbath School, in training up their children.*

It may be that the early education of the parents, their acquired habits, or their circumstances put it out of their power to teach their children to be punctual. And yet it is of unspeakable importance to the child that he have these habits. He is sent to the Sabbath School, and there he learns what punctuality is, and conforms to it. The machinery is put in motion at such a moment, and it closes at a particular moment, and multitudes of children have not only here obtained their first ideas of punctuality, but have here acquired the invaluable habit of being punctual.

Is it of great consequence that your child have the spirit and the habit of subordination? Perhaps there

is far too little of family government under your roof.
But your child can never govern himself, unless he
be taught to obey now, while a child. In the Sabbath School he has this discipline. Every week he
submits his will to the will of his teacher, submits to
restraints and to government. This is a great blessing to a child who is not sufficiently governed at
home. And what is better than all, is, that children
in the Sabbath School are subdued by the law of
kindness. It is well known that a savage is softened
by being taken and dressed up and for a few times
introduced into genteel society. And can kindness
and love,—disinterested love ever be brought to bear
on a human being, and that being a child, without
softening him? Never. And every week your child
is chained down by the bonds of love. Do you wish to
have your child disciplined,—I mean, to have his attention arrested and frequently riveted, till he can hold his
mind down to a single point? The Sabbath School
does this, and is a very powerful instrument by which
to cultivate the power of attention. Do you wish to
have the memory of your child strengthened and
cultivated, so that he can compare and reflect, till he
can, by himself, draw conclusions and correct inferences? If well and properly taught, he learns to
do this in the Sabbath School. You wish your child
to have the power of manly and rational conversation, so that when he talks, it shall be with propriety,
without diffidence, or impudence. He learns how to

THE SABBATH SCHOOL TEACHER   285

Duties of the church.   First duty,—*understand the system.*

do this at the Sabbath School. You wish him to have a conscience that is cultivated, that he may do his duty to man, and his duty to God, and thus walk in the path that leads to eternal life and glory. You would have him learn "what is the chief end of man," that his soul may at last be saved, and shine in the everlasting kingdom of God as the sun in the firmament forever and ever. The Sabbath School is pledged to aid you in all this. The better teachers that church brings into the school, the more prayer she throws around it, the more intense interest she takes in this young garden of the Lord, the more is she doing to aid every family in training up their children for the honors and rewards of heaven. And the father who understands the subject, will see that it is a most wise and wonderful instrument by which he may be aided in the great work of leading his children to God. Every effort of his will be seconded, every impression which he makes will be deepened, and every prayer which he offers for the salvation of his child will find a response from the teacher.

I must now turn to the consideration of the DUTIES which the church owes to the Sabbath School.

1. *The system ought to be thoroughly understood by every church.*

Let me lean to the side of charity; and I think I can do that while I say that many who patronize the Sabbath School, and who speak well of it, seem to feel as if it were something in which they have little

or no interest.   It is a kind of appendix to the Sabbath,—a very good thing indeed, since it keeps the
children from being at play, or relieves them from the
wearisomeness of the Sabbath, and it furnishes the
teachers with something by which to occupy their
thoughts and their time.   I am not sure that many
might not be found even in the ranks of teachers whose
views of the subject are such, that they would draw
back the hand at once, were it not that they can do
the work on the *Sabbath*, and thus not lose any time
which is so precious to devote to business or to the
world.   Would it not be so, that but few of these
schools would be kept in operation, even if all the
children would attend them, were the teachers under
the necessity of doing the work on any other day?
Is this a true and correct estimate of the value of
the system?

All allow that before Sabbath Schools were so
multiplied, it was a good thing in the minister to
meet, catechise, and instruct the children under his
charge: all allow too, that the Sabbath School is a
much more valuable way of educating the rising
generation for God, inasmuch as a whole church can
do more for her children than a single mind can do.
It follows, then, that if Sabbath Schools could not be
held on the Sabbath, they ought to be held some day
during the week, and the church ought to do the
work.   But have our churches such views of this
subject?   Do they feel, and try to make all around

feel, that it is, next to the ministry, by far the mightiest lever put into the hands of God's people, by which to raise the world? Some will praise the system, perhaps contribute a part of a dollar annually for its benefit, perhaps now and then step into it; but they do not understand its design, its power, or its usefulness. They do not know how it is a grand improvement upon the old system of education, when the children of the church were suffered to grow up almost without religious instruction and religious impression; and when the field ought to have been bringing forth fruit, it was found to be full of tares. Weeping parents often bent over their unconverted children in anguish, and cried, " an enemy hath done this ;" but they overlooked the grand secret, that the ground must be preoccupied. 'It is now beginning to be found that it is easier and wiser to preoccupy than to dislodge; that it is infinitely important that the soul should hear the voice of God, before the syren song of the great deceiver.' This system gives the child the solemn voice of a powerful guardian, and thus hushes the voice of temptation, and breaks the charms that would delude and seduce. It holds a brazen shield over the immortal being even from his childhood, against the fiery darts of the wicked one. It holds the misguided youth even when driven by the winds of temptation from rushing off the precipice into the gulf of despair.

2. *The church ought to be careful to speak respect-fully and affectionately of the teachers.*

You send your child to the Sabbath School. He watches you to know why you send him, and what you think of the school. Perhaps, as parents, you give your approbation to the school; but it is that *languid, heartless* approbation, which is worse than silence. ' They are friendly to the cause. They can use freely the language of approbation; but the *heart* is not in it. There is no deep emotion on the subject. The head is indeed near the equator, but the heart is at the poles. A man's tongue may be loose, while his soul is ice-bound. The lack is not that of praise, but of self-denying energy. They are not prepared to encounter the obstacles in bringing the influence of the Sabbath School over their children. If suita-ble apparel is not provided, no pains are taken to fur-nish it. If a little reluctance is manifested by the children, the question of their staying at home is easily settled in their favor. They are not strongly and earnestly urged to this duty. This languor and indifference are imbibed by the children : their attend-ance on the Sabbath becomes a mere whim. They are their own masters. There is no steady, strong, decisive parental influence. The children, when they come to the school, have the family likeness, and are as cold and uninterested there, as are their friends at home. Thus do parents multiply the sorrows of the faithful teacher, and thus do they lay up a fearful account to be rendered at last for the consequences.'

You know a teacher in the school, perhaps more than one, of whom you do not think very highly. He is not qualified for his station. But whose fault is it? The church have put the best in the office to be found; and till you have done all within your power to raise up good teachers, you ought not to complain. Now will you destroy the whole influence of that school over your child, by your prejudices, your un-kind remarks,—by your uncharitable insinuations, by your unmanly, as well as unchristian thrusts? No child goes to the Sabbath School without knowing precisely what his parents think of the school, and of his teacher in particular. A few words incau-tiously dropped, a few improper remarks, may coun-teract all that can be done for your child at school, and perhaps ruin his soul forever. What shall you do? Would I have you *speak* well of a teacher, when you do not think well of him, and thus play the hypocrite before your child? No. But I would have you *think* well of the teacher, believe that he does the best he can; and remember that if the teachers are not qualified, it is a matter of humilia-tion to you that you have not labored and prayed more to raise up good teachers.

Besides, the teacher is doing the work of the pa-rent,—he is doing the hardest, most difficult and responsible work of the parents every week; he is

trying to aid you without fee or reward, and will *you,*
can you throw so much responsibility upon him, and
then add insult to ingratitude, and do all that you can
to crush his hopes of usefulness, and destroy all his
means of doing good to your child?

3. *The child ought to have the assistance of his
parents at home in understanding the Sabbath
School lesson.*

The lesson of the Sabbath School is, or ought to
be, short.   It is almost uniformly on some interesting,
useful, instructive, and practical part of the Bible.
Every member of the church ought to study so much
of the word of God every week, as to obtain a full,
clear, and thorough knowledge of this single lesson.
No man can hope to grow in a knowledge of the
Scriptures, who does not do as much as that.   For
their own improvement, then, every man, woman,
and child, ought to study the lesson of the Sabbath
School.   But what is the fact?   Excepting those who
are compelled to study in consequence of being
teachers, how few even try to keep up with the children in the Sabbath School!

Your child comes into the room with his Bible in
his hand to get his lesson; he has no helps but his
question-book.   He soon comes to a question which
he cannot answer.   He looks up.   His mother is too
busy to give him her eye.   He asks a question, and
is told, in a cold, indifferent tone, 'I don't know any
thing about it,'—or, 'don't trouble me now,'—or, 'I

wish you would go into your room, and study your lessons by yourself,' or, 'you must ask your teacher, it is not my business to teach you the lesson,'—or, 'you will have it all explained to you, I presume, on the Sabbath.' That child must be very remarkable indeed, who, under such circumstances, can help feeling discouraged. On the contrary, let the child see that his parents know, that his parents honor the lesson, that they will study it with him, and will aid him to understand it, and he stands on very different ground. The following beautiful picture of what I could wish every family to be, is so appropriate, that I do not think my reader will regret to see it. It is a true narrative.

'It was Saturday evening when I arrived at the house of my friend, in a retired village in Massachusetts. The family had just risen from the table, and the little ones were retiring to rest, when one of the elder children requested their mother's permission to attend the teacher's meeting that evening.'

" The rain will prevent a meeting to night," replied her mother, " but we will not be denied the *privilege* of studying the lesson."

Accordingly, the table was soon covered with books, and surrounded by the happy family.

" This is our usual custom," said the mother, " when the weather deprives us of the assistance of our minister, whose kind instructions have for many years greatly assisted the teachers in their benevolent work."

I declined an invitation to join the interesting circle, but was a highly gratified spectator. Here were the father and mother, with three lovely children, together with a modest young woman residing in the family, with their Bibles open. Each one was questioned in turn, references were found and impressively read, maps consulted, and the Bible Dictionary often referred to. The intelligent and unrestrained questions of the children, clearly manifested that it was no new employment. The Bible seemed to them not only a familiar, but a beloved book. While looking at this animated scene, my mind unconsciously glanced back over a period of sixteen years, which I have been permitted to spend as a Sabbath School teacher, and I could not but reflect, oh! had I thus been aided by Christian parents, cheerful and effectual had been my labors, where now, I fear, they were lost!

After the lesson was concluded, family prayer offered, and the children had retired, the following conversation took place.

"I am delighted to find your children engage with so much pleasure in studying the Bible. How have you managed to make it so agreeable?"

"We have never found any difficulty in making the word of God a pleasant study. In the first place, my little children are taught many of its stories before they can read. And as soon as they become

Sabbath scholars, we make it a point to study the lesson *with* them. I believe they were never sent away to get it by themselves; this would seem too much like a task. Either one or both of us always take the lesson and show them that we cannot be denied the privilege. We ask, and in our turn an swer the question, talk over the scene, imagine our- selves in the very spot, and endeavour as much as possible to interest and impress our young scholars. This is done on Saturday evening, or Sabbath morn- ing. But there is another method adopted by their mother, which I think still better. Every morning during the week after family prayer and breakfast, the children have always been accustomed to read with her a chapter, which is talked over in the same way. Questions are continually arising while it is read, and thus the habit is formed, of *daily reading the word of God with pleasure and attention.*"

"Your method is certainly a very simple one, and how easily might every Christian parent adopt it!"

"Yes, for although the Holy Spirit alone can take of the things of God and show them to our dear children, yet I am confident that parents can do much to render this blessed volume a precious book to their children. If with a countenance beaming with plea- sure, they would say, ' come, let us read it together, my children,' instead of assigning it as a daily task to be run over alone, the time might not be distant when it would be to both better than "gold, even fine gold,

sweeter than honey and the honey-comb;" and I
think it would essentially aid *you*, who are Sabbath
School teachers, for I know you must have your
trials as well as your pleasures, and many of the
trials must arise from the negligence of parents. God
forbid that such negligence be laid to *Christian* parents, and yet is it not a sad truth, that the children
of many of them have not learned to esteem this
holy book as their necessary food ?'

Alas! why is it that many parents prefer that the
teacher explain the lesson to their children, or that the
minister explain it from the pulpit, or that it go
unexplained, to becoming scholars themselves and
aiding their children to understand it? Let those
of my readers who are parents, pursue the course
followed by the parents, as described above, only
for a single term of three months, and if at the
end of that period they do not feel that they and
their children are abundantly benefited, then I
will neither venture to prophesy again, nor be a
troublesome reprover of their negligence, and criminal
neglect of their offspring.

4. *It is the duty of the church to give her countenance, support, and interest to the school ; and if
possible, every member should have something to do
with it, either as a teacher or a scholar.*

The Library should be revised, enlarged by new
books, and the church ought to do it cheerfully and
abundantly The parents ought to take particular

pains to read the books of the Library, for their own improvement, for an example to their children, and in order to be able to talk with their children about the books which they read. Many occasions in reading these books would undoubtedly arise, by which deep and lasting impressions might be made on the memory and on the heart. Truths might be pressed upon the conscience under circumstances which would cause them to abide in consequence of the associations with which they are indissolubly connected.

Besides, if the church were to do her duty, almost all of the congregation would be connected with the Sabbath School in some relation or other. In some of our congregations this is already the case. I could mention several village-congregations in New England in which the Sabbath School numbers between five and six hundred, or nearly all of the congregation. These are the most interesting schools I have ever seen. I have seen a class of old ladies,—probably all over fifty years of age, who sat down to the recitation of the lesson with as much interest as any class of children could. I do not intend to say that all, without exception, can do so. Mothers with young children cannot, and fathers sometimes cannot be connected with the Sabbath School. But these cases are exceptions to the rule, when I say, that the church and congregation can profitably belong to the school. How often do we hear people lamenting that

they could not have enjoyed the benefits of the Sabbath School when they were children! Do they forget that they can *now* go, and enjoy all these benefits? Do they forget that the Sabbath School would
actually do them more good now than when they
were children? But it is hard to begin now, they
cannot bring themselves up to the point of doing it.
I ask, if it be so hard for you, who profess to love
the Bible, who love religion, who feel your need of
light and instruction, if it be so hard for *you* to study
the Bible, what must your children suffer in doing it?
They do not profess to love the Bible: they do not
feel their need of its light and instructions,—and yet
you feel that it is their duty to go to the Sabbath
School. May I ask a plain question? Is it not *pride*
which prevents you from belonging to the Sabbath
School? I ask it, because I have known many who
wished the privilege of being at the teachers' meeting with a view of hearing the lesson explained, who
could not be induced to belong to the School itself.

It is impossible for any mind, not absolutely un-
balanced by disease, not to be benefited by studying
and talking about the word of God. I could wish to
see all our congregations belonging to the Sabbath
School. Good rooms should be provided, and the
adult classes, by *all means*, should be separated from
the children. It is from negligence of this simple
rule that so many attempts to induce the whole congregation to unite in the Sabbath School have failed.

It is in vain to try to have all in the same room. But different rooms can be provided, the adult classes can each select their own teacher, and the object so desirable can be accomplished. In the Tabernacle in New-York, they have a room for each adult class separate from the rest,—an admirable plan. But you can never expect a congregation to come into the system, if the church stands aloof. They cannot be induced to give up their conversations, and their resting seasons, if the people of God refuse to do it. Few have any conception of the sins which are committed on the Sabbath by the tongue. I was once acquainted with a devoted Superintendent who had one of the fullest and most prosperous schools. One Sabbath morning he went out to get in the wandering, straggling boys who did not come into their several classes. He found two groups of boys standing under different horse-sheds, listening to the conversation of two groups of professors of religion. On coming up he found them in quite animated conversation, the one discussing the price of wood, and the other computing the prices of rye, in a season in which the crops had fallen short! These were members of the church talking together, and the children had run away from their Sabbath School to listen to them! When the Superintendent kindly stated these facts to the church, though no names were called, these individuals were highly offended. Can any faithfulness on the part of the Superintendent or teacher cause the children

25 *

to love the school, so long as members of the church do thus ?

5. *It is the duty of the church to pray and labor for the immediate conversion of the children in the Sabbath School.*

Perhaps it is sometimes the case that the church feel that if the teachers were Judges, Rulers, or Ministers of the Gospel, or were filling some high and responsible station, they should be made the objects of prayer; but as it is, they are only teachers in the Sabbath School, and it is of little consequence. But do not forget that every prayer that you offer for the teacher, is a prayer for the salvation of your child placed under his care; that the truth of God may impress his heart. and that thereby he may be made wise unto eternal life. You wish that your child may drink in the pure truth and in right proportions; then ask God that the teacher may have wisdom so to teach him. Pray that he may be a pious man, a holy man. Arguments from the wants and condition of your child press you to add your prayers with those of the teacher, and that too daily, in the closet, at the family-altar, and especially on the morning of the holy Sabbath.

The Bible and our own observation abundantly show us that children can be converted at a very early age. Multitudes of such cases might be adduced. The most eminent men who have ever lived for God and for the salvation of the world, have been converted in the morning of life. Children may thus early be brought in,—they ought to be. The church ought to pray for it,—to labor for it. I have more than once had the pleasure of welcoming to the table of Jesus Christ, those who were under twelve years of age. They were like the early, small stars of evening,—very small, but pure and bright and beautiful. They held on their way too, gloriously. I have not half the fears that a converted child will dishonour religion, that I have that the aged sinner, who has lived in the iron habits of sin for half a century, will do it. With him it is the work of life and death to break off those old habits. His thoughts, wicked and vile, will, ever and anon, flow back into the old, deep-worn channels. But piety in the child gushes up like the breaking out of a new spring, making its own new channel, growing, and widening, and beautifying as it flows. The Bible has promised that the time shall come, when the child shall die an hundred years old. It can be brought about. Every church must aim to bring it about in regard to the children committed to her, whom she places in the Sabbath School. Most stupid, negligent, and guilty will she be, if she does not gird herself to this work. Oh! were I to take my choice for helpers in the labors of the kingdom of Jesus Christ, I would rather have a church committed to me, made up of converted children from the Sabbath School, and thus trained up for the service of God, than to have a church of a thousand members, formal, stiff, cold and barren as the aged oak. Blessed is the man who shall be the instrument of the conversion of a single child ; he adds a bright star to the moral heavens. Here must we raise up our pillars, here our polished stones, here our strong men, and here those who, on seraph-wing, will hasten to declare the name and love of Christ to the very ends of the earth.

6. *The ministers of the Gospel should make the Sabbath School an important part of their pastoral charge.*

Ministers have done much to rear up and sustain the institution of the Sabbath School. That they have not done more, and all that might be reasonably expected of them, I impute in part to the pressure which this age brings upon them, and partly to the fact that they have never examined to see precisely on what ground they should stand in regard to it. I do not believe any deficiencies on their part which might be pointed out, are the result of design.

Almost every Sabbath School contains hundreds of children, in the morning of their being, open to the best impressions, and rapidly forming characters which will abide with them forever. These hundreds of immortal beings are placed in the hands of some thirty or forty teachers,—the best probably to be obtained : but all the minister is supposed to know of

them is, that they are members of his church, and
are people of common abilities. I ask now, if he
would be willing to have as many adults taken from
his pastoral charge, and once a week instructed in
religion by those of whom he knows nothing, except
that they are professors of religion? Would he be
wise, or safe, judicious or justifiable in so doing? I
think not. But are not these children as liable to be
led wrong, biassed wrong by any want of judgment
or piety on the part of the teachers, as the adult
part of the congregation would be? It seems to me
that the Pastor ought to know, intimately know who
and what the teachers are, how they teach, what
they teach, and what impressions they are making.
Each teacher has some six or eight children committed to him, and he can teach them and form their
characters as no other human being can. Ministers
may preach well, eloquently, learnedly, and power-
fully; but in the pulpit, they reach not the child. All
goes over him. But the teacher can reach him and
make impressions and aid in forming his character
every Sabbath. Were it only for the safety of the
individual church, the minister ought to become deeply interested in the Sabbath School. But more. Let
the teachers be neglected, let them pick up knowledge as they are able here and there, let them
teach error and feed from the vine of Sodom, and
pluck clusters from the vineyard of Gomorrah, and
we have a power growing up which is irresistible.

Our churches are already in the hands of Sabbath
School teachers. They give character and create
the fashions and feelings of our churches. Let them
believe and go wrong, and we cherish an infant Her-
cules whose club will shortly be used in beating and
killing his own mother. Teachers must be taught,
indoctrinated, that they may feel that the ground on
which they tread is firm, and that their path is
through light and under sunshine. If our teachers
are not held responsible for what they do and what
they teach, to the Pastor and to the church, woe be
to the hopes of stability in the walls of our Zion. In
order to meet the case, the minister must not be cold,
formal, indifferent, but his heart must warm over the
school as over his own children. The safety of our
churches, their stability, permanency, order, purity,
knowledge, all, under God, depend upon the character of our Sabbath Schools. That character cannot
be what it should and must be, if there is any deficiency on the part of our ministers.

Teachers are men,—good men, I will suppose,—
but men who want improving, enlightening, and instructing. They are ready to admit this. Left to
themselves, they grow discouraged, and droop. They
do as well as they can. The minister and the church
stand off, they receive no countenance, no encouragement, no sympathy. . They bring such explanations
of Scripture as their limited means will allow, and
thus each one explaining and teaching in his own

Can have time.

way, they plod on from year to year. Is this right? Ought not the minister to meet his teachers once a week as a father,—feel that they are colleagues with him in aiding him to take care of the lambs,—instruct them in the lesson which they are to teach the ensuing Sabbath, giving them his warm sympathy and co-operation? Ought not the Sabbath School to be made an integral and an important part of his pastoral charge, so that the minister shall feel that he is to be the guide of the teachers, and that he is to keep the church awake and alive to the interests of the school,—that he is to do what he can, to create an interest in the parents, in the congregation, and in all classes of his charge, so that it shall be cherished by all as the dearest boon committed to the church? If it is said that he has not time for all this, I answer, it be true ;—*but he must take time.* There is no part of his work that is more important than this. He had better have fewer weekly meetings, make fewer pastoral visits, than to neglect the School.

I cannot dismiss this topic without once more urging that the Pastor meet his teachers once a week, and instruct them in the lesson. They would gladly have him the fountain whence they draw their knowledge, and by him they are willing to have their opinions shaped. They feel, too, their need of mental discipline their poverty of thought or illustration, and especially, they feel their inability to obtain and grasp those

great principles and views of the whole plan of re-
demption which are so desirable, and which, once
obtained, give a religious teacher such power. Ministers do not get this great system fully before the
mind till after years of study. Is it any wonder that
teachers cannot? The doctrines of the Bible, the
great foundation-stones of the moral temple, are what
they want to measure and examine, to lay their
hands upon, to rest their hopes upon, and by which
they wish to teach better. The Pastor only can
thus instruct them.

By meeting the teachers weekly, too, the minister
would preach better! And how? Because he would
be continually studying to simplify truth, and thought,
and language, so that the children may understand
what is taught them. In this way he will preach
with more simplicity, more nature, more ease, more
directness, and more illustration. So great a part
of his instructions will not go over the heads of his
hearers.

I plead for this close connexion between Pastor and
school, once more, because it will create a strong, a
sweet, and a delightful tie between the Pastor and
his flock. The children will feel that their privileges
are great, because the minister of God is so frequently
present, and takes so deep an interest in the school.
The teachers feel that they labor not in vain; and
that however discouraging their prospects may be,
there is one heart that will never grow cold, never lose

Conclusion.

its sympathy for them. The parents will feel that the piety and the intelligence of the church are enlisted in behalf of their children, and will be encouraged to co-operate. The church will feel that she must go with her leader, and will gather her sympathies around the vineyard of the Lord ; and the minister himself will feel that when no success attends his labors, he has a cohort in his church, who, by experience, have learned what it is to labor in vain, and who will not be backward to sympathise with him. And when the holy man of God dies, there will be tears from the eyes of those in the Sabbath School room who have looked upon him as their best friend.

26

CHAPTER XI.

DISCOURAGEMENTS are inseparable from every attempt at being useful. I had thought of devoting this chapter to the consideration of those which attend the faithful teacher in the Sabbath School. But they need not be pointed out, nor dwelt upon. They will come of their own accord; but the wisest way is to think as little of them as possible, and to resolve that they shall never retard or stop our efforts. The world is at war with the kingdom of holiness, and in whatever shape effort is made to reclaim it from the dominion of the prince of the power of the air, there will be obstacles and difficulties. Ever since the first promise that the seed of the woman should crush the serpent's head, it has been so. It is a part of the moral discipline through which the people of God must pass. No class of active, devoted Christians has ever met with so much opposition, as did the Apostles and early Christians. But

302

they neither stopped nor turned aside for such opposition.

" About one hundred and twenty disciples, after the death of their master, were gathered together for prayer, and the Holy Spirit descended upon them; and then they all spake with tongues, and preached the Gospel to the people of many different languages. The consequence was a great excitement: a crowd collected; some mocked, and then Peter preached to them a sermon, *with an application*, and three thousand were converted. Then they had time enough for prayer and religious duties, and money enough for benevolent purposes; for each " sold his possessions, and parted them to all men as every man had need, and continued daily with one accord in the temple." Then the lame man was healed; a crowd collected; Peter preached another sermon with an application, and five thousand were converted. The High Priest and nobles are alarmed and indignant at all this excitement; they seize Peter and John, and demand of them by what authority they did so; and then Peter preached the Gospel faithfully to the High Priest and nobles. The Apostles are commanded to hold their peace, are threatened and dismissed; and they immediately return to their work of preaching to the people. Again they are seized and imprisoned; but an angel releases them, and they continue to preach. A third time they are taken and beaten; but they rejoice that they are counted worthy to suffer; and without delay resume their work. The excitement spreads and increases, Jerusalem is filled with their doctrine, the opposers are in great perplexity what measures to take to stop it; till at length, in a paroxysm of popular fury, Stephen is seized and stoned to death.

Here we may suppose there was a pause. The disciples probably met to consider what should be done, and to pray for divine guidance. Imagine them assembled, many countenances indicating anxiety and alarm. At length one speaks: 'Oh! the torrents of ridicule with which we are assailed! How shall we ever stand before it? Another remarks, 'I can bear the ridicule very well; but they tell such falsehoods about us, they will utterly ruin our reputation, and destroy all our influence among the people!' A third feels it most deeply that they should be hated for the *good* which they were doing, and that these false-hoods are invented to make them odious on account of their usefulness. A fourth cannot bear the thought of being charged with wrong motives, and having all his efforts charged to the desire of building up a party. A fifth feels himself disheartened because their success is principally confined to the poor, that none of the great, and the rich, the priests and nobles, lend them their name and influence, but do all in their power to crowd them down. A sixth is disturbed that there should be so much noise and excitement, such a tumult that there can be no living in the city, if

THE SABBATH SCHOOL TEACHER. 305

The true spirit of primitive Christianity.   Reasons for faithfulness.

---

these efforts should go on. Another regrets the disunion of families occasioned by their preaching, and another points to the blood of Stephen, and hints at a little more prudence, lest they should all be massacred together.

Now what shall they do in all this trouble? They kneel down and pray together; they continue for some time earnestly engaged in the exercise; and the clouds begin to clear away, the heaviness is removed from their heart, they are in an entirely different atmosphere. Now one and another begin to recollect the words of Christ, how he had foretold that all this would happen in just this manner;—how he had commanded, warned, and encouraged them; promised them a mansion in his Father's house; he had gone to prepare a place for them, and send the Comforter to be with them till his return. And now they have only to do their duty, and leave the consequences with their Master. They see things in an entirely different light, their despondency is all gone; they go again to their work with more resolution and earnestness than ever.

Such was the spirit of primitive Christianity; this is the spirit that should animate *us* in all our well-directed efforts for the salvation of the soul."

Let those who engage in teaching and raising up Sabbath Schools, meet opposition, and discouragements in *this* way, and the cause of Jesus Christ can never suffer from the efforts of men.

I must now proceed, briefly to mention a few motives which God, in his providence, holds out to the Sabbath School teacher to be faithful and untiring in the cause in which he has engaged.

1. *The teacher will himself receive benefit in proportion to his faithfulness.*

The providence of God seems to design the Sabbath School to be the place where the teacher shall have all his Christian graces continually called out and exercised. The man who is faithful in his station as a Sabbath School teacher, can hardly fail of having his Christian character improved.

Are you naturally proud ? Who is not ? You must here associate with ignorance, stupidity, prejudice, and it may be, with filth. Like your Master, you must associate with the poor. Your intellect must be exercised by coming down to the capacity of the child. You must visit the poor, listen to their tales of sorrow, sympathize with their condition, put yourself, in some measure, on their level, and encounter any prejudices, however vulgar, which they may entertain. Can this be done without calling the grace of humility somewhat into exercise ?

Are you naturally selfish ? You must go to your school, and visit the families, at the time appointed, let the weather be what it may, your own ease and comfort making what demands they may ; you must enter the dwellings of sorrow, of woe, of wretchedness : you must forego seasons of visiting, social interviews with friends, leisure for reading, thinking, and on the Sabbath especially, even a part of your hours of secret meditation and devotion in the closet. It is a constant call for self-denial; and you cannot be happy without its exercise.

Do you in any measure lack patience? You will meet with the stupid and the dull, whom you must instruct; with the stiff-necked and the stubborn, with whom you must bear and forbear; with ingratitude which at times seems too much for poor human nature to bear. You will have to follow your scholars from week to week—sometimes discovering that they are wearied with your teachings, sometimes that they would gladly get away if they could. Can you do all this, and endure all this, without a patience constantly increasing?

'Are condescension, affability, meekness, gentleness, goodness, long-suffering, Christian love that hopeth all things, endureth all things, required? They are all called into daily exercise, and all, if asked of the Giver of all goodness, will freely be given, and abundantly strengthened and increased, by the blessed spirit of consolation, until every precious stone in the diadem of Christian graces be set in its place, and burnished, and made fit, for Christ's sake, to be added to those which evermore shall burn and blaze around the throne, and brighten and brighten, throughout eternity, in the pure and holy splendors of the glory of God and of the Lamb.'

Thus, they " *that be wise shall shine as the brightness of the firmament, and they that turn many to righteousness, as the stars forever and ever.*"

2. *The faithful teacher will have the thanks of his scholars in after life.*

Few teachers are aware how long they are remembered, and, if faithful, with how much affection, by their scholars. More than twenty years ago, a lady, in a destitute neighborhood, opened in her own house, what she called a Sabbath School. The Bible and the catechism were recited by quite a number of children who united in the school. This teacher was a mother, and often has been known to hear thirty or forty recitations with an infant in her arms. These self-denying labors were not overlooked by the Great Head of the church. Those who attended her school grew up altogether unlike others in the same neighborhood, who did not attend. The moulding of their minds and the forming of their characters seem to have been done by her, and that too, in some instances, when the almost omnipotent example of parents was directly opposed to her influence. Three of her scholars were the daughters of profane and intemperate parents. Such was the hold which this devoted teacher obtained over their affections and confidence, that she rescued them from the ruinous influence of these parents, and trained them to be ornaments in society. They were respectably settled in life.

Several of her scholars who had removed to other places, and who had grown out of her recollection, have been known to return and extend the warm hand of greeting, and hail her as their former teacher and friend.

One of her pupils who had taken up her residence in a new and remote section of the State, was induced, by a remembrance of the example and influence of this teacher, to go and do likewise. She also collected children around her, and taught them the things which pertain to their eternal welfare.

One scholar while on her death-bed sent a messenger from the town in which she was residing, to request this teacher to come and see her. She was unable to go; but just as the young lady was going into eternity, leaning upon the staff of the Redeemer, she left a special message for her teacher: "*Tell her that her instructions in that little Sabbath School were blessed to the salvation of my soul.*" Such was the influence of one teacher, and she a mother at the head of a family! Such were the rewards which she lived to receive. All may not see the results of their labors so clearly. Sometimes, for wise reasons, the teacher will not be permitted to see the results, and to hear the offerings of the grateful scholar in this life. But the word of God shall not return to him void. The seed may seem to die; but it will, in God's own time, spring up, and bear fruit unto eternal life. As an illustration of this, I have often been

affected at an incident connected with Henry Mar·
tyn. If I mistake not, my reader will be also.

Some years since an English gentleman spent
several weeks at Shiraz, Persia. He attended a
public dinner with a party of Persians, among whom
was one who took but little part in the conversation.
He was below middle-age, serious, and mild in countenance. His name was Mahomed Rahem. In the
course of a religious conversation, the Englishman
expressed himself with some levity; at which Mahomed fixed his eyes upon him with such a look of
surprise, regret, and reproof, as reached his very soul.
Upon inquiry, the gentleman found that he had been
educated as a Mollah, (Priest,) though he had never
officiated; that he was much respected, was learned,
retired in his habits, and was drawn out to attend
that party only by the expectation of meeting an
Englishman—to whose nation and language he was
much attached. In a subsequent interview, Mahomed
Rahem declared himself a Christian, and gave the
following account of the happy change in his views
and feelings.

" In the year 1223 (of the Hejira) there came to
this city an Englishman, who taught the religion of
Christ with a boldness hitherto unparalleled in Persia, in the midst of much scorn and ill-treatment from
our Mollahs, as well as the rabble. He was a beard-
less youth, and evidently enfeebled by disease. He
dwelt among us for more than a year. I was then a

decided enemy to Infidels, as the Christians are termed
by the followers of Mahomet: and I visited this
teacher of the despised sect, with the declared object
of treating him with scorn, and exposing his doctrines
to contempt. Although I persevered for some time
in this behavior toward him, I found that every interview not only increased my respect for the individual, but diminished my confidence in the faith in
which I was educated. His extreme forbearance
towards his opponents,—the calm and yet convincing
manner in which he exposed the fallacies and sophis-
tries by which he was assailed, (for he spoke Persian
excellently,) gradually inclined me to listen to his
arguments, to enquire dispassionately into the subject
of them, and finally to read a tract which he had
written in reply to a defence of Islamism by our
Chief Mollahs. Need I detain you longer? The
result of my examination was a conviction that the
young disputant was right. Shame, or rather fear,
withheld me from avowing this opinion. I even
avoided the society of the Christian teacher, though
he remained in the city so long. Just before he quit-
ted Shiraz, I could not refrain from paying him a
farewell visit. Our conversation—the memory of it
will never fade from the tablet of my mind—sealed
my conversion. He gave me a book—it has ever
been my constant companion—the study of it has
formed my most delightful occupation—its contents
have often consoled me." Upon this, he put into

his hands a copy of the New Testament in Persian.
On one of the blank leaves was written—" *There is
joy in heaven over one sinner that repenteth.*—
HENRY MARTYN."

3. *The faithful teacher will have the consciousness
of carrying light, and hope, and mercy into many
families where they would otherwise be excluded.*

The faithful teacher will be a blessing to all,—the
rich as well as the poor. But the greater part of
this world are poor ; and the Gospel is emphatically
designed for the poor. Every ray of light which you
carry into the dark bosom, cheers, elevates, and
blesses. Every family with whom you come in contact, you can aid, you can cheer, you can comfort.
And mercy too, the richest mercy of God, can by you
be conveyed to the heart over which none that is merely earthly can shed her beams. Let a few teachers meet,
who have been faithful a few years, and let them tell
over the scenes through which they have passed, and
your heart would not only ache over the misery
which sin every where produces, but it would also
rejoice at the power which the teacher has óf doing
good. I should like to mention examples, did circumstances allow it ; but I may be allowed to select a
single instance of the results of the system, out
of scores of examples at hand, all of which are
equally interesting. This little scene took place in
Europe.

" At the foot of a lofty hill, crowned to the summit with the richest verdure, peeped out from among encircling bush-wood and straggling elms, a miserable mud cabin. A streak of smoke rolling up through the green trees, was the only sign that met my eye of its being inhabited. The sun was up, and over the deep blue heavens the thin cloud lay sleeping. It was the hour between sunrise and the full blaze of day. A stillness seemed to lie around the spot, and I felt an indescribable sensation creep over me as I drew near the house of mourning. I paused at the entrance. A low, murmuring kind of sound stole upon my ear, and again all was hushed. The apartment on the threshold of which I now stood was one of the meanest construction. It was without a single piece of furniture that deserved the name. In one corner of it a dead body lay stretched out, very slightly covered with a tattered coat, and a cold kind of horrible feeling crept through my very soul, and I should probably have shrunk away from any further investigation, if I had not been suddenly arrested by a soft, sweet voice, mingled with a low groan, somewhat like a death-rattle, that seemed to issue from the same apartment. I turned my head around and beheld a sight that chained me, as if by magic, to the ground. It was heart-thrilling to behold it. On a bundle of straw, a woman somewhat in years lay apparently in the agonies of death. Near her head hung, reclining in deep sorrow, a beautiful little half-naked child. On one side a lovely girl, about thir

27

teen yea.·s of age, knelt ;—a Bible clasped in her thin,
slender hands, with which she was endeavoring to
comfort her dying mother! I instantly recognized
them,—twc of my Sabbath School children! The
meeting was affecting. They had been without food
for some days. The mother died the next day in
the triumphs of that faith which her little daughter
taught her out of the Bible. The girls grew up to
be respectable members of society, and one of them
has been a teacher in a Sabbath School for a number of years."

4. *It is an encouragement to be faithful, that you
are engaged in a system of usefulness by which the
whole world is to be benefited.*

There is something disheartening to work alone,
and to feel that you have not any one to sympathize
in your trials and difficulties. It is not thus with the
Sabbath School teacher. He can hardly go to any
part of the wide world, without finding fellow-laborers.
And the system, improved by the experience and the
prayers of God's people, will yet reach every tribe
of men under heaven, and become one of the most
efficient means in the hands of the church by which
to fill the earth with the salvation of the Gospel.
How soon would the Sabbath School cause the Sabbath to be sanctified and hallowed through the world!
How soon would it do that for slavery which nothing
has as yet done, or is soon likely to do, in this land!
How soon would it redeem a community so that our

prisons would be almost entirely empty! Mark the following testimony of the Chaplain to the great State Prison at Sing-Sing, (New York.) " I have lately made pretty thorough inquiry among the convicts here, for the purpose of learning who, and how many, have ever enjoyed the advantages of a Sabbath School. The result is, that out of more than *five hundred convicts*, not *one* has been found who has ever been, for any considerable time, a regular member of a Sabbath School; and not more than two or three, who have ever attended such a school at all."

Most of the missionaries of the present day were faithful and indefatigable teachers in the Sabbath School at home. The consequence has been that they have uniformly introduced the system into the heathen countries where they have gone. Those from London early introduced it into the Society Islands. It is the testimony of Mr. Ellis, that the Sabbath School is a vital principle in their system of operations, and that God has so abundantly blessed them, that their schools are now almost wholly taught by those who were formerly scholars. ʻOften has my heart rejoiced to see, early on the Sabbath morning, the little Islanders running to school at the sound of the iron suspended from a cocoa-nut tree, and struck by a stone, which told them that the hour for instruction had come,—often when the second summons from this substitute for a bell intimated that public worship was about to commence, have I heard their voices mingling in sweet melody to the Savior's praise,—then arranged to attend the several places of worship, with their clean cheerful faces, their neat attire, made from the products of the islands, each with a little basket in one hand, and in the other their books,—when the service began I have observed them quiet in prayer,—attentive to the discourse, and ready on their return to school to meet the questions of their teachers from the sermon just heard, with intelligent and appropriate answers, I have been unfeignedly thankful to God, and delighted with the influence of these nurseries for his church.

Here also they hold their Sunday School Anniversaries. When a deputation from the Missionary Society were there, (Huahine,) more than 1200 adults and 350 children were present on such an occasion; —the scholars were examined, and indications of intellect were afforded which showed, not that mind, but cultivation was required. They acquitted themselves most creditably, and showed their acquaintance with the principles of the Christian religion to the surprise and gratification of all. Nor could their neat appearance escape notice. After whole chapters, portions of catechism, and various hymns, had been recited, some books as rewards were distributed, which added not a little to the interest of the occasion. Particularly in the instance of one scholar, a boy, who, for his diligence and good conduct, received the Gospel of St. Matthew bound in morocco. From

amidst the admiring multitude stepped forth this
child: with beating heart and smiling face, he reached
forth his hand to take the book, put it into his bosom,
and could hardly return to his seat, his little heart
was so full of joy. It was a scene in which it was
hard to tell whether children or parents shared the
most pleasure; — but there was one present,—a
mother,—in whose sad countenance was depicted the
deepest grief, now suppressed by covering her face
with a cloth, and wringing her hands amidst heavy
sighing and sobbing, till overcome by the emotions of
her soul, it burst forth in touching exclamations.
"Oh, that God had sooner taken away our hard
hearts! Oh, that the light of his word had sooner
come to these islands,—then my poor, poor child had
not been gone,—she too might have been here to-
day!" This woman once had a daughter, and had
offered her as a sacrifice to the idols of the islands,
previous to the Gospel being made known to them
by the missionaries."

5. *You are encouraged to be faithful, because in
a short time those whom you instruct will become
fellow-laborers with you in the cause of Jesus Christ.*

The best teachers in our schools are those who
were educated in the Sabbath School. They probably remember their own modes of conceiving of truth,
their difficulties and perplexities, besides, they have a
kind of tact which a long acquaintance would naturally give them. We hope the time is near when we shall

27 *

have no teachers but those of this description. But what is peculiarly encouraging, we do not have to wait till the child is matured sufficiently to become a teacher. As soon as he is converted to God, he at once becomes a little laborer in the vineyard. I have marked a multitude of instances which might be adduced to illustrate this point,—instances, in which a child had been the means of leading parents, friends, and companions, to a knowledge of the Savior. In looking over these cases,—all of which are well authenticated,—I am at a loss which to select. I can take but a single case,—one that was pointed out to me by a most esteemed friend, who, as I suppose, was the writer of the interesting narrative. Should my conjecture be right, I shall have the strongest assurance that there is nothing like exaggeration in the account. Perhaps every reader could recite narratives of the labors of these young disciples of Christ, equally interesting, and equally a reproof to those who have a name to live, while they are dead.

'Some years since a Superintendent was walking out at the edge of evening, in one of the pleasant villages of Massachusetts. By some providence he turned out of his accustomed walk, and was accosted by a child, who inquired if he were not a Sabbath School teacher. On being told that he was, she sighed, and said that she had long been wishing to go to the school, but that her parents forbade her. On being asked the reason of their objections, she wept profusely, said that her father was intemperate, and her mother so wicked, that when she asked to go to the Sabbath School, they would chastise her for it, and make her work all the Sabbath.

"Oh! if my parents were willing, how glad I should be!"

"Will you direct me, my child, to your home? I will have some conversation with your parents respecting your coming to the school."

"O yes, and will thank you too."

On entering this dwelling, I breathed forth a prayer to God that my visit to this family might be long remembered by me, and by them. The child introduced me as one of the Sabbath School teachers, who wished to have some conversation with her father on the subject of his permitting her to attend the school.

"You wretch!" he exclaimed to his child, "have I not forbid your going to such places?"

He then called for the rod to chastise her. I felt that I was in a delicate position, and at first stood amazed at such unnatural cruelty. I remarked that I hoped he would not punish the child, particularly as on this occasion I had been the cause of exciting his anger.

"Your little daughter is kind, Sir, and obedient, is she not?"

'Yes. But who are you?"

" I am your friend, and wish to have a little conversation with you, if you please."

" Well, talk on."

" I hope you will not correct your child on account of my calling to see you, as I was pleased on meeting her, with the simplicity of her conversation, and thought I should be pleased to see her father."

" Sir, I will take your advice: Jane, you will attend to your evening's business."

After conversing with this man for nearly two hours on the subject of Sabbath Schools, and the propriety of his sending Jane, he partially promised that she might go. " What say you, *mother*, to our Jane's going to the Sunday School?" The mother refused with an oath! My heart began to despair, for I thought I had succeeded, and was now disappointed from a quarter which I did not expect. I continued my entreaties for a short time to no purpose, and promised that I would call again.

On the day following I called again, and after three hours of painful and laborious conversation, gained the consent of these parents that Jane might come to our Sabbath School.

The next Sabbath, with gratitude to God, I had the pleasure of introducing Jane into the Sabbath School. After supplying her with books, I placed her under the care of Miss D——, one of the most faithful teachers in our school. Jane had not been long with us, before it was plain that she had serious thoughts and feelings; and in a few Sabbaths after, her countenance indicated that a change too pleasing and too visible to be concealed, had taken place.

At the close of the school one Sabbath, Miss D. requested me to remain, that I might have some particular conversation with Jane. We tarried after the school was closed, and I turned to the little girl, who said,—

'Oh, Mr. ——, you are the kindest of friends in this world: you have, by bringing me into this school, taught me how to worship God. Before I came here I used to feel bad, but could not help it. Miss D. has told me that sin is the cause of all our bad feelings,— that we are all sinners in the sight of God. I have also learned in this school that we must pray to God that he would forgive us our sins. Oh, Sir, a few Sabbaths since I felt that there was no peace to my poor soul, and saw, that if I should then die, I must go to hell with the wicked. On leaving the school, I resolved to pray God that he would give me a heart to love and serve him; a heart to fear and obey my parents; a heart to love *everybody*. And, you cannot know what a weight my sins were to me: I could get no sleep on account of my sins. But I have longed for the last few days to see you. I have had such new feelings,—my load is removed,—I could hardly wait for the Sabbath to come, that I might tell you what a Savior I have found. I trust I have given myself entirely to God. I feel that

there is something in my heart which I cannot express. O how thankful to God I am for your care
and attention,—for the instructions of Miss D.,—for
ever coming to the Sabbath School ;—for here I have
found the Savior who loves me, and who hath said to
me, Seek *me* early,—seek me *now*, and you shall find
me ! Oh ! will you pray for me,—pray for my father,
mother, brothers, and sisters ;—I have prayed for
them,—I will continue to pray for them.'

This account, which I have related in her own
language as nearly as possible, was almost too much
for me. She was then only thirteen years of age.
She was not only happy herself now in the enjoyment of religion, but it was her heart's desire that
all her father's family might enjoy the same religion.
While she did not forget to pray for them, she often
introduced topics in conversation, to interest them in
religion.

From continued dissipation, the father induced a
disease, which brought him near the gates of death.
One morning, on Jane's visiting him, while very weak
and low, he asked her if she thought he would get
well ? She replied, with tears, that she hoped he
would,—' but if it is God's will, *dear father*, that you
should soon die, where will your soul be when you
enter upon eternity ?' He gazed at her in silence :
she then asked if he wished to have the good Sabbath School teacher call to see him ?—he will pray
for and with you. He then said, 'oh ! my child, will

you pray for me?' and do you think God would hear prayer for such a wicked man as I am? The weeping child knelt by the bed-side of her sick father, and breathed out her soul to God in prayer, that he would pardon her dear father's sins, and prepare him for the events of the future. The unkind father was melted into contrition, on hearing such importunity to God, to bestow blessings from the throne of his grace upon such a sinner as he had been. The old man now prayed,—felt the efficacy of prayer,—felt that he was a sinner against God,—yes, the aged sinner prayed; and his prayer, we believe, was heard. Under God, Jane was the instrument of her father's conversion. God in mercy restored him to health, *a new man,*—an humble Christian. On his recovery, he was soon seen in the Sabbath School which he had so long opposed, where he then confessed, before teachers and scholars, how much he then felt on account of his past conduct to the school. He asked the forgiveness of all.

He is now an active teacher, in the fifty-eighth year of his age, in the Sabbath School. The mother soon became serious, her brothers and one sister were also anxious for the salvation of their souls, and to make their peace with God. In a few months from the time that Jane entered our school, she came forward with her father, mother, four brothers, and a sister, who all joined the church of God! Thus she was instrumental, in one short summer, in the con-

version of seven immortal souls, and all of her own
family. Where formerly oaths were daily heard, now
morning and evening prayer is offered, and the blessing of God supplicated to rest upon Sabbath Schools,
to which, through the goodness of God, eight undying
souls ascribe their conversion.'

I cannot leave this beautiful narrative without re-
minding teachers of two suggestions which arise on
reading it. One is, that teachers should not value a
little time when necessary to meet prejudice, combat
error, or persuade obstinacy. A few hours of faithful
labor may save a whole family. The other suggestion is, that when we have once led those who are
opposed, to become friends, they are among our
warmest friends, and labor with a zeal and an earnestness corresponding to their previous prejudices
and opposition.

6. *The faithful teacher will be the means of preparing many for an immortality of blessedness.*

A beloved member of my church once came to me
with a discouraged heart. She had, I believe,
twelve young ladies in her class; she had taught
them, she had prayed for them, and had apparently
done all for them that she could. Not one was
savingly converted, not one was anxious, or even serious; what could she do more? I recollect saying
what little I could to encourage her,—which was not
much, for I have too often had the same feelings in
regard to my ministry, not to be aware that no hu-

Illustration

man sympathy can reach the case. But she continued faithfully to instruct them. In a little while God poured out his Spirit upon us, and that teacher has since sat down at the table of Christ, with every one of that class,—celebrating the love that redeemed them. Who would not prefer the rewards which a faithful teacher will at last receive from the great Redeemer, to all the honors which this world can bestow? To lead one soul to the Lamb of God,—to be the benefactor of one immortal mind, will cause you to shine as the sun in the firmament forever and ever. But the faithful teacher will do more than this; he will lead several to the waters of life, and to the river of God.

There are no situations in which the teacher may not, and should not labor faithfully, devotedly, and prayerfully; for there are none in which his labors will not do good. I introduce the following narrative to illustrate the point, that a single teacher, under the most unfavorable circumstances, may be a worker together with God. I trust, too, that the reader will think as I do on this point, after having read it.*

---

* Perhaps this narrative may have met the eye of the reader before. It has frequently been published as the production of a pen in England. I have three several copies now before me, each ascribing it to different English periodicals, in each of which, it was inserted as original. The author begs leave to say, that the facts were communicated to him some years

A few years since, a man and his wife arrived in the town of M——, N. Y., as permanent residents. They were young, lately married, and their prospects for the future were bright and cheering. They purchased a farm in M——, which was then a new country,—and had happily spent two or three years in this situation, when, by a mysterious providence, the young man was called from this world.—With his surviving widow, he left two lovely twin infants, to deplore a loss which time could not retrieve. The widow sought comfort in vain from the limited circle of her acquaintance. There was no minister of the Gospel in that region to direct her to the great source of comfort, nor was there a pious friend who could direct her trembling footsteps to the cross of Jesus. But she went to her Bible, and by the assistance of the Spirit of truth, found that consolation which a selfish world can neither bestow nor taste. She mourned indeed a husband who was no more, but she was cheered by the hope that God would protect her and hers. She wept over her innocent babes, and resolved that while she lived, they should never need a mother's care. As they grew up, she endeavored to teach them the first principles of religion. but they received only her instructions. One week after another rolled away,—one Sabbath after another

since, while on a journey in the State of New York, and that it first came from his pen.

dawned upon the wilderness, but they brought none of its privilege. The wilderness had never echoed with the sound of the church-going bell. The solitary places had never been gladdened by the sound of the footsteps of him who proclaims glad tidings of great joy. The feeling mother clasped her little boys to her aching bosom, and sighed and wept for the opportunity of taking them by the hand, and leading them up to the courts of God. In the days of her childhood she had possessed great advantages, and she now mourned that her babes could only receive instruction from *her* lips. Alas! no man of God came to instruct,—to cheer,—to gladden the bosom of her, who, for years, had never heard the whispers of love from the servants of her Savior. When the little boys were five years old, and before they were old enough to be sensible of their loss, a consumption had fastened upon their tender parent, and she was soon encircled in the cold arms of death. She steadily watched the certain issue of her disease, and even in her last moments, commended her children to Him who is "a Father to the fatherless." A few moments before she expired, she kissed her little boys, who wept, almost without knowing why, on feeling the last grasp of the clay-cold hand of their mother. "It is hard," said she to a neighbor who was present, "it is hard for a mother to leave two such helpless babes without friends, and without any one to protect them; but I leave them in the hands of God,

Narrative continued.

and I *do* believe he will protect them. My last prayer shall be for my poor, destitute orphans."

After the death of their mother they were received into the house of a neighbor,—a poor widow. In less than a year, one of them was stretched beside his mother beneath the sods.

About this time a pious young lady arrived in the place. She too was an orphan, but was not comfortless. It was her first inquiry how she could do good to the spiritually destitute villagers around her.

In the course of one of her afternoon walks, she met a little boy straggling by the side of the road. There was a something in his countenance which excited interest at once, though he was exceedingly ragged The young lady was struck with his appearance, and immediately entered into conversation with him.

"What is your name, my little boy?" said she, gently.

"James."

"Where do you live?"

"With widow Parker, just in the edge of the wood, there, in that little log-house; can't you see it?"

"I see it; but is widow Parker your mother?"

"No: I had a mother last year, and she loved me. She used to take care of *me* and of my brother *John*. She made our clothes, and taught us to say our prayers and catechisms. Oh! she was a most good mother."

Narrative continued.

"But where is your mother?" said the lady, as soothingly as possible.

"Oh, madam, she is dead! Do you see that grave-yard yonder?"

"Yes"—

"And the great maple-tree which stands in the further corner of it?"

"Yes, I see it."

"Well, my poor mother was buried under that tree, and my brother John lies there too. They were both buried deep in the ground, though my mother's grave was the deepest. I shall never see them again, never, never, as long as I live. Will you go with me and see the graves?" continued he, looking at the lady with great earnestness and simplicity.

The short account which the little boy gave of himself awakened the best feelings of the young lady, and she had been devising some plan by which to do him good. For the present, she declined visiting the grave, but continued to converse with him, and to gain his confidence. She found him very ignorant, having never been at school, and the instructions of his pious mother, not having her to repeat and enforce them by precept and example, were nearly forgotten.

A Sabbath School had never been established in the place, and whether it was practicable to establish one, was doubtful,—but she was determined to make the experiment. Accordingly, she visited every little cottage in the village, and urged that the children

28 *

Narrative continued.

might be assembled on the next Lord's day, and a school formed. A proposal of this kind was new, was from a new-comer, and was unpopular. All the old women in the place entered their protest against such innovations. For the first three Sabbaths, the young lady had no other scholar besides her little James. But she had already been taught, that however faint our prospects of doing good at first may be, we should not be discouraged. Our labor may not be lost, though the first blow may not produce much effect. She was sorry that she had so few scholars, but she bent all her energies to the instruction of her little boy, and afterwards felt that Providence had ordered it wisely.

But in a few weeks the prejudices of the people began to wear away, and before the summer closed, this school embraced every child whose age would allow it to attend.

It was the second summer after the establishment of this school, and after little James had become well acquainted with his Testament and catechism, that his health also began to fail. This good young lady beheld his gradual decay with anxiety, visited him frequently, and always wept after having left him. She used often to walk out with him, and to endeavor to cheer him by her conversation.

One pleasant afternoon she led him out by the hand, and at his request visited the spot where lay his mother and little brother. Their graves were botr covered with grass, and on the smaller grave were some beautiful flowerets. It was in the cool of a serene summer's day, as they sat by the graves in silence; neither of them feeling like speaking. The lady gazed at the pale countenance of the little boy, upon whose system a lingering disease was preying, while he looked at her with an eye that seemed to say, 'I have not long to enjoy your society.' Without saying a word, he cut a small stick, and measured the exact length of his little brother's grave, and again seated himself by the lady. She appeared sad while he calmly addressed her.

"You see, Miss S——, that this little grave is shorter than mine will be."

She pressed his little, bony hand within her own, and he continued—

"You know not how much I love you,—how much I thank you. Before you taught me, I knew nothing of death,—nothing about heaven, or God, or angels,— I was a very wicked boy till you met me. I love you much, very much, but I would say—something else"—

"And what would you say, James?" inquired the lady, trying to compose her own feelings.

"Do you think I shall ever get well?"

"Indeed I hope you will; but why ask that question?"

"Because I feel I shall not live long,—I believe I shall soon die,—I shall then be laid beside my poor

mother,—and she will then have her two little boys,
—one on each side of her.   But do not cry, Miss S.,
I am not afraid to die.   You told me, and the Testament tells me, that Christ will suffer little children to
come unto him, and though I know I am a very sinful little boy, yet I think I shall be happy, for I love
this Savior who can save such a wicked boy as I am.
And I sometimes think I shall soon meet mother and
little brother in happiness.   I know you will come
too, won't you ?   When I am dead I wish you to tell
the Sabbath scholars how much I loved them all,—
tell them they must all die, and may die soon, and
tell them to come and measure the grave of little
James; and then prepare to die."

The young lady wept, and could not answer him
at that time.   But she was enabled to converse with
him many times afterwards on the grounds of his
hope, and was satisfied that this little lamb was indeed of the fold of Jesus.   She was sitting at his
bed-side, and with her own trembling hand, closed
his lovely eyes as they shut in the slumbers of death.
He fell asleep with a smile,—without a struggle.
The lady was the only sincere mourner who followed
the remains of the child to the grave, and while she
shed many tears over that grave, which concealed
his lovely form, she could not but rejoice in the belief that God had permitted her to be the feeble instrument of preparing an immortal spirit for a man-

sion in the skies, where the wicked cease from troubling, and where the weary are at rest.

7. *Once more,—the teacher is urged to faithfulness, because it will add to his own eternal blessedness.*

The death-beds of many of the most active and devoted servants of Jesus Christ within a few years have proved to us, that the spirit and the consolations of the Apostolic times have come down to us. The days of martyrdom, for the present, have gone by; but the labors of martyrs, and the dying triumphs of martyrs are still left. A host of bright stars have set upon this land within a few years,—and they went down growing brighter as they set. The light of eternity came through the gloom of the grave, and threw glories even into the dominions of death. The song of angels was heard even here, and the tongue began to unite in these songs before it became silent. These men have gone to their rest. In their lives and deaths, God has seemed to say that he will honor those who honor him. But the work of converting the world to God, is yet to be done. One agent and another is raised up, and then removed, and yet the plans of the Infinite One still move onward. They will go on, let men be faithful or otherwise.

Teacher! your day will soon be over. The night cometh, in which no man can work. You will soon be called away to pass beyond the shores of time; that which will then press your conscience will be,—

not how much of this world you have gotten in any shape,—but how much have you been a co-worker with God! If faithful in your sphere, however humble, you will be acknowledged as a co-worker. You will go into eternity conscious that you have served Jesus Christ, and that you have been laboring to bring souls to his cross. He will welcome you, he will crown you, he will own you as his dear friend in the day when he shall come in the glory of the Father.

On the hill of Zion above, you will, too, see a glorious sight. That bright one who shall accompany your wearied spirit even from the bed of death, who shall lead you up to the regions of everlasting blessedness, may be the redeemed spirit of that dear scholar whom you taught in the school, whose soul you led to Jesus, and whose body you followed to the grave. You had almost forgotten his name,—but *you* had not been forgotten; and he was the sweet messenger sent down to guide your soul from earth to heaven. As you see that glorious spirit, as you hear his song of redeeming love, will you ever regret your labors, prayers, tears? And when your feet have become familiar with the golden streets of the New Jerusalem, you may hereafter hail one and another whom you instructed in the Sabbath School, but whom you left on the earth completing their day of probation. They will come, and with you, forever become learners in that glorious school of Christ above.

There will be gathered, converts, a great multitude, ministers who have been most faithful and laborious and successful, and churches who have been lights in the world, all of which may be traced back to the little class which you once taught; and to ages untold, you will see the results of your labors here on earth.

Reader! before rising from my chair, I expect to write the last paragraph of this book,—a book which has cost me much labor, many fears, and much deep anxiety. A book may be written for reputation, for pecuniary profit, or to gratify earthly feelings. I do believe I have not been led to write from either of these motives. If motives as pure as our sinful hearts will permit us to feel, could secure me from having said what would make bad impressions, or lead to any other than good results, I should lay down my pen with more satisfaction than I now do. If in any remarks I have exhibited any other than the kindest feelings, I beg my reader to believe that it was wholly unintentional. I have not felt any other. In very many cases the reader will doubtless dissent from what I say. Let him do so, feeling that his experience may have been different from my own, or that I have been laying down general rules, while his was an exception. I have been on ground new, and to a great degree, unexplored; and if the reader feels that he discovers great deficiencies, or great defects, he will remember that I have had great difficulties to encounter.

Many unknown friends will read these pages, upon whom this will be the first and the last impression which I can ever make. May I not hope that they will at least gather one hint, and one impression from this little volume which will quicken them in duty, make them more devoted to their work, more laborious and more faithful in their Master's service ?

The writer and the reader are both passing to the grave. The providence of God which has brought their minds into contact by means of these pages, lays them both under new and heavier responsibilities to be devoted to the salvation of men. Those of the reader cannot be small : those of the writer immeasurably great. May we sow beside all waters ; in the morning scattering the seed upon the earth fresh with the dews of heaven, in the evening withholding not the hand,—for we know not whether the one or the other shall prosper. And when the toils and anxieties of this life shall be over, may we rejoice together with the ten thousand times ten thousand, who without ceasing day or night, praise God and the Lamb forever and ever !

THE END.